School–University Partnerships

School–University Partnerships

The Professional Development Schools (PDS) Approach

KELI GARAS-YORK

SUNY
PRESS

Published by State University of New York Press, Albany

For information, contact State University of New York Press, Albany, NY
www.sunypress.edu

Library of Congress Cataloging-in-Publication Data

Name: Garas-York, Keli, author.
Title: School-university partnerships : the professional development
    schools (PDS) approach / Keli Garas-York.
Description: Albany : State University of New York Press, [2024]. | Includes
    bibliographical references and index.
Identifiers: LCCN 2024012265 | ISBN 9781438499932 (hardcover : alk. paper) |
    ISBN 9781438499956 (ebook)
Subjects: LCSH: College-school cooperation—United States. | School
    improvement programs—United States. | Teachers—In-service
    training—United States.
Classification: LCC LB2331.53 .G37 2024 | DDC 378.1/03—dc23/eng/20240814
LC record available at https://lccn.loc.gov/2024012265

Contents

Foreword

Since first learning about Professional Development Schools (PDS) as a faculty member at Buffalo State, I have been amazed by the limitless possibilities of PDS to strengthen teacher education and P–12 learning through collaboration. School–university partnerships (with PDS being one approach) provides a framework that benefits all stakeholders in the enterprise of education. This book helps to explain the power of PDS and its potential to address the challenges we face while also identifying practices and policies that will improve teacher preparation to enhance P–12 experiences for children and adolescents.

This book serves as an important roadmap to understand the ways in which school–university partnerships can utilize collaboration to reach these goals through the approach of the PDS model. In Dr. Keli Garas-York we have a wonderful guide due to her extensive experience with PDS that began when she was a classroom teacher invited to join the PDS work of her school. She then became a teacher educator who, along with her teacher candidates, participated in another PDS site. She moved on to become the director of the Buffalo State PDS, co-edited two books on PDS, and took on leadership roles in the national PDS organization, while also helping to extend PDS into the international arena through the Buffalo State International PDS (IPDS) program. From these personal, local, national, international, and scholarly perspectives, Garas-York helps us more fully understand what PDS is and what it could be.

This journey takes readers through a historical overview of the PDS approach to school–university partnerships. We learn about ways to formalize and govern school–university partnerships and then explore the roles and responsibilities of each stakeholder group. Next, suggestions are offered for creative and innovative ways to use the flexible and versatile structures of PDS to meet the needs of each reader's context. Our journey ends (or really starts!) with information about the assessment and evaluation of PDS.

Incorporated throughout is the research associated with PDS to ground readers in the study and exploration of PDS and to identify new areas of scholarship. Helpful suggestions and templates are provided, and additional features include the clever "PDS: Pause, Deliberate, and Share" to embed opportunities for reflection as well as a spotlight feature to provide examples of concepts related to each chapter.

This book will serve readers well, whether they are new to school–university partnership or have many years of experience with this collaborative model. When reading the book, I found myself thinking about ways to improve, extend, and innovate my own collaborative practices. You have in your hands a great guide to invigorate your work as an educator.

Dr. Pixita del Prado-Hill
Professor, SUNY Buffalo State

Acknowledgments

I would like to acknowledge all those who supported me during the writing of this book. Thank you to Richard Carlin and the folks at SUNY Press for their help and encouragement.

I am grateful to my friends and colleagues from the National Association of School–University Partnerships (NASUP) for their knowledge, resources, and feedback, especially JoAnne Ferrara.

I truly appreciate my colleagues at Buffalo State University for allowing me to be the director of our amazing PDS consortium. Thank you for your support and encouragement during the writing of this book, especially Pixita del Prado Hill, Julie Henry, and Wendy Paterson.

Finally, I am very thankful for the constant love and support of my family: Tena Garas, Richard York, Atticus York, Alexander York, and Bailey York. This project would not have been possible without your patience and encouragement.

Introduction

My PDS background goes back many years. Almost 20 years ago, I was teaching reading at a small suburban elementary school. The principal asked me if I could work with some teacher candidates who were in a literacy methods course at SUNY Buffalo State. My colleagues who were classroom teachers also had pairs of teacher candidates placed with them. The teacher candidates spent the morning with me two days a week for a semester. Initially, they observed my lessons, and then we gradually began to co-plan and co-teach, and eventually, they planned and taught small-group lessons on their own. The teacher candidates were also able to participate in school activities and classroom management, and to get a general feel for the culture of the school.

Their course instructor was always in the building when the teacher candidates were there. She sat in on our school literacy committee meetings and helped to plan a literacy night at the school for preschool parents and their children. The course instructor also met with the whole group of teacher candidates from her course at the school. She asked various faculty and staff from our school to come and speak at these meetings, so the teacher candidates could further learn about the inner workings of a school.

I was fascinated by this approach and appreciated the collaboration with the course instructor. My principal was invited to a Professional Development School (PDS) meeting by the course instructor held at another area elementary school, and the principal let me come along. We met other school representatives who mentored teacher candidates. There was a presentation by the host school and a lively related discussion among the attendees who were administrators, teachers, faculty members at the college, and teacher candidates.

On the final day of the semester, we celebrated the accomplishments of the teacher candidates with a breakfast in the school cafeteria. The course instructor asked me if I would like to come teach at Buffalo State. They had an opening for a literacy professor. I quickly declined as I could not envision myself teaching anywhere else but at my then current elementary school.

The relationship between the elementary school and the university continued to grow, and we collaborated on a project funded by a PDS action research mini-grant. I found this work extremely rewarding and started to think about teaching at Buffalo State.

I became part of the SUNY Buffalo State Elementary Education and Reading department about 16 years ago. I was mentored by the university's PDS director at the time. We visited the school where I was to bring my methods students to engage in authentic teaching experiences with young learners. I told myself, in this way, I was still able to work with children. teacher candidates, and teachers as part of my new position. The principal of my PDS and I collaborated on an early literacy project with teacher candidates and presented our results at the SUNY Buffalo State PDS fall conference, so that other PDS stakeholders could learn from it. These PDS experiences made such an impact on the teacher candidates in my classes and became some of the highlights of my career. Through these experiences, the teacher candidates were not only able to practice literacy instruction in an authentic setting but also many of the skills and techniques it takes to be a teacher.

Now, I am the director of the SUNY Buffalo State Professional Development Schools (PDS) Consortium. I still have a PDS site where I take literacy specialist candidates for a summer practicum, but I am also fortunate enough to work with all the PDS stakeholders (teacher candidates, college faculty, school administers, teachers, and sometimes P–12 learners and their parents) in the consortium. I help to develop and maintain relationships, facilitate meetings, and implement professional development or professional learning initiatives with the goal of preparing teacher candidates to positively impact P–12 learning. I have also served as a board member and on various committees for the National Association for School–University Partnerships (NASUP), formerly the National Association for Professional Development Schools (NAPDS). I feel fortunate to have had such a variety of valuable experiences related to PDS. The more I became involved in PDS, the more I learned about the genesis of this approach to school–university partnerships. The more

I learned, the more appreciative I became of the folks who recommended, organized, researched, developed, implemented, and improved this remarkable approach for school reform with a focus on improving teacher preparation and P–12 student learning. This is especially true at my own institution. The founder of the PDS consortium at Buffalo State was Leslie Day. She built the Buffalo State PDS on such a solid foundation, using carefully researched methods and innovative ideas in every aspect of the program. As the current director, I was fortunate to inherit such an effective PDS consortium. With a strong foundation and flexible procedures in place, the Buffalo State PDS affords the consortium more time and energy to focus on the improvement of teacher education and P–12 learning while trying to address the needs of all PDS stakeholders.

This book is an attempt to provide a reader-friendly historical and procedural overview of what it means to be a PDS. All aspects of the text are situated in current or seminal research in the areas of PDS and school–university partnership scholarship. I hope the information in this book will provide readers with ideas to either begin or refresh PDS relationships between schools and universities.

The first chapter provides a historical overview of the PDS approach to school–university partnerships. Chapter 1 also addresses the flexible frameworks that serve as the foundation for PDSs. Chapter 2 provides information on formalizing school–university partnerships, including developmental stages and governance. The third chapter lays out general roles and responsibilities of PDS stakeholders and situates them in PDS and school–university partnership research. In Chapter 4, I offer suggestions on how to branch out and consider creative ways to meet the needs of stakeholders while adhering to the recommended 9 Essentials of being a PDS. Finally, Chapter 5 provides information on the assessment and evaluation of PDSs and why it is important. Additional research findings about the impact of PDS on various stakeholders is also included.

Each chapter ends with a spotlight section. In these sections, I dig a little deeper into the people and concepts related to the chapter. The spotlight section at the end of Chapter 1 provides an extensive overview of John Goodlad, his work, and his role in PDS. At the end of Chapter 2, you will find a brief interview with a faculty chair of a teacher education department who provided her initial perspectives on PDS. Chapter 3 ends with a spotlight on a very specific stakeholder group, PDS student representatives. Details about this unique teacher candidate leadership program are presented. Chapter 4's spotlight details an International

Professional Development Schools (IPDS) program, while Chapter 5 concludes with a spotlight on overall reflection.

Reflection is an important part of PDS. There are opportunities throughout the book to stop, think about what you are reading, and make connections. The reflection areas are, of course, called PDS—here, PDS stands for Pause, Deliberate, and Share. Take advantage of these opportunities to reflect on your own, in writing, or as a group about how the ideas and concepts in the text apply to your situation or school–university partnership. If you are already part of a PDS or PDS network, consider how what you are reading could take your school–university partnership to the next level, or maybe piggyback on ideas presented in the text to continue to best meet the needs of the stakeholders in your PDS.

There is a lot of research presented in this book. You will find that researchers tend to use different but related terms when writing about PDS. Again, PDS is an approach to a school–university partnership—a term that is used more generically, at times, throughout the text. You will also see the terms "consortium," "network," and "collaborative" to describe an overall partnership or group of partners. The term "teacher candidate" is used to describe undergraduate or graduate students in an education or teacher preparation program. They may also be called interns or preservice teachers. The people from the university who supervise the teacher candidates in partner schools are referred to as university faculty members, teacher educators, or supervisors. Throughout the text, the children or youth who attend elementary, middle, or high school are often called P–12 learners or P–12 students. Finally, the teachers who work in the partner schools and open their classrooms up to teacher educators and candidates at various levels in their teacher preparation programs are called mentor teachers, cooperating teachers, in-service teachers, veteran teachers, seasoned teachers, or practicing teachers.

One aspect of this book needs clarification here. The National Association for Professional Development Schools (NAPDS) changed its name in 2023 to the National Association for School–University Partnerships (NASUP). You will still see NAPDS used in aspects of the text that refer to the history of PDS. As well, 9 Essentials (two editions) were published under the name NAPDS, so those continue to use the name NAPDS.

I hope you enjoy this text and gain a deeper understanding of the possibilities of PDS and how this approach can help you improve teacher education and P–12 learning while meeting the unique needs of the particular stakeholders with whom you work. Best wishes on this complicated and challenging—yet extremely rewarding—journey!

Chapter 1

Introduction to the Professional Development Schools Approach to School–University Partnerships

As the title indicates, this book is about a specific approach to school–university partnerships. A school–university partnership is any union of a school or school district and a university or college. Typically, these partnerships are formed with a P–12 institution and a university's teacher preparation program. School–university partnerships can be formed for any number of reasons, such as finding placements for student teachers, developing pipelines for future teachers, proximity, or professional learning, to name a few (Castle & Reilly, 2011; Clark, 1999).

Typically, the structure of professional development schools (PDS) consists of a school (elementary or secondary) and a university teacher education program. Interns or teacher candidates are in schools for extended periods of time learning to teach with support from a university faculty member and a mentor teacher from the school through an immersive experience. This is where connections between theory and practice are made through a university and school collaboration. "In their most developed form, PDSs embody fundamental changes in the basic assumptions about knowledge, teaching, and learning, and they support these new assumptions with organization, roles, and relationships" (Levine, 1997, p. 2). PDSs align with the notion that knowledge about pedagogy resides in both practice at a school and at the university level, making the school–university partnership a necessity, with the assumption that learning for teacher candidates, university faculty, mentor teachers, and students should be contextualized.

The partnerships might be one-sided or for only one reason, and when that endeavor or initiative has been completed, the relationship may fizzle and end. There are also long-lasting, thriving school–university partnerships, due primarily to personal relationships among people from each institution, funding, or ongoing initiatives that do not necessarily adhere to the main tenets of PDS. School–university partnership is a general term and can be used to describe a myriad of connections between some sort of school entity and a college or university.

The PDS approach is a very specific type of school–university partnership. The overall goal of the PDS approach is to positively impact student learning (Teitel, 2003). Snyder (1999) stated, "Determining an exact definition of PDS is difficult. It does not require much scratching beneath the surface rhetoric to realize the situation here is that having a PDS can mean anything and therefore means nothing. An idea, institution, or person has to stand for something, or it will fall for anything" (p. 137). Zenkov et al. (2016) discussed the importance of those who have been part of a PDS and have a great deal of experience with the approach be the determiners of the definition. The thinking was, basically, that if those involved in PDS don't decide on the meaning of PDS, someone else will. For instance, as previously mentioned, there are many types of partnerships for many different reasons, but many of them do not fall into the category of a PDS. Even so, the term "professional development school" has been used to describe almost every form of partnership between P–12 schools and other schools, colleges, or departments of education (SCDE). What is or is not a PDS can depend on the eye of the beholder (Brindley et al., 2008a, p. 71). Such broad generalization can dilute the original purposes of PDSs and what signifies a PDS relationship. Zenkov et al. (2016) stated, "Little sense of the history of PDSs, coupled with the tendency to include all who wish to participate in such structures, has resulted in a tradition of calling virtually every such organization a PDS and in confusion between institutions, within institutions, and even within teacher education departments" (p. 6). To avoid some of this confusion, let's delve into the history of the approach to gain a better understanding of the original thoughts and purposes behind the PDS approach.

The History of Professional Development Schools

The history of the concept of professional development schools began well before their inception, going all the way back to John Dewey. Dewey

(1859–1952) was a progressive thinker with a philosophical outlook on life called pragmatism. Typically, when progressive education is discussed, Dewey is referenced as one of the main players. His pragmatic theory of inquiry sought to provide intelligent methods for the purpose of social progress. Dewey saw human experience as an influence on education as well as social reform. "Dewey's work was centered on the role of education in helping to assure that the highest form of democratic society could be promoted" (Shaw, 2002, p. 29). He saw the schools as a prime location for fostering conditions for social change (Shaw, 2002).

Dewey illuminated the importance of experiential learning and problem-based learning, more specifically learning by doing or hands-on learning. Dewey expounded the significance of learners' interactions with reality with no modifications. He had an optimistic outlook on education and was the author of many writings on the state of education throughout the progressive education movement. He and his wife started a laboratory school in 1896. Dewey's ideas were pervasive and adopted (or adapted) by many aspects of society (Cremin, 1959).

In 1908, Abraham Flexner wrote a report on the medical field, and progressive influences were the impetus for his creation of teaching hospitals. Surgeons are in hospitals practicing techniques under the guidance of mentors (expert doctors) who carefully scaffold their development until they are ready to perform surgeries on their own. Flexner was greatly influenced by the ideas of John Dewey, particularly the connection between research and practice. Flexner designed teaching hospitals based on Dewey's perspectives, making practice in clinically rich environments an ideal model for doctors—and, eventually, for teachers. Just as you would not want your surgery performed by a novice with little training or practice on the operating table, you probably would not want your child's teacher to be someone with no, or little, classroom experience, having learned only the theoretical aspects of teaching in their college courses. It took decades, but in time Dewey's experiential learning notions were finally applied to the field of education.

Teacher candidates must have opportunities to practice teaching, and to reflect on their practice, early on and unceasingly in their teacher education programs and as novice teachers (Darling-Hammond & Baratz-Snowden, 2007; Sosin & Parnham, 1998). Sykes (1997) stated that learning to teach should happen in the setting where teaching occurs. However, the weakest area of teacher education has typically been the clinical aspect, which is tragic because most teachers will reflect that the clinical portion was the most crucial part of their teacher preparation. "[T]eaching, like medicine, is a profession of practice, and prospective teachers must be prepared to become expert practitioners who know how to use the knowledge of their profession to advance student learning and how to build their professional knowledge through practice" (NCATE, 2010, p. 2).

Soard (2018) has described the top 10 qualities of a teacher candidate. These qualities included a positive attitude, good communication skills, organization skills, a forgiving heart, brilliance in their subject area, a willingness to communicate with parents, respect for students, value for inquiring minds, dependability, and a liking of children. These are not necessarily qualities that teacher candidates can pick up while taking a course on children's literature or how to teach elementary mathematics on their college campus. Many of these are traits developed through actual work with children. "Although dispositions cannot be directly taught, they can be acquired in settings where they are regularly acted out, with opportunities to practice them" in clinically rich programs (Holmes Group, 1986, p. 60).

"Clinically rich programs have strong school–university partnerships and intentional and scaffolded clinical practice throughout the curriculum" (National Association for Professional Development Schools [NAPDS], 2021, p. 11). You will find, throughout this book, the importance of defining terms. What one school calls a clinically rich program may differ greatly from another. For instance, what one program calls a *clinically rich* program might actually be a *clinically accompanied* program, where the student-teaching experience, which usually falls at the end of their program, is their first, and often only, opportunity to be in a school interacting with children in a classroom. "Clinically accompanied programs have clinical practice usually positioned as a capstone experience and detached from the rest of the educator preparation curriculum" (NAPDS 2021, p. 11). Clinically rich programs provide authentic experiences for teacher candidates to work with students throughout their teacher preparation program.

OK—now that you know how the term "clinically rich," in terms of teacher preparation, came about, let's situate the PDS approach to school–university partnerships historically for a deeper understanding. Many would say that there have been iterations of school–university partnerships for decades, with the current approach having the most potential for success. Throughout history, many attempts have been made to unite schools and universities to work together to reform the field of education. In 1892, the Committee of Ten brought together university faculty and teachers at a conference to discuss ways to reform education. This working group determined that universities needed to take more of an interest in what was going on in secondary and elementary schools (Clark, 1988; Cohen, 1974; Winitzky, Stoddart, & O'Keefe, 1992).

This leads us back to John Dewey. Around the same time that the Committee of Ten was discussing reform, John Dewey became an important voice for the restructuring of schools. As noted, Dewey and his wife started a laboratory school in 1896. Many thought laboratory schools would fit the bill as far as the need for educational reform. Laboratory schools can be called the predecessors to PDS. Dewey envisioned laboratory schools as research sites where school and university faculties could work together to prepare teachers (Stallings & Kowalski, 1990).

"Laboratory schools reached their peak in the 60s, but even at their height they failed to bring the research component of Dewey's ideal into existence" (Winitzky et al., 1992, p. 2). Lab school leaders did not prioritize research. Instead, the focus was on student learning and new teacher learning. Eventually, as the demand for teachers grew, there was not enough room in the lab schools, and teacher candidates were frequently placed in public schools to do their student teaching (Winitzky et al., 1992).

The convenience of the lab schools did not outweigh the criticisms, such as the cost and lack of diversity of these institutions. Many also thought that lab school settings were not realistic and did not particularly mirror what was going on in public schools at that time. They were very expensive and often viewed as elite schools for the children of university faculty and not reflective of real-world public schools (McIntyre & McIntyre, 2020). The drawbacks of laboratory schools eventually led to their downfall, beginning around 1969, and diminished the obvious direct connections between schools and universities (Stallings & Kowalski, 1990).

In fashion for a short time in the 1970s were portal schools, intended to serve as "a point of entry for promising new curricula and practices" (Chambers & Olmstead, 1971, p. 2). The goals of portal schools were to provide environments for educating new teachers, serve as research sites for university faculty, and provide real-life situations for trying out new practices and curricula. Different from laboratory schools, portal schools had advisory committees comprised of representatives from both schools and the university. They had a collaborative selection method and carved out planning time for developing and planning based on goals. The demise of portal schools was complete by around 1980 (Stallings & Kowalski, 1990).

Despite all the criticisms of laboratory schools, relationships between schools and universities continued to be viewed as beneficial (Zenkov et al., 2016), which provided part of the impetus for the onset of professional development schools.

John Goodlad began publishing books containing his ideas on school reform, such as 1959's *The Nongraded Elementary School*. Goodlad's ideas sparked discussions and debates about the status and future of schools in the United States. While education in the early part of the 20th century focused a great deal on progressive ideals, the 1960s was an era of educational reform. The civil rights–related Elementary and Secondary Education Act was signed by President Johnson in 1965, when the United States was embroiled in the Vietnam War. As far as schools were concerned, "Energy that might have gone to innovation shifted to evaluation. That is where significant federal dollars were spent in the late 1960s and early 1970s" (Goodlad, 1993, pp. 27–28). Schools were not characterized by a process of renewal. "There were not in place the processes and structures through which teachers were engaged in continuously inquiring into and thoughtfully effecting changes" (Goodlad, 1993, p. 28). Central to Goodlad's beliefs was this concept of renewal.

The term "partner school" was introduced as the "concept of a school where personnel from both sets of institutions join in the renewal and the socialization of teachers-to-be in the process" (Goodlad, 1993, p. 29). Goodlad, Sirotnik, and Soder initiated efforts in support of simultaneous educational renewal through teacher preparation programs as part of school–university partnerships. They created the Center for Educational Renewal (CER) in 1985 at the University of Washington, Seattle, to work toward simultaneously improving teacher preparation and schools to foster educational renewal (Paufler & Amrein-Beardsley, 2016). For more on Goodlad and his contributions, see our "Spotlight on John Goodlad" at the end of our chapter.

Reform movements of the 1980s set the stage for the PDS concept (Levine, 1997). *A Nation at Risk* by the National Commission of Excellence in Education was released in 1983 and called for education reform (Ferrara, 2014). A report from the Ford Foundation in 1985 entitled *Teacher Development in Schools* included very specific ways to move the field of education forward. "Contributing to an emerging conception of professional development schools, this report spoke directly to how these more dynamic schools would enable the preparation, induction, and socialization of prospective and novice teachers" (Howey, 2011, p. 326 in Neapolitan (Ed). Taking Stock of Professional Development Schools: What's Needed Now). The Carnegie Forum on Education and the Economy (1986) released

A Nation Prepared: Teachers for the 21st Century. The Report of the Task Force on Teaching as a Profession, which called for a major restructuring of teacher education. To raise teacher education standards, the Carnegie Forum recommended improving educational preparation by requiring a bachelor's degree as a prerequisite for the professional study of teaching. These professional education courses could then be situated at the graduate level, with teacher candidates participating in clinical internships (Burton & Greher, 2007). In the same year, the Holmes Group (later renamed the Holmes Partnership) also reported on the preparation of teachers (Howey, 2011).

The idea of Professional Development Schools emerged from *Tomorrow's Teachers* by the Holmes Group (1986). This was a group of deans from across the United States who sought to find ways to improve teacher education programs and the teaching profession in response to the criticism in *A Nation at Risk*. The PDS approach was conceptualized by the Holmes Group as a way to strengthen ties between public schools and institutions of higher education, and thus improve education (Darling-Hammond, 1994; Ferrara, 2014; Holmes Group, 1986; Klingner Leftwich, & van Garderen, 2004; Kochan & Kunkel, 1998).

The goal of the Holmes Group was to change teacher education and professionalize teaching (Johnston-Parsons, 2012). The Holmes Group agenda included an action plan with five goals for schools and universities (Ferrara, 2014). PDS stemmed from the group's agenda item number four, "To connect our own institutions to schools" (Holmes Group, 1986, p. 12). This item recognized that college faculty and teacher experts could work together in schools to study and improve teaching. The Holmes Group argued that all "aspects of professional studies must be integrated into the clinical experience where formal knowledge must be used as a guide to practical action" (p. 58). And so, PDS was born. Similarly, around the same time, John Goodlad and colleagues began to advocate for *centers of pedagogy* and created the National Network for Educational Renewal (NNER). Along with the Holmes Group, NNER moved the focus to the universities in partnership to make teacher preparation more rigorous and clinically rich (Howey, 2011).

The Holmes Group released another report in 1990 entitled "Tomorrow's Schools: Principles for the Design of Professional Development Schools." This report offered a different perspective on teachers and how they fit into school reform. In the Group's 1986 report, the university was deemed the lone source of educational wisdom, and teachers were called on to become standard educational researchers for the sake of educational practice improvement (Howey, 2011). But by 1990, the idea of PDS was becoming more widely accepted, and the report provided more specific information on the attributes of PDSs and highlighted the role of universities. The report helped center universities in partnerships with schools to move toward more rigorous teacher preparation and moving the perception to teachers as professionals. "The report called for a subset of schools focused on teacher education, akin to a medical school's teaching hospital" (Howey, 2011). Teachers were also viewed as co-researchers. The report explained this as teacher-centered inquiry, and this would prompt some structural changes in higher education (Whitford & Villaume, 2014).

During the same time period, Darling-Hammond and Lieberman (1990) sought to promote clear connections between the schools and the reform of teacher education. They created the National Center for Restructuring Education, Schools, and Teaching at Teachers College. One of the center's initiatives was the PDS Network. This brought together representatives from schools and universities from approximately 30 to 40 PDS partnerships a few times a year for reciprocal learning in support of professional development school partnerships while making improvements to the PDS partnerships to have a significant impact on educational reform (Howey, 2011; Lauter, 1998).

According to Levine (1997), the idea of PDS can be attributed to the following three concepts: (1) an image of teaching as a profession that includes a direction of inquiry along with knowledge-based practices coupled with interaction with colleagues; (2) collaboration between the school and university, which includes both the knowledge and expertise regarding teaching based on the needs and practices of the other institution; and (3) the notion that teacher education and staff development and research must be aligned to new professional and curricular standards. PDSs support these three concepts by developing school–university partnerships in school settings with the goal of supporting teacher preparation, staff development, research, and quality education for all children.

Use of the transformative PDS approach would likely require many changes for the institutions involved in the partnership. For instance, a school's mission needed to change, along with the manner in which a school functions in such a way created to execute a certain interaction conveyed as praxis. Praxis is the interaction between theory and practice. "The concept of a Professional Development School where teaching and learning are subjects of both inquiry and practice embodies this idea of praxis. The Holmes Group, a group of elite schools of education, adopted praxis when it presented the PDS concept in *Tomorrow's Schools* (1990), and pressed for the PDS as a commitment by schools of teacher education in *Tomorrow's Schools of Education* (1995)" (Sosin and Parham, 1998, p. 3).

Both partners needed to link to the field in ways that concurrently enrich both inquiry and practice, which demonstrates the concept of praxis. "Praxis is reflexive and evaluative. It influences and shapes the bases of knowledge that, reciprocally, influence and shape human action. It is influenced by underlying beliefs, values, and human interests, and it must therefore make such normative content manifest and subject to critical inquiry and action. It is knowing in action a dialectical process of reconstructing knowledge in the context of practice" (Soder & Sirotnik, 1990, pp. 402–403).

Not only do these partnerships foster increased educational experiences, but they also allow teacher candidates to decide early on if being a teacher is the right path for them. Once a teacher preparation program is dedicated to providing these authentic experiences for teacher candidates across the program, they can move to building school–university partnerships and eventually professional development schools (PDSs). "Unique and particularly intense school–university partnerships, PDSs should be built upon four pillars: (1) the improvement of P–12 student learning; (2) the joint engagement in teacher education activities; (3) the promotion of professional growth of all its participants; and (4) the construction of knowledge through intentional, synergistic research endeavors" (Holmes Partnership, 2007, as cited in the NAPDS, 2021, p. 6). Professional development schools allow teacher candidates to have increased time in schools with children, scaffolding from experienced teachers, and an authentic way to practice their teaching skills (Darling-Hammond, 2005).

The Holmes Group's (1987) report is a seminal work in the PDS field. You will see it cited many times in this text, particularly in this first chapter. Although it was written so many years ago, it illustrates the initial goals of PDS and the contexts in which it derived. Sadly, some of the challenges facing the educational field in 1987 remain problems today. "Professional Development Schools, the analogue of medical education's teaching hospitals, would bring practicing teachers and administrators together with university faculty in partnerships that improve teaching and learning on the part of their respective students" (Holmes Group, 1986, p. 62).

There are so many things to learn when becoming a teacher. Varying by state, some teacher education programs can only mandate teacher candidates to take a certain number of courses in education, for instance, a 4-year teacher education program in Texas may mandate fewer courses than a 4-year program in other states (Cochran-Smith et al., 2008). As well, changing licensing standards to address new standards in content areas (Darling-Hammond & Baratz-Snowden, 2007) make it almost impossible for teacher preparation programs to teach everything needed to become a successful teacher in college courses. "Clearly, there is much more to effective teaching than standing in the front of the room giving information to students. And there is much that teachers need to learn in order to do this complex job well" (Darling-Hammond & Baratz-Snowden, 2007, p. 113).

Acknowledgment that teacher candidates should be working in schools or community organizations (Boyle-Baise & McIntyre, 2008) with children and teachers at the very early stages of their teacher preparation program is a clear impetus for the development of school–university partnerships (Darling-Hammond & Baratz-Snowden, 2007; NAPDS Nine Essentials, 2021).

Now, you might be thinking back on your preservice experiences in a school in your teacher preparation program, but it was not called a PDS. There is a difference between a PDS and a school at which your professor used to teach and would ask former colleagues to help them out and work with their students. PDS is not placing a group of students across multiple buildings where the college faculty member must drive around and is not able to spend a good amount of time building relationships in one school. PDS is not just a school close to the university. "[T]here has been a coalescence and a codification of what it means to be a PDS along with a growth in networks to support and help develop PDSs" (Teitel, 2004, p. 402). Although PDS relationships can be quite different, they are built on the same basic characteristics.

The main characteristic of a PDS is a mutually beneficial partnership between a school and university. The teacher education program is not just dropping pre-service teachers off at a school and hoping for the best. The university course instructor is present at the PDS when the teacher candidates are at the school working in classrooms. "PDSs are designed to be those funded, designated sites where clinical practice is centralized in the teacher preparation curriculum and embedded in the P–12 setting" (NAPDS, 2021, p. 11). Some PDS programs will have a clinical faculty or professor in residence right at the school site. The college faculty member teaches courses at the school site and might even have an office there to meet with teacher candidates. As well, the college faculty member also works with the school administration and teachers to complete action research and/or provide professional development based on the school's needs. PDS configurations can vary based on the partners (Doolittle, Sudeck, & Rattigan, 2008; Myers & Price, 2010).

The PDS relationship involves leveraging the resources of both the university and schools to educate and support teacher candidates and serve the needs of P–12 learners. Partners can share resources such as money, space, time, expertise, and materials. The pooling of resources among partners allows for shared initiatives, programs, research, or professional development or professional learning based on the needs of school partners (Yendol-Hoppey & Smith, 2011).

After the Holmes Group moved on to other initiatives, there was a core group of people doing PDS work. In 2000, the group held a conference sponsored by the University of South Carolina, and that grew into a national professional organization. It became a national yearly conference called the Professional Development Schools National Conference. The National Association of Professional Development Schools (NAPDS) was formed in 2005, stemming from the work of approximately 75 PDS directors and college of education deans in order to continue their dialogue and construct a means by which this could occur throughout the year as opposed to once a year at an annual conference. The group's communication across two years led to the creation of NAPDS at the PDS National Conference in 2005. NAPDS still exists today; however, in July 2023, the organization voted to change the name to the National Association for School–University Partners (NASUP) in order to be more inclusive of all kinds of school–university partnerships, not just PDSs. Since its inception, the goal of NAPDS has been to have equal representation from the P–12 universe and from university/college teacher education programs on the Executive Council and Board of Directors.

NAPDS tackled questions about what is and what is not a PDS. In 2008, the NAPDS Executive Council and Board of Directors released "What It Means to Be a Professional Development School." Brindley et al. (2008a) stated, "It takes the very hard work of multiple people with multiple perspectives. This is what allows each PDS to be unique while still holding firm to the essentials" (p. 74).

What Is PDS?

While there are a number of definitions of the PDS approach, the most commonly used was formulated by the Holmes Group as a "school for the development of novice professionals, for continuing development of novice professionals, and for the research and development of the teaching profession" (p. 1). According to Goodlad (1988), the strength of such a model is that by combining and focusing resources to support a mutual concern, opportunities for real reform are increased.

What makes a partnership a PDS remains actively discussed today. The National Association of School University–Partnerships (NASUP) sought to determine the differences among PDSs, school–university partnerships, community schools, service learning, and other kinds of partnerships that can influence teacher preparation and schools. Ideas suggested to define a PDS include the following:

- Levine (1997) stated, "PDSs weave together the strands of teacher education and school reform" (p. 63).

- A PDS is any school–university partnership that adheres to the NAPDS Nine Essentials (Brindley et al., 2008a).

- The professional development school (PDS) is a place where preservice teachers spend much of their time and preparation on-site in a school that is affiliated with a university (Wong & Glass, 2005, as cited in Walmsley et al.).

- "The mission of the PDS partnership is integrated into the partnership institutions. PDS work is expected and supported and reflects what is known about best practices" (NCATE, 2001, p. 67).

- "The purpose of professional development schools is to promote student learning" (Teitel, 2003, p. xvii).

- "PDSs aim to provide new models of teacher education and development by serving as exemplars of practice, builders of knowledge, and vehicles for communicating professional understandings among teacher educators, novices, and veteran teachers" (Darling-Hammond, 2005, p. 1)

- "Professional development schools (PDSs) are innovative types of school—college partnerships designed to address this disconnection and finger-pointing and bring about the simultaneous renewal of schools and teacher education pro- grams—restructuring schools for improved student learning and revitalizing the preparation and professional development of experienced educators at the same time" (Teitel, 2003, p. 2).

- "Professional development schools are special cases of school–university collaboration in which the experience in partnership formation provides a rich background for the efforts to 'grow' PDSs" (Teitel, 2003, p. 3).

- "The PDS partnership differs from traditional university–school partnerships because the two groups share interaction and decision making on an equitable basis with a long-term commitment" (Walmsley et al., 2009).

- PDS is "developing and implementing improved approaches to teaching, learning, and leadership" (Teitel, 2003, p. 57).

- "Two institutions engaged in mutual renewal that are simultaneously trying to expand professional development opportunities" and engage in research and development in order to improve education (Teitel, 2003, p. 57).

- "Professional development schools are special schools where there are unique university-school relationships that can change a school culture and add value to students and the community" (Basile, 2009, p. 2).

- "The most comprehensive partnership arrangement with a variety of integrated components is the professional development school (PDS). PDSs offer an innovative strategy to create thoughtful collaborations between schools or school districts and institutions of higher education, seeking novel ways to respond to the needs of their respective organizations" (Ferrara, 2014, p. 5).

Brindley et al. (2008a) described that PDSs were meant to mentor new teachers, but most of the focus became centered on professional development or professional learning for teacher candidates as well as teachers, which may have led to the labeling of any school–university partnership as a PDS. Basically, PDSs strive for the best in the preparation of teachers and school environments to positively impact P–12 learners.

In almost 40 years, the initial idea of the Holmes Group has blossomed into countless PDS sites across the United States and internationally

(NAPDS, 2021). The foundation for these PDS sites involves some important frameworks.

Frameworks That Support PDSs

Many frameworks help guide the work of school–university partnerships and how they support clinically rich experiences for teacher candidates in teacher preparation programs with the hope of positively impacting PreK–12 learners. These frameworks will be discussed at length in the following subsections.

NAPDS NINE ESSENTIALS

NAPDS collaboratively developed the Nine Essentials (https://napds.org/nine-essentials/) that serve as a framework for what it means to be a PDS (2008, 2021). "The Essentials are one of the core contributions of NAPDS to the field of teacher education in the association's less than two decade long existence" (Zenkov et al., 2021, p. 21). These essentials are broad and somewhat flexible to guide a school–university partnership to be a PDS. The foreword of the second edition of the Nine Essentials states, "NAPDS invites individuals involved in school–university partnerships to share this statement with colleagues in the spirit of continuous improvement. By coming to terms with the challenges and opportunities inherent in this statement, we can collectively fulfill the vision of this remarkable and distinct partnership we call PDS" (2021, p. 5). The NAPDS Nine Essentials along with other frameworks and standards provide guidance to PDS participants for successful partnerships. Listed below are the Nine Essentials with examples from the SUNY Buffalo State PDS Consortium:

Essential 1 encapsulates, "A PDS is a learning community guided by a comprehensive, articulated mission that is broader than the goals of any single partner, and that aims to advance equity, antiracism, and social justice within and among schools, colleges/universities, and their respective community and professional partners" (Zenkov et al., 2021, p. 22).

NAPDS Essential 1 calls for a comprehensive mission. The mission should clearly state the promises made to each of the stakeholders in a community that promotes collaboration (NAPDS, 9 Essentials, 2021). The mission should also contain the four PDS pillars from the Holmes Partnership (2007), which include: (1) the improvement of P–12 student learning; (2) the joint engagement in educator preparation activities; (3) the promotion of professional growth of all participants; and the construction of knowledge through intentional, synergistic research endeavors (Ferrara, 2014; Zenkov et al., 2021).

The first of the Nine Essentials calls on PDS stakeholders to vehemently support antiracism endeavors, along with equitable and rightful teaching in an effort to address students' opportunity gaps (Zenkov et al., 2021).

The National Association for School–University Partnerships (NASUP) wrote the following mission statement:

> The National Association for School–University Partnerships advances the education profession by providing leadership, advocacy and support to sustain professional development schools as learning communities that improve student learning, prepare educators through clinical practice, provide reciprocal professional development, and conduct shared inquiry. (https://nasup.org)

The SUNY Buffalo State PDS Consortium's mission encompasses similar characteristics.

The Professional Development Schools Consortium (PDS) partnership between the School of Education (SOE) and the Teacher Education Unit (TEU) at SUNY Buffalo State and participating schools is a collaborative effort. The partnership is dedicated to college faculty, school administrators, practicing teachers, and teacher candidates exploring effective practices to:

> (1) cooperatively mentor teacher candidates and provide close connections to authentic classroom practice;
>
> (2) promote shared professional development for all constituents;
>
> (3) impact student learning; and
>
> (4) research innovative and best educational practices. (https://pds.buffalostate.edu/what-pds)

The mission of the PDS Consortium explains the organization's purpose or reason for being in existence. The first essential stresses that the goals of the group must be broad and not align with the goals of a small group of people or single PDS (Duffy, 1994; Lefever-Davis et al., 2007).

Both the NASUP mission statement and the mission of the SUNY Buffalo State PDS Consortium contain a version of the four PDS pillars (Holmes Group, 2007). These pillars involve improving student learning P–12, collaborative efforts to prepare educators, professional development for all, and the building of knowledge through research. However, currently, both mission statements are missing the other piece of the first NAPDS Essential (2021) that calls for a focus on advancing social justice and anti-racism. In 2004, Teitel stated that "there has been an increase in attention and some slow movement toward using professional development schools to address the diversity and equity challenges of the country" (p. 402). This was 20 years ago, and these mission statements still do not reflect an initiative toward advancing social justice and antiracism. Teitel (2004) also stated, "The challenges of changing society around the deep-seated issues of race and class are both daunting and essential. The current high level of focus on the achievement gap in many sectors of the educational community and society can provide important support for ensuring that PDSs move this way" (p. 413). Current achievement gap data should be seriously considered as part of the continuous renewal of PDS.

Initially, PDS sites were to be committed to overcoming various social and educational barriers to promote better teaching and learning for all students in an unequal society (Holmes Group, 1987). "The Holmes Group, whose reports—especially *Tomorrow's Schools* (1990)—provided powerful intellectual impetus for PDSs, makes very clear the commitment of the PDS as an institution to remedy the inequities of the society, as they get played out in education. Nonetheless, there are often differing views among PDS participants of what equity means" (Teitel, 2004, p. 411). The original intent of the PDS approach included school renewal and improvement of PDS which is mentioned in another essential. The advancement of social justice and anti-racism was given a place of prominence in the first NAPDS Essential (2021), but PDS advocates and researchers need to study and provide more specific information or data on how the advancement of social justice and anti-racism is actually being implemented within school–university partnerships. "[E]ven when understandings and purposes of the diversity and equity agenda are clear, the underlying challenges of implementation still remain high. In large measure, this is because really addressing issues of diversity and equity requires deeper, more fundamental change than almost anything else on the table in professional development schools" (Teitel, 2004, p. 14). The collaborative nature of PDS relationships make them an ideal space to cultivate ideas around teaching for equity (NAPDS, 2021).

Essential 2 focuses on clinical preparation. It states, "A PDS is committed to nurturing and developing the next generation of educators by engaging candidates and valuing them as active members of the school and PDS communities. In a PDS, educator preparation is a joint responsibility involving all partners in shared decision making. PDSs serve as authentic educational preparation setting where coursework and clinical experiences are closely coupled, ensuring that educators are profession ready" (NAPDS, 2021, p. 15). Simply put, "A Professional Development School (PDS) embraces the preparation of educators through clinical practice" (Burns et al., 2022, p. 39). In the first edition of Essential 2 (2008) there was no explicit connection related to PDS's long history with clinical practice. In the second edition, Essential 2 states, "PDSs clearly stand for what they have long been doing—attending to the intentional and thoughtful clinical preparation of educators through partnership between schools and universities" (Burns et al., 2022, p. 39).

Having teacher candidates in schools early in their teacher preparation program is a main component of PDS. The American Association of Colleges for Teacher Education (AACTE) (2018) Clinical Practice Commission defined clinical practice as, "a model to prepare high quality educators with and through a pedagogical skill set that provides articulated benefits for every participant, while being fully embedded in the P–12 setting" (p. 6, as cited in NAPDS, 2021). This was echoed by the National Research Council (NRC) report *Preparing Teachers: Building Evidence for Sound Policy*, which identifies clinical preparation (or "field experience") as one of the three "aspects of teacher preparation that are likely to have the highest potential for effects on outcomes for students, along with content knowledge and the quality of teacher candidates" (2010, p. 180). Learning to teach in the authentic setting of a classroom equals more successful teachers.

Other national groups weighed in on characteristics of effective clinical practice. Here is a summary of *10 Design Principles for Clinically Based Preparation* provided by the National Council for Accreditation of Teacher Education (NCATE) (2010). In clinically based situations, the main focus should be on student learning. Clinical preparation is dynamically woven into every aspect of teacher education. Data is used to examine the progress of teacher candidates and their teacher education programs. Teacher education programs produce teachers who are content area experts and how to teach the content area with a focus on innovation, collaboration, and problem solving. An interactive, professional community is provided in which teacher candidates learn and grow. The clinical educators from higher education and P–12 schools must be effective practitioners and are carefully chosen and prepared. There are sites designated and funded to provide for the clinical preparation of teacher candidates. Technological tools should be utilized to nurture impactful teacher preparation. Improvement in teacher education is driven by data gathered systematically as part of a collaborative research agenda. Effective clinical preparation is based on strategic partnerships. To achieve clinically based preparation that completely incorporates content, pedagogy, and professional coursework, it is important to overhaul existing models of clinical practice using the 10 aforementioned principles.

At SUNY Buffalo State, teacher candidates go into schools to observe as part of their early coursework. They also partake in service learning as part of their coursework in schools or working with children. In methods courses, teacher candidates are in classrooms teaching small groups of students. As student teachers, they employ a co-teaching model with their mentor teachers. Coordinators work hard to ensure that teacher candidates are having these experiences at rural, suburban, and urban schools. Teacher candidates put into practice what they learn as part of their coursework with guidance from mentor teachers and college faculty. They also obtain the experience of being in schools and the daily procedures and routines that come with the career of being a teacher.

Essential 3 of the NAPDS relates to professional learning and leading. It states: "A PDS is a context for continuous professional learning (PL) and leading for all participants, guided by need and a spirit and practice of inquiry" (NAPDS, 2021). A PDS is the hub of professional development for all stakeholders based on the needs of those same stakeholders. A PDS should foster an atmosphere of co-learning and professional development for all. Because PDS brings together a variety of stakeholders with equal voices in the partnership, no matter what their position, each stakeholder provides input and has the opportunity to be a leader.

Professional development, or professional learning (PL), has been found to have a positive impact on teaching and learning. Successful professional development should be situated in the authentic settings of the learners, the topics should be of interest to the participants, there should be a mix of both knowledge and pedagogies, it should occur over a long span of time, and the PL should be comprised of both collaborative and engaging experiences for attendees (Polly et al., 2022).

Doolittle et al. (2008) shared the results of projects to foster school improvement undertaken by PDS schools with the help of faculty liaisons using a systemic change model. They championed PDS has a key component to the learning, working, leading, and changing of three school learning communities. "Because educational change is complex, PDS partnerships can provide a supportive yet rigorous structure with attention centered on research-based models and systems" (Doolittle et al., 2008, p. 309). They concluded that an effective PDS can assist schools to function as successful learning communities.

The SUNY Buffalo State PDS has an advisory board comprised of teacher candidates, college faculty, and school partners. Board members bring forth needs, questions, problems, and challenges that occur among the partners. For instance, a few years ago, administrators on the advisory board expressed the need for teacher candidates to know more about social emotional learning. One partner school hosted a PDS meeting and brought in an expert on trauma with whom the school's faculty often worked to speak to stakeholders. A taskforce was started by faculty members on campus and provided various events for faculty, teacher candidates, and school partners pertaining to social emotional learning. Taskforce members helped plan how more content on social emotional learning could be embedded in the courses that teacher candidates were required to take. The PDS obtained funds to pay experts to come to campus and speak to all the consortium members from grants. Since this was brought to the PDS Advisory Board, PDS has led the way with professional development on social emotional learning for teacher candidates, college faculty, and school partners.

Essential 4 deals with reflection and innovation. It states: "A PDS values and respects professional knowledge that is practical as well as theoretical and that recognizes the influence of context and culture. PDSs are living laboratories for creating, implementing, refining, and sharing innovative approaches to teaching and learning. Any PDS participant may initiate innovations, and everyone should have the opportunity to serve in the role of leader and learner. Through innovation and reflection, PDSs generate new knowledge about teaching and learning" (NAPDS, 2021, p. 15). All voices in the partnership are respected and valued for their contributions to the collaborative effort. The positions of stakeholders in the partnership are fluid, and roles can fluctuate from leader to learner, with all contributing to the group's understanding of teaching and learning (Stoicovy et al., 2022).

The structure of the PDS affords opportunities for reflection for all stakeholders. The PDS provides a space where reflection of teaching and learning is valued and practiced. For instance, Shandomo (2010) used critical reflection with teacher candidates enrolled in a methods course situated at a PDS. She stated: "Critical reflection blends learning through experiences with theoretical and technical learning to form new knowledge constructions and new behaviors and insights" (p. 101). Reflection allows teacher candidates to process their clinically rich experiences with the content of their education courses. Freese (1999) discussed the value of reflection and a consistent framework for reflecting for teacher candidates along with other stakeholders to follow over the course of their program in a PDS setting. A repetitive framework for reflection can encourage the use of this valuable practice throughout the PDS community.

The SUNY Buffalo State PDS consortium is continuously reflecting on its practices and initiatives with a focus on the impact on teacher candidates and ultimately P–12 learners. PDS leadership often sends out surveys to stakeholders to check in and obtain feedback on the activities of the consortium overall. As well, stakeholders are asked to complete an evaluation form after all PDS events, so PDS leadership and participants can reflect on what worked and what did not work. At the end of each academic year, the liaison committee at each PDS develops a report or some kind of representation, such as a slide of what occurred at their PDS that year.

Innovation is coupled with reflection in the NAPDS Essential 4. Due to the constant changes in schools and the field of education, innovation in all areas and for all stakeholders is key. Groth et al. (2017) detailed how their elementary PDS program embraced innovation. They have different "Pathways to Partnership" at George Mason University (p. 3). Their innovative and flexible structure allowed PDS partners to select how they wanted to participate by selecting one of the three pathways, "partner school, clinical practice school, or collaborative inquiry school" (p. 3). The first level of partner school hosts teacher candidates engaging in clinical field hours. At this level, the partner school is still eligible for all the benefits of the PDS, including participation in stakeholder meetings, and are provided with scaffolding to work their way up to a clinical practice school (final internships) or a collaborative inquiry site where there is a college faculty member at the school collaborating with the school partners on research and projects. Other innovative efforts included using a video tool for collaboration and reflection on instruction, creative use of year-long teacher candidates to help school partners with substitute teacher shortages, and a grow-your-own program with teacher candidates hired by the partner schools.

The PDS frameworks foster an environment for the creation of innovative approaches to solving problems of practice (del Prado Hill & Garas-York, 2020). Along with reflection, the Buffalo State PDS is also dedicated to innovation. During times when in-person professional development was not possible, PDS leadership made sessions available synchronously and asynchronously online. At the onset of the academic year in 2021, the consortium sponsored an initiative called "All Hands on Deck" to prepare teacher candidates, college faculty, and school partners to work with P–12 learners who were coming back to school full-time after a prolonged period of online and hybrid learning. Based on the needs of the stakeholders, sessions were planned and held online in the areas of social emotional learning, equity, learning acceleration, tutoring, co-teaching, classroom management, math, and literacy. Being innovative helped the PDS reach even more stakeholders by offering professional development in flexible ways.

Essential 5, which encompasses research and results, states: "A PDS is a community that engages in collaborative research and participates in the public sharing of results in a variety of outlets" (NAPDS, 2021, p. 4). Typically, in a PDS, the topics of research stem from the questions or needs of school partners as opposed to research ideas from the college being foisted on the schools which occurs more often than not. "The people most intimately responsible for children's learning in elementary and secondary schools are not sufficiently valued by the education school. Schoolteachers and young learners, who should be the focus of the education school's concern, are kept at arm's length. They are a sideshow to the performance in the center ring, where professors carry out their work insulated from the messiness and hurly-burly of elementary and secondary education" (Holmes Group, 1987, p. 35). On the contrary, as part of PDS, school challenges, questions, and ideas are tackled by all stakeholders.

Stakeholders in a PDS collaboratively work together on research and its dissemination. PDSs are inquiry based for the purpose of improving mutually agreed upon areas of the PDS community that ultimately lead to well-prepared teachers and positively impact P–12 learners. PDS research can also contribute to the educational field and policies.

The SUNY Buffalo State PDS values action research and views research as a kind of professional development. Action research mini grants are awarded to collaborative groups of college faculty and school partners for projects in schools involving teacher candidates. The projects and results are often published or presented to all stakeholders who attend an annual PDS conference. Some teacher candidates also take part in PDS research and have opportunities to present at local and national conferences.

In addition, PDS research serves to renew schools, districts, and teacher preparation programs. The NAPDS Nine Essentials (2021) define simultaneous renewal as "the continuous process of getting better together" (p. 14). Remember, renewal was at the core of Goodlad's ideas relating to school–university partnerships (Goodlad, 1994). Polly et al. (2022) stated: "It is not feasible to engage in deep simultaneous renewal and processes of continuous improvement if participants in PDS or school–university partnerships are not collaborating and involved in the research and examination of teaching and learning related to the partnership" (p. 43). Renewal occurs when PDS stakeholders change and grow together for the sake of improvement. They collaboratively study and adjust the facets of their relationship(s), such as goals, structures, and duties within the PDS community as part of this renewal.

Essential 6 is articulated agreements, stating that "PDS partners collaboratively create, review, and renew written articulated agreements. The documents (1) identify the commitment of each entity, (2) articulate the expectation that each partner will have an equal voice in decision making including in determining the content of the agreement(s), describe the roles and responsibilities of various individuals, and (3) outline processes for developing, maintaining, and identifying, desired shared outcomes to promote sustainability and renewal" (NAPDS, 2021). The revision of Essential 6 underscores the importance of the articulated agreement as a critical aspect of PDS (Goree et al., 2022). When entering a PDS partnership, it is important to lay out the roles and responsibilities of each stakeholder. As well, the updated Essential 6 stresses the addition of clearly focused commitments and expectations in the articulated agreement (Goree et al., 2022). The agreement should ensure that the needs of all parties are being met to form a mutually beneficial relationship with clear expectations. "If schools and universities can work together to identify partnership sites and express that commitment through formal agreements, transforming teacher education becomes more possible" (Burns et al., 2016, p. 9). As well, these agreements should evolve as the partnership evolves (NAPDS

Nine Essentials, 2021). The agreements can change as far as the level of participation and based on the changing field of education (Groth et al., 2017).

The agreements used by SUNY Buffalo State demonstrate different levels of participation (initial, beginning, developing, and at-standard); in this instance, the school gets a small stipend from the university, with the amount depending on the level of participation, and the agreement is signed by university faculty and administrators and school administrators and liaisons. The structure of these relationships can vary. There are PDS relationships where the school district pays the college, or they pool their money together to better meet the needs of all stakeholders based on an agreed-upon set of expectations.

Essential 7, governance structures, states: "Shared governance is the collective oversight and responsibility of and to the partnership. It involves joint decision making and leadership. It recognizes and values each partner's perspective in the collaborative process. Partnerships must be strategically based on the recognition that none can fully do the job alone" (NAPDS Nine Essentials, 2021, p. 14). A sustainable foundation is needed for a successful PDS to guide the work of the partnership. The governance structures should allow for collaboration and reflection with a means by which all stakeholders' voices are heard. The governance structures should also allow for shared decision making in various areas of the partnership, such as goals, evaluation of outcomes for constant improvement, and how resources will be leveraged. Participation in these relationships must be mutually beneficial for all the stakeholder groups (NAPDS Nine Essentials, 2021). "PDS partnerships include structures that not only guide the work of the partnership, but also enable collaboration, ongoing communication, and reflection among all participants" (Coler et al., 2022, p. 42).

Governance between a college and a school involves four critical tasks. First, the governance structures must bring together two organizations and iron out any differences and the delineation of responsibilities. Second, to support mutual renewal, the governance structures must detail the roles of the stakeholders and provide pathways for change and a means by which the partnership can exist among other structures that govern the partners individually. A third critical task is managing the resources of the partnership, such as money and time. Finally, the fourth critical task is that governance structure should provide for long-term goal setting and evaluation that meets the needs of all stakeholders to implement the renewal process (Teitel, 1998). The specifics of the governance structures will vary from partnership to partnership. For instance, special area or secondary teacher preparation programs may need to enter into partnerships with a district as opposed to one school because individual schools may have only a couple teachers or just one teacher in the program's content area, such as art education (Wolf, 2021). "It is impossible to have a shared governance without equity and social justice" (Coler et al., 2022). The necessity of these concepts is more explicitly stated in the updated NAPDS Nine Essentials (2021) based on the requirement that all voices are to be heard for shared governance (Coler et al., 2022).

The SUNY Buffalo State PDS governance structure begins with a PDS director or co-directors. The director works to make PDS a collaborative space for all PDS stakeholders by determining and executing the most beneficial ways to obtain feedback from teacher candidates, college faculty, and school partners. Each PDS site has a liaison committee or team comprised of a college faculty member, the school administrator, and usually a teacher or other school representative. They meet across the year to determine placements, reflect on the PDS relationship, collaborate, and plan next steps or future projects. Members of the liaison team represent each school site at PDS meetings during the year. The PDS advisory board meets three to four times a year and provides a space for all stakeholders to express views, needs, and information. This structure allows for the communication of ideas, collaboration, and shared decision making.

Essential 8 deals with boundary-spanning roles. It states: "PDSs—figuratively the spaces between schools and universities-are conceived of as places of discovery and experimentation, governed by ideas and ideals and not bound by the traditions of any one institution. They are designed to renew a culture of teaching, learning, leading, and schooling. PDS participants span boundaries between university and P–12 settings; thus, their work is situated in the 'third space,' which distinguishes it from work occurring solely in school or only in university organizations. PDS participants assume a variety of boundary-spanning roles, defined by each respective PDS. These boundary-spanning roles incorporate necessary functions and are integral to the operations of each PDS" (NAPDS, 2021, p. 16). This essential focuses on the work of individuals in the space between the school site and the college. NAPDS labeled it the "third space." The work of PDS is situated in that space, not solely on the college campus and not only at the school site. The third space can be depicted as the middle, overlapping part of a Venn diagram where the two circles represent the university and the P–12 school and the overlapping part represents PDS (Consenza et al., 2021; NAPDS Nine Essentials, 2021). "The PDS is a unique kind of community that lies between two or more organizations" (NAPDS Nine Essentials, 2021, p. 9). This space is an area of collaboration and experimentation. It is a space for discovery and the exchange of ideas not holding to the ideals of one particular stakeholder group or PDS site. These spaces can invigorate teaching and learning between the college and school sites.

This third space allows for individuals who are part of the PDS community to become boundary spanners. These people link the college and P–12 schools based on their understanding of the culture of both organizations. The work of these hybrid educators spans the boundaries of both the university and P–12 institutions (NAPDS Nine Essentials, 2021). Regarding boundary-spanners, Consenza et al. (2022) stated: "They are unique roles as compared to other positions at schools and universities because they are only necessary for the PDS. These roles can also develop as boundary spanning roles where the individual doing the work bridges both partners or represents both institutions concurrently. Whether they emerge on their own, or created in a formal way, these new roles typically concentrate on better teaching, better learning and provide educators more opportunities to for leadership" (p. 44).

Burns and Badiali (2020) described three important components that describe hybrid educators (boundary spanners). The first component called for a description of the educator's original role in either a university or P–12 school and their role in the third space (PDS). The second component involves the definition of role characteristics. This includes how long they will be in the role and primarily where they work. Finally, the third component calls for the definition of the role responsibility as supervisory tasks. This entails the nature of the hybrid educator's responsibilities as they relate to supervisory tasks.

Burns and Badiali (2020) also described the transformation that a hybrid educator can undergo while working in the third space as a boundary spanner. The subject of their study reflected more deeply, helped to preserve relationships, prioritized the students, and worked to distribute leadership across the partnership. The implications are that being more reflective, preserving relationships, and prioritizing the students are all characteristics of a leader. They found, "that powerful and transformative professional learning can occur through hybrid roles in PDSs" (p. 23). The hybrid educator role not only helps to prepare teacher candidates but also serves as an impactful professional learning event that can transform the hybrid educator into a teacher leader.

In Garas-York et al. (2017), PDS stakeholders from the SUNY Buffalo State PDS consortium shared stories and strategies pertaining to boundary-spanning roles, such as creating a Global Book Hour at school and community PDS sites. The college faculty member involved in this project took on a boundary spanning role as she helped to prepare teacher candidates while working as part of a PDS to impact P–12 learners and their parents.

Finally, NAPDS **Essential 9** concerns Resources and Recognition. "A PDS provides dedicated and shared resources and establishes traditions to recognize, enhance, celebrate, and sustain the work of partners and the partnership" (NAPDS Nine Essentials, 2021, p. 16). Because a PDS requires substantial resources above what is allocated at individual universities or schools, partners can each dedicate resources to support the work of the PDS (NAPDS Nine Essentials, 2021). These resources include time, money, space, and expertise, to name a few. For instance, Marchand et al. (2013) described how they were able to pool valuable resources, such as time and expertise, to conduct a rigorous evaluation of their PDS that might not have occurred without this community of sharing. Leveraging resources for renewal and professional development is vital for the success of a PDS.

As previously mentioned, a key attribute of a PDS is the leveraging of resources. Again, the SUNY Buffalo PDS consortium advisory board decided to delve more deeply into the topic of social emotional learning. One PDS site provided a space for the group to meet and brought in a speaker to help deepen the knowledge of all stakeholders. The college, in turn, sponsored sessions on campus for all stakeholders to learn more about social emotional learning using grant money to bring in national experts in the field. When a PDS school was receiving online professional development related to social emotional learning, college faculty were also invited to participate. The sharing of space and expertise allowed all stakeholders to learn more about an important topic to better prepare teacher candidates and positively impact P–12 learners.

"Essential Nine concerns two separate, but related ideas. We have discussed resources that support and maintain partnerships. Now we turn to celebratory traditions that enhance a partnership community by pulling partners closer together" (Badiali et al., 2022, p. 51). The cohesion that special traditions foster can add to the longevity of a partnership.

Perhaps the most joyous facet of the NAPDS Nine Essentials is recognition. PDS should have ways to celebrate, recognize, and award PDS-related activities and accomplishments aside from the those typically awarded by the college and school districts. "Taking the time to plan and implement forms of recognition and incentives can lead to long-term sustainability, community building, and partnership strength" (NAPDS Nine Essentials, 2021, p. 14). The National Association for School–University Partnerships (NASUP) provides many opportunities for individuals and entire PDS partnerships to be recognized yearly. NASUP has awards for Emerging PDS Leaders, Jason Kinsey Award (given to an individual for outstanding service to NAPDS), Outstanding Dissertation Award, Exemplary PDS Award, Exemplary Mentor Teacher Award, and Exemplary PK20 Boundary Spanner Award.

The Buffalo State PDS consortium has multiple ways to recognize the achievements of stakeholders. The PDS newsletter often features the successes of participants in the PDS realm. School partners are highlighted on the consortium's website. PDS-related publications and presentations are listed on the website as well. Awards are given out at the annual PDS Conference. Some teacher candidates who participate in the PDS are awarded scholarships. The Buffalo State PDS has also won awards from NASUP, such as the 2018 Exemplary PDS Achievement Award.

"The NAPDS expects only that each PDS relationship in some way or another addresses all nine *essentials*. The association recognizes that there is no 'magic bullet' to make a strong school–university relationship become a PDS. It takes the very hard work of multiple people with multiple perspectives. This is what allows each PDS to be unique while still holding firm to the *essentials*" (Brindley et al., 2008b, p. 74). The NAPDS Nine Essentials are broad and flexible. They provide a structure that allows for each PDS to make them their own. "Each PDS develops as a result of local needs and conditions. Partner educators interpret and implement PDS principles according to the needs of their contexts. Therefore, the PDS is not a model, but a set of community agreements arrived at through collaboration and sustained by a respectful, fair, and reciprocal approach to addressing priorities" (NAPDS Nine Essentials, 2021, p. 10). The flexibility of the NAPDS Nine Essentials allows for continuous renewal and the ability to meet the changing needs of all PDS stakeholders.

The SUNY Buffalo State PDS Consortium learned just how flexible these structures were during the COVID-19 pandemic. The important relationships we built with school partners were in jeopardy. Interactions with school and community partners went through multiple stages during that trying time. During the first stage, we found there was panic, uncertainty, and a need for empathy. Communicating effectively was vital not only to maintain relationships but to move forward with partnerships. Stage 2 focused on needs and priorities and the sharing of information. We were all in the crisis together. Stage 3 was responding and planning forward, while stage 4 centered on the call to action (Kindzierski et al., 2021). We had to stretch the PDS structures and rethink how we had always done things. With guidance from the NAPDS Nine Essentials (2008), we were able to maintain and even build partnerships in an online or remote environment.

We listened to the needs of the PDS stakeholders, canceled our annual conference, reallocated funds, and found ways to deliver the professional development needed at that time remotely. The focus on social emotional learning became even more vital. We also addressed equity, accelerated learning, tutoring, behavior management, co-teaching, math, and literacy as part of our All Hands on Deck initiative to prepare for the 2021–2022 school year. While our PDS had to pivot and change, we relied on the NAPDS Nine Essentials to guide us and inform our plan to move forward (Kindzierski et al., 2021). Other principles and standards provide a foundation and guidance for PDS communities.

National Council for the Accreditation of Teacher Education's (NCATE) Blue Ribbon Panel 10 Design Principles for Clinically Based Preparation (2010)

Another framework that helps to provide guidance and structure for school–university partnerships is the NCATE Blue Ribbon Panel on Clinical Preparation and Partnerships for Improved Student Learning (2010). This panel sought to shift teacher preparation to include more school-based experiences for teacher candidates. The Blue Ribbon Panel Report on Clinical Teacher Preparation (2010) is a seminal publication in the PDS world. It took a close look at the shortcomings of current teacher education programs and how school–university partnerships might address flaws in schools of education (Zenkov et al., 2016).

There is overlap between the 10 NCATE Design Principles for Clinically Based Preparation and the NAPDS Nine Essentials (2008) in four categories. Both of these frameworks provide guidance pertaining to rich school–university partnerships that concentrate on improving teacher preparation and the learning of P–12 students. Van Scoy and Eldridge (2012) found that although they have different purposes, both documents focused on "deliberate planned partnerships, comprehensive clinical preparation, high standards for all, and data driven practice" (p. 7). The NCATE Blue Ribbon Panel released 10 Design Principles for Clinically Based Preparation (pp. 13–14).

The first principle is **student learning is the focus**. Clinically based teacher preparation programs need to focus on the learning of P–12 students. Teacher candidates should provide instruction that advances the knowledge of the students.

The second principle is **clinical preparation is integrated throughout every facet of teacher education in a dynamic way**. Clinical practice is at the heart of the teacher preparation experience. Opportunities for teacher candidates to work in authentic settings with P–12 learners are embedded throughout the program.

The third principle is **a candidate's progress, and the elements of a preparation program are continuously judged on the basis of data**. The teacher candidates' educational practice must align with the Interstate Teacher Assessment and Support Consortium (InTASC): Model Core Teaching Standards (these will be discussed later in the chapter) as well as state standards for P–12 students. Candidate evaluation should be based on both teaching observations and student data (artifacts, assessments).

The fourth principle is **programs prepare teachers who are expert in content and how to teach it and are also innovators, collaborators, and problem solvers**. The expectation of this principle is that teacher candidates must build up a core knowledge base with a variety of instructional practices and the ability to use both to assist with expert decision making. In addition, teacher candidates must be able to use a variety of assessments to inform their teaching and further P–12 student learning and also use that data to differentiate instruction to aligns with the needs of the students. Candidates must be innovative, collaborative, and willing to look for fresh and unique ways to reach struggling students.

The fifth principle is **candidates learn in an interactive professional community**. Teacher candidates need a collaborative environment to nurture and review rigorously their teaching as it relates to student learning with a great deal of feedback.

The sixth principle is **clinical educators and coaches are rigorously selected and prepared and drawn from both higher education and the P–12 sector**. Teacher candidates need effective educators to usher them through their teacher education program. Those who prepare teacher candidates should be exemplary teachers themselves who can differentiate instruction, monitor students' learning through assessment and feedback, and lifelong learners who seek best practices for students while possessing the skills necessary to be an effective clinical educator. These educators must hold themselves responsible for the performance of teacher candidates and their P–12 students' learning.

The seventh principle is **specific sites are designated and funded to support embedded clinical preparation**. Teacher candidates must have clinical experiences in schools that are carefully structured and embedded throughout the teacher preparation program. The school experiences should be properly staffed and provided with ample financial support to foster teacher candidate and P–12 student learning.

The eighth principle is **technology applications foster high-impact preparation**. The most up-to-date technologies should be embedded in teacher preparation programs to foster productivity and collaboration throughout the learning environment. Technology should be a means by which best practices and professional development are shared.

The ninth principle is a **powerful research and design agenda and systematic gathering, and use of data, supports continuous improvement in teacher preparation**. Clinically based preparation programs must collect and use data regarding the effectiveness of teaching, practices, and performance. There must be a robust research and design plan that includes both the teacher education programs and the school partners in order to foster development in the areas of knowledge, innovation, and renewal to grow a body of evidence that provides a deeper understanding of the education field.

The tenth principle is that **strategic partnerships are imperative for powerful clinical preparation**. Clinically based teacher preparation program development and execution should be viewed as the shared responsibility of teacher education programs, school districts, and state education departments.

This Blue Ribbon Panel called for "clinically based preparation, which fully integrates content, pedagogy, and professional coursework around a core of clinical experiences" (2010, p. 8). SUNY Buffalo State has designed teacher preparation programs with this in mind. Teacher candidates begin with doing observations at partner schools in their very first education courses. As they progress through the program, teacher candidates are required to complete a service-learning project with school or community partners. This allows teacher candidates to get to know children outside of the school setting and to work with families (Orellana et al., 2017). Many of those are related to exposing P–12 learners to global books and literacy strategies. As the teacher candidates move into their methods courses, they are required to spend two days a week at a professional development school working with small groups of P–12 learners under the guidance of a mentor teacher and college faculty member. They have two of these methods placements at a PDS. Finally, teacher candidates are required to student teach for one semester. These core clinical experiences allow teacher candidates to grow their understanding of content, pedagogy, and professionalism in a scaffolded, authentic school setting with P–12 learners.

"The NCATE Blue Ribbon Panel report suggested that teacher preparation be redesigned to include more clinical experiences embedded in school–university partnerships" (Howell et al., 2013, p. 48). This solidified the need for thriving professional development school networks.

A Report of the American Association of Colleges for Teacher Education Clinical Practice Commission

The NCATE Blue Ribbon Panel (2010) report remains a valuable document that highlights the importance of school–university partnerships to promote opportunities for clinical practice in teacher education programs. However, in many of these programs, the recommendations have not been fully realized or have been implemented inconsistently. In 2018, the American Association of Colleges for Teacher Education (AACTE) released a report on clinical practice with the purpose of advancing the operationalization of the recommendations of the NCATE Blue Ribbon Panel and subsequent research. Stemming from the ideas of Goodlad related to clinical practice, the AACTE report was situated as part of a democratic agenda and highlighted the importance of flexibility in the implementation of clinically rich practices that benefit all the stakeholders in a partnership in various contexts. The proclamations that follow are guided by this notion that clinical practice and school–university partnerships in teacher education programs lead to successful and responsive teachers.

Initially, the AACTE report on clinical practice demonstrated efforts to advance the implementation of these ideas by defining key terms on which to build guiding principles and promote a common understanding. "This is a framework to build, maintain, and sustain a clinical partnership, which joins the needs of a college or university and local PK–12 schools in the preparation of highly effective educators to meet the needs of all learners" (p. 4). At the center of the AACTE report are 10 proclamations that spell out the critical elements of clinical practice.

First contained in the AACTE report is a Central Proclamation under which there are five tenets:

- The key framework for teacher preparation programs is clinical practice.

- The basis for high quality teacher education programs stems from the joint forces of clinical practice and research.

- Based on teaching standards, articulation of effective practice and how it can be measured help to create the conditions necessary for clinically based teacher preparation that allows for time for teacher candidate development with support from effective practitioners.

- The benefits of clinical practice partnerships in both schools and teacher preparation programs are supported by research that helps to improve teacher preparation and ultimately the success of PK–12 learners.

- Clinical practice must occur in teacher preparation programs to provide for experiences that afford teacher candidates opportunities for practice in authentic school settings.

Beneath this Central Proclamation are other proclamations on pedagogy, skills, partnership, infrastructure, developmental, empowerment, mutual, common language, and expertise. The AACTE report hoped to accentuate the importance of clinical practice to effective teacher preparation programs and how quality partnerships lay the groundwork for continuous renewal of teacher preparation programs and the development of the veteran educators who support teacher candidates. The AACTE committee charged with the development of this report accomplished the aim of examining the path to becoming an effective teacher.

National Council for the Accreditation of Teacher Education's (NCATE) Five Standards for Professional Development Schools

The goal of the NCATE PDS Standards Project was to determine what it means to be a professional development school. The development of these standards and peoples' knowledge of them was evidence of growth in the PDS movement. The difficulty with these standards was that they may have been well respected, but they are voluntary. There were no consequences for not aligning to them (Teitel, 2004).

After over a decade of school reform initiatives related to school–university partnerships, NCATE established standards for PDSs in 2001. The notion of school–university partnerships had spread across the nation, but the types and forms of partnerships tended to look very different. NCATE was pleased with the growth of school–university partnerships and their potential to fuel school changes and positively impact student learning. However, there were negative aspects of the steady pace at which this collaborative answer to many issues concerning schools spread, such as the formation of partnerships for the sake of being able to say your institution is part of a partnership. Advocates of school–university partnerships did not want this to become an educational fad that spread quickly and then disappeared when the pendulum swung the other way. For these reasons, NCATE developed standards to rigorously formalize the concept of PDS. NCATE synthesized PDS research and the work of organizations such as the National Network for Educational Renewal (NNER), as well as the American Federation of Teachers, and, of course, the Holmes Group and conducted field tests. NCATE searched for most important components of PDS and came up with five standards: (1) Learning Community, (2) Accountability and Quality Assurance, (3) Collaboration, (4) Diversity and Equity, and (5) Structures, Resources and Roles (Nolan Jr. et al., 2011). The five standards that professional development schools should meet are described in more detail below:

> **Learning community**—At the heart of the PDS, the learning community standard represents the teaching and learning activities, philosophies, and environments created in these partnerships. As part of this standard, multiple learners are supported, both work and practice are inquiry-based and focused on learning. There exists a shared vision of teaching and learning that is grounded in research and the knowledge of practitioners. The learning community also serves as an instrument of change.

> **Accountability and quality assurance**—This standard covers the assessment of the partnership and its outcomes, in ways that address the PDS's accountability to its various stakeholders and the public. PDS participation criteria are set up as part of the development of assessments that are followed by the collection of information and the use of the findings in the PDS context.

Collaboration—This standard addresses the partnership's formation and its development of an increasingly interdependent committed relationship. As part of this standard, stakeholders work together with certain roles and structures to strengthen cooperation and work toward equality among stakeholders.

Diversity and equity—This standard focuses on how the PDS prepares a diverse group of educators to provide equitable opportunities to learn for all students. Under this standard, partners work to evaluate the policies and procedures of the PDS to ensure equitable learning outcomes and recruit and support diverse participants.

Structures, resources and roles—This standard relates to how the PDS organizes itself to support and do its work. Governance and support structures are established to ensure the PDSs progress toward its goals through the creation of PDS roles and effective leveraging of resources and use of communication (NCATE, 2001, as cited in Teitel, 2004).

As most educators agreed that teacher candidates need to have clinically rich experiences as part of their teacher preparation programs, a more centralized view of what teacher candidates needed to know as far as knowledge, skills, and dispositions emerged. "In 1987, standards for novice teachers were developed by the Interstate New Teacher Assessment and Support Consortium (InTASC) as a project of the Council of Chief State School Officers" (Whitford & Villaume, 2014, p. 431). These general standards for educators also serve as a framework for teacher candidates in professional development schools.

INTERSTATE NEW TEACHER ASSESSMENT AND SUPPORT CONSORTIUM (INTASC) STANDARDS

The 1987 InTASC core teaching standards provided a consolidated overview of a long list of teacher competencies. "These were updated in 2011 using four headings: the learner and learning, content knowledge, instructional practice, and professional responsibility" (Whitford & Villaume, 2014, pp. 431–432). This iteration of the standards is not just for novice teachers. More advanced teachers will apply the standards in more sophisticated ways. The updated standards are also organized under four categories.

The Learner and Learning

Standard 1: Learner Development. The teacher understands how learners grow and develop, recognizing that patterns of learning and development vary individually within and across the cognitive, linguistic, social, emotional, and physical areas, and designs and implements developmentally appropriate and challenging learning experiences.

Standard 2: Learning Differences. The teacher uses understanding of individual differences and diverse cultures and communities to ensure inclusive learning environments that enable each learner to meet high standards.

Standard 3: Learning Environments. The teacher works with others to create environments that support individual and collaborative learning, and that encourage positive social interaction, active engagement in learning, and self-motivation.

Content

Standard 4: Content Knowledge. Teachers understand the central concepts, tools of inquiry, and structures of the discipline(s) they teach and thus create learning experiences that make the discipline accessible and meaningful for learners to ensure mastery of the content.

Standard 5: Application of Content. The teacher understands how to connect concepts and use differing perspectives to engage learners in critical thinking, creativity, and collaborative problem solving related to authentic local and global issues.

Instructional Practice

Standard 6: Assessment. The teacher understands and uses multiple methods of assessment to engage learners in their own growth, to monitor learner progress, and to guide the teacher's and learner's decision making.

Standard 7: Planning for Instruction. The teacher plans instruction that supports every student in meeting rigorous learning goals by drawing upon knowledge of content areas, curriculum, cross-disciplinary skills, and pedagogy, as well as knowledge of learners and the community context.

Standard 8: Instructional Strategies. The teacher understands and uses a variety of instructional strategies to encourage learners to develop deep understanding of content areas and their connections, and to build skills to apply knowledge in meaningful ways.

Professional Responsibility

Standard 9: Professional Learning and Ethical Practice. The teacher engages in ongoing professional learning and uses evidence to continually evaluate his/her practice, particularly the effects of his/her choices and actions on others (learners, families, other professionals, and the community), and adapts practice to meet the needs of each learner.

Standard 10: Leadership and Collaboration. The teacher seeks appropriate leadership roles and opportunities to take responsibility for student learning, to collaborate with learners, families, colleagues, other school professionals, and community members to ensure learner growth, and to advance the profession (Council of Chief State School Officers, 2011, pp. 8–9).

Each of these standards is broken into the three areas of performances, essential knowledge, and critical dispositions. Criteria are listed for each standard in all three areas. SUNY Buffalo State uses the InTASC standards to guide curriculum and assessment planning. As well, the evaluation forms for student teachers are comprised of these standards. Student-teaching supervisors and mentor teachers complete an evaluation of each student teacher based on the InTASC standards.

Association of Teacher Educators (ATE) Clinical Experience Standards, Third Edition (2023)

The 11 standards presented by the Association of Teacher Educators (ATE) detail how this organization promotes effective teacher preparation through clinical practice and research. Each of the standards provide more specific indicators to comprehensively describe effective clinical practice to illustrate the components of high-quality clinical practice in an aspirational way. In other words, the ATE Clinical Experience Standards provide those involved in education with what could picture of what teacher preparation could be. The 11 standards are listed here:

Standard 1: Collaboration
Standard 2: Coherence
Standard 3: Organization of Clinical Experiences
Standard 4: Quality Placements
Standard 5: Communications
Standard 6: Resourcing, Reviewing, and Renewal
Standard 7: Clinical Educators
Standard 8: Seminar
Standard 9: Clinical Coaching and Formative Assessment of Teaching
Standard 10: Teacher Candidate Evaluation
Standard 11: Virtual Supervision

These standards help showcase the value of clinical practice and reify the elemental components of clinical experiences in teacher education to prepare high quality teachers who positively impact the lives of students.

So, that is a lot of information to digest regarding the different essentials, principles, and standards that guide the establishment of a solid and successful school–university partnership. Table 1. Guiding Frameworks helps you to distinguish among the various reports that support and drive the need for clinical practice in teacher education programs. There are similarities among them, but remember they were established by different entities for different purposes and the combination of them helps to encompass much of what is necessary for the formation and sustainability of a PDS that positively impacts student learning. The NAPDS Nine Essentials, NCATE 10 Design Principles for Clinically Based Preparation, NCATE's Five Standards for Professional Development Schools, the AACTE Clinical Practice Commission Report, the ATE Clinical Experience Standards, and the InTASC Standards are all frameworks that help provide guidance and structure for school–university partnerships to become professional development schools producing well-prepared teachers while positively impacting P–12 learners. These are crucial documents to review with stakeholders if you are planning to develop your own professional development school network. They will help to ensure quality and organization across your PDS community.

As you begin to form PDS relationships, or even a consortium, please remember that PDS have no police. Burgeoning PDSs are not expected to excel in all areas of the NAPDS Nine Essentials or other frameworks all at once (NAPDS, 2021). "The major purpose for developing standards for professional development schools is to help PDSs achieve their potential" (Levine, 1997, p. 63). They provide a loose framework with aspects that can be easily tailored to the needs of your particular PDS. No PDS relationship is the same. Each school site and college faculty member brings different advantages and challenges to the "third space" for deliberation, creative problem solving, and dreaming big! As Snyder (1999) points out, PDS work, though not easy, is extremely beneficial and rewarding. Start small and design your PDS collaboratively based on the perspectives and needs of your stakeholders.

Reflection Time

Pause

Deliberate

Share

Based on these PDS-related frameworks, in what areas are your partnerships already excelling? What are some areas that are not as fully developed? How might your responses to these questions inform your PDS goal setting?

Spotlight on John Goodlad

BACKGROUND

In the PDS world, John Goodlad is a well-known name. Let's take a few minutes to learn more about Goodlad, the man, his accomplishments, and his impact on the PDS approach of school–university partnerships.

John Goodlad was born on August 19, 1920, in Vancouver, Canada. He attended graduate school in Canada and then worked as a teacher in a one-room school in British Columbia. Goodlad taught at every grade level throughout his career. Goodlad attended the University of Chicago for his doctoral work and earned a PhD in 1949.

According to his Wikipedia page (en.wikipedia.org/wiki/John_Goodlad), Goodlad was known as an educational researcher and theorist. He disseminated his models for school renewal through his many publications and other initiatives. He wrote more than 30 books, approximately 80 book chapters, and over 200 journal articles.

Along with his many publications, John Goodlad held many prestigious positions throughout his life, such as president of the American Educational Research Association (AERA) from 1967–1968. He was a faculty member at Agnes Scott College, Emory University, University of Chicago, and the University of California at Los Angeles, where he was also the dean of the graduate School of Education. In addition, Goodlad was a professor emeritus of education at the University of Washington beginning in 1984. It was there that he served as a co-director of the Center of Educational Renewal (Durden, 2005).

John Goodlad received honorary doctorates from 20 institutions of higher education in the United States and Canada. He was also the recipient of many awards, including the Harold T. McGraw Prize in Education in 1999, the James Bryant Conant Award for Outstanding Service in Education from the Education Commission of the States in 2000, the first Brock International Prize in Education in 2002, the New York Academy of Public Education Medal in 2003, and the American Education Award from the American Association of School Administrators in 2004 (Durden, 2005).

Goodlad's best-known book is *A Place Called School*, published in 1984. It won the first Distinguished Book of the Year Award from Kappa Delta Pi and AERA's Outstanding Book Award in 1985 (Goldberg, 2000). The book debuted Goodlad's notions about simultaneous renewal as well as the education of educators. He also touched on the importance of school–university partnerships. Here is that PDS connection!

Some of Goodlad's other well-known books were *Teachers for Our Nation's Schools* (Jossey-Bass, 1990); *In Praise of Education* (Teachers College Press, 1997); *Romances with Schools: A Life of Education* (2004); *Education for Everyone: Agenda for Education in a Democracy* (written with Corinne Mantle-Bromley and Stephen J. Goodlad, 2004); *The Teaching Career* (co-edited with Timothy J. McMannon, 2004); a 20th anniversary edition of *A Place Called School* (2004); and *Education and the Making of a Democratic People* (co-edited with Roger Soder and Bonnie McDaniel, 2008). Believe it or not, these are just a few of his books!

Goodlad helped start the Center for Educational Renewal (CER) at the University of Washington in 1985, the National Network for Educational Renewal (NNER) later that year, and the Institute for Educational Inquiry (IEI), which was a nonprofit organization started in 1992. The CER conducted research. The NNER worked on implementation. And the IEI conducted leadership training. These three organizations helped promote the Agenda for Education in a Democracy (Goodlad, 2000).

THE AGENDA FOR EDUCATION IN A DEMOCRACY

The Agenda for Education in a Democracy was the product of 20 years of research on educational change, schooling, and teacher education by teams from the Institute for Development of Educational Activities in Los Angeles and at the Center for Educational Renewal (CER) in Seattle (Goodlad, 2000).

The Agenda sought to stir up the priorities of education. It held to the position that students should be educated broadly and deeply for an uncertain future without reliance on previous research. Goodlad viewed teacher education programs and schools as partners in the change process. However, he noted that "substantial immersion of groups of future teachers in partner schools is becoming commonplace. But this immersion is taking place less than we would wish in schools that are busily renewing their practices in line with the Agenda's mission" (Goodlad, 2000, p. 88).

Goodlad's Agenda for Education in a Democracy was comprised of a mission, The Four Pillars to Advance Education in Democracy (not to be confused with the four pillars established by the Holmes Group):

1. Provide access to knowledge for all children ("equity and excellence").

2. Educate the young for thoughtful participation in a social and political democracy ("enculturation").

3. Base teaching on knowledge of the subjects taught, established principles of learning, and sensitivity to the unique potential of learners ("nurturing pedagogy").

4. Take responsibility for improving the conditions for learning in P–12 schools, institutions of higher education and

communities ("stewardship") (https://nnerpartnerships.org/about/four-pillars-twenty-postulates).

There were also conditions necessary for carrying out the mission. These conditions were contained in Goodlad's 20 propositions or postulates for teacher education. They show the circumstances needed to prepare teachers, so they are ready to ease students into a democratic society while giving them access to knowledge, at the same time building solid relationships with students and preparing them to be good future stewards of democracy (Goodlad, 1990a, 1990b). The 20 Postulates can serve as building blocks for an educational renewal agenda that creates real-life experiences to help prepare teachers to educate children, particularly children in high-needs schools (Paufler & Amrein-Beardsley, 2016).

Based on the NNER website, the Twenty Postulates are listed here:

Postulate 1: Programs for the education of the nation's educators must be viewed by institutions offering them as a major responsibility to society and be adequately supported and promoted and vigorously advanced by the institution's top leadership.

Postulate 2: Programs for the education of educators must enjoy parity with other professional education programs, full legitimacy and institutional commitment, and rewards for faculty geared to the nature of the field.

Postulate 3: Programs for the education of educators must be autonomous and secure in their borders, with clear organizational identity, constancy of budget and personnel, and decision-making authority similar to that enjoyed by the major professional schools.

Postulate 4: There must exist a clearly identifiable group of academic and clinical faculty members for whom teacher education is the top priority; the group must be responsible and accountable for selecting diverse groups of students and monitoring their progress, planning, and maintaining the full scope and sequence of the curriculum, continuously evaluating and improving programs, and facilitating the entry of graduates into teaching careers.

Postulate 5: The responsible group of academic and clinical faculty members described above must have a comprehensive understanding of the aims of education and the role of schools in our society and be fully committed to selecting and preparing teachers to assume the full range of educational responsibilities required.

Postulate 6: The responsible group of academic and clinical faculty members must seek out and select for a predetermined number of student places in the program those candidates who reveal an initial commitment to the moral ethical, and enculturating responsibilities to be assumed, and make clear to them that preparing for these responsibilities is central to this program.

Postulate 7: Programs for the education of educators, whether elementary or secondary, must carry the responsibility to ensure that all candidates progressing through them possess or acquire the literacy and critical-thinking abilities associated with the concept of an educated person.

Postulate 8: Programs for the education of educators must provide extensive opportunities for future teachers to move beyond being students of organized knowledge to become teachers who inquire into both knowledge and its teaching.

Postulate 9: Programs for the education of educators must be characterized by a socialization process through which candidates transcend their self-oriented student preoccupations to become more other-oriented in identifying with a culture of teaching.

Postulate 10: Programs for the education of educators must be characterized in all respects by the conditions for learning that future teachers are to establish in their own schools and classrooms.

Postulate 11: Programs for the education of educators must be conducted in such a way that teachers inquire into the nature of teaching and schooling and assume that they will do so as a natural aspect of their careers.

Postulate 12: Programs for the education of educators must involve future teachers in the issues and dilemmas that emerge out of the never-ending tension between the rights and interests of individual parents and interest groups and the role of schools in transcending parochialism and advancing community in a democratic society.

Postulate 13: Programs for the education of educators must be infused with understanding of and commitment to the moral obligation of teachers to ensure equitable access to and engagement in the best possible K–12 education for all children and youths.

Postulate 14: Programs for the education of educators must involve future teachers not only in understanding schools as they are but in alternatives, the assumptions underlying alternatives, and how to effect needed changes in school organization, pupil grouping, curriculum, and more.

Postulate 15: Programs for the education of educators must assure for each candidate the availability of a wide array of laboratory settings for simulation, observation, hands-on experiences, and exemplary schools for internships and residencies; they must admit no more students to their programs than can be assured these quality experiences.

Postulate 16: Programs for the education of educators must engage future teachers in the problems and dilemmas arising out of the inevitable conflicts and incongruities between what is perceived to work in practice and the research and theory supporting other options.

Postulate 17: Programs for the education of educators must establish linkages with graduates for purposes of both evaluating and revising these programs and easing the critical early years of transition into teaching.

Postulate 18: Programs for the education of educators require a regulatory context with respect to licensing, certifying, and accrediting that ensures at all times the presence of the necessary conditions embraced by the seventeen preceding postulates.

Postulate 19: Programs for the education of educators must compete in an arena that rewards efforts to continuously improve on the conditions embedded in all of the postulates and tolerates no shortcuts intended to ensure a supply of teachers.

Postulate 20: Those institutions and organizations that prepare the nation's teachers, authorize their right to teach, and employ them must fine-tune their individual and collaborative roles to support and sustain lifelong teaching careers characterized by professional growth, service, and satisfaction. This postulate was added to the list of postulates in 2000 (https://nnerpartnerships.org/about/four-pillars-twenty-postulates).

Goodlad (1994) described his notion of educational renewal through the 20 Postulates, which are grouped sequentially based on the specifications needed for teacher preparation: (1) structural, (2) faculty responsibilities, (3) programmatic responsibilities, (4) curricular, and (5) regulatory and policy. He saw educational renewal as a joint process in which "colleges and universities, the traditional producers of teachers, join schools, the recipients of the products, as equal partners in the simultaneous renewal of schooling and the education of educators" (p. 2). In the realm of pedagogy, educational renewal strives to represent the mission of teacher preparation in a democracy. "Although recent reforms have been implemented to hold teachers and, by extension, the teacher education and school district partnership programs that prepare them, accountable for their students' learning and achievement, often in high-stakes ways, many of these reforms are arguably working against the late John Goodlad's (1987, 1988, 1990b, 1994) notion of educational renewal" (Lewin, 2015, p. 251). His vision for teacher preparation was somewhat brushed to the side due to recent accountability programs. Discussions have changed from the creation of better schools through simultaneous renewal to accountability approaches that demand that teachers improve using evaluative and punitive practices. Higher test scores are not an indicator of educational renewal (Paufler & Amrein-Beardsley, 2016).

Recent reforms based on accountability have been problematic. "[M]any policy makers remain transfixed in their preoccupation with test scores as indicators of teacher and teacher education effectiveness and quality, regardless of Goodlad's or many other influential scholars' prior and current works" (Paufler & Amrein-Beardsley, 2016, p. 256). From Goodlad's perspective, a focus on test results negatively affects novice teachers and teacher preparation programs.

The Agenda for Education in a Democracy focuses on renewal and responsibility as opposed to reform and accountability that has been the direction of years of attempted school improvement. "It should come as no surprise that most people who choose to work in education are motivated and challenged by an agenda of renewal but are scarcely moved by still another round of reform" (Goodlad, 2000, pp. 86–87).

Goodlad espoused that the renewal of schools, teachers, and teacher preparation programs needs to occur simultaneously (Goodlad, 1990b). As part of this undertaking, Goodlad declared that collaboration among schools of education, arts and science schools or departments, and schools should be hubs for teaching with three main functions. They need to prepare preservice teachers to be able to teach in a variety of types of schools. They should participate in inquiry related to school settings, what teacher candidates need to learn in their teacher preparation programs as far as knowledge and skills to be effective teachers. Finally, they should be participating in research and other forms of scholarship pertaining to the art and science of teaching (Goodlad, 1994).

This can be accomplished as part of a school–university partnership. Goodlad viewed "the concept and creation of school–university partnerships as a strategy for school improvement" (Goodlad, 1993 p. 25). Goodlad explained that early on he believed the partnership of university and school would be beneficial. He and his colleagues had in mind from the beginning that the joining together of university and school environments would positively impact both institutions. At the heart of this relationship was the concept of partner schools: school settings in which school-based and university-based partners gather together for the simultaneous renewal of both the school and the teacher education program. The partner school was Goodlad's idea of a professional development school (Goodlad, 1993). These are "schools in which school and university personnel join in renewing schools where a significant part of the preservice teacher education program is carried out jointly" (Goodlad, 1993, p. 20).

Across partnerships, there are four main features that indicate how they are organized. The first feature is theory which is grounded in the idea of a mutually beneficial partnership between a school and university. The second feature relates to purposes which includes an approach based on three aspects: preparation of educators, the support of schools, and a collaborative effort to promote the previous two aspects to improve performance. The third feature is agenda which centers around the simultaneous renewal of schools and teacher preparation programs. The final feature related to the organization of partnerships is structure. Structure refers to governance, leadership, budget, working groups, processes, and a time commitment (Paufler & Amrein-Beardsley, 2006). Despite these challenging features of partnership formation, Goodlad found a way to model and support school–university collaborations.

The National Network for Educational Renewal (NNER) was created by Goodlad, Sirotnik, and Soder to provide a crucial structure to support the Agenda for Education in a Democracy. The NNER is a group of school–university partnerships that came together to improve schools. The goals of these partnerships consisted of fostering effective performance by teacher education programs to educate the educators, to foster effective performance by the schools as they educated the country's young citizens and developing collaboration between universities and schools to foster excellent performance of mutually beneficial aspects like simultaneous renewal (Goodlad, 2004). Within 10 years after its creation in 1985, the NNER was made up of 25 different colleges and universities that partnered with almost 100 school districts all over the United States (Paufler & Amrein-Beardsley, 2006). NNER participants are invested in implementing the conditions encompassed by Goodlad's Postulates via inquiry managed through the CER (Goodlad, 1990).

SIMULTANEOUS RENEWAL

Goodlad (2004) posited that meaningful improvements to schools cannot occur without simultaneous efforts to the settings that prepare teachers. This brought about his idea of simultaneous renewal. A key facet of simultaneous renewal includes the development of partnerships between schools and teacher education programs to improve schooling as well as to develop a setting where both teachers and teacher candidates learn together in mutually beneficial ways.

Teacher candidates will be made aware of expectations from the beginning to foster interactions as part of cohorts. Their placements should provide experiences throughout the school, not just in one classroom. The school partners should be engaged in the process of renewal due to the collaboration between individuals from the school and university. It is this that helps to make real the simultaneous renewal of schools and the education of educators (Goodlad, 1993).

Paufler and Amrein-Beardsley described the need for research that examine ways to reaffirm teacher education, to help foster stewardship in teacher preparation programs, and call on in-service teachers to be agents of change while affording spaces for university faculty to collaborate on research with school partners (Paufler & Amrein-Beardsley, 2006).

In 1999, Goodlad and his team published four books related to the NNER partnerships and Agenda for Education in a Democracy. Along with these books, Goodlad and his team engaged in a formal evaluation of the execution of their effort. Goodlad cited a range of data that were collected across a span of 10 years. Interestingly, the data listed was all qualitative, such as fieldnotes, participant evaluations, self-assessments, and interviews, to name a few. This lack of quantitative research continues to be a criticism of the effectiveness of school–university partnerships to this day.

In an interview with Goldberg (2000), Goodlad stated, "Over more than 60 years, the problems remain essentially the same, and the solutions remain essentially the same" (p. 82). In a discussion later with Durden (2005), Goodlad explained that educators are the main obstacle to educational renewal. The Center for Education Renewal's research about the education of educators drew attention to the area of teacher education. Goodlad's *Teachers for Our Nation's Schools* (1990) was "based on the assumption that America will not have better schools without better teachers, but we will not have better teachers without better schools in which teachers can learn, practice, and develop" (Durden, 2005, p. 349). The politicizing of education was the second major obstacle to educational renewal. Goodlad described how in the late 1990s there was an emphasis on standards, tests, and accountability on the part of politicians. At about the same time, the country experienced economic issues. This is when governments at both the state and federal level started pressing for a workforce that was better educated as American students' test scores were lower than their counterparts in other countries. This tied education reform to the economy which was closely aligned with the conservative political agenda (Durden, 2005).

Until the three groups related to schooling—the local community school culture, the culture of the College of Education, and the College of Arts and Sciences—get together and come up with a common understanding of the responsibilities of each entity in the preparation, mentoring, and sustaining of teachers, efforts will not lead to progress in the field of education. As well, a political culture that comprehends and supports the idea of education in a democracy must be valued over an education system that serves as neoliberal means to improve the economy (Durden, 2005).

Goodlad's *A Place Called School* highlights that schools should be reviewed by the compilation of thick descriptions to examine each individual school holistically, such as comparison of the perceptions of stakeholders, school climate, student support, teacher expectations, collegiality, and leadership, to name a few. Attention should be focused on the collecting, sorting out, and analyzing data at the local levels. This would provide insight into and understanding of practices in local schools, which are the site of change in education (Durden, 2005).

Goodlad believed educational change would arrive when the culture and practice of local schools became the primary focus of discussions and change efforts. He emphasized that this should be top priority, and that other priorities would follow in time. For a democratic school, education-related cultures, such as the political culture, the culture of inquiry, and the main culture of schooling, must blend together to support the renewal of local schools (Durden, 2005).

Goodlad reflected that just as democracy is a work in progress, the same goes for education within a democracy. If America is to fulfill the dream of our Founding Fathers, we must understand that democracy requires active participation; it is not self-perpetuating but needs constant and active involvement in shaping the anticipated paths and expectations of human interaction, interdependence, and the evolution of democracy. Also, as our Founding Fathers envisioned, education is the way to prepare future citizens to move forward and to mold the purpose of this work to progress toward what we call a democracy. We must come together to support renewal of the local school, and with the students, teachers, parents, and community. This pursuit should still be viewed as a work in progress, as it likely always will be.

Goodlad had a major impact on the field of education in many areas. He contributed a great deal to formation and sustainability of school–university partnerships and how they could improve student learning. On November 29, 2014, Goodlad died in Seattle, Washington, at the age of 94 (Lewin, 2015).

Reflection Time

Pause

Deliberate

Share

Now that you know a bit about John Goodlad, try putting yourself in his shoes. What might Goodlad think about schools today? Why do you think so? Reflecting on your present school environment, what conditions might be necessary for simultaneous renewal? Does something need to change? Does something need to be added?

Chapter 2

Formalizing the PDS Relationship

Now that you know about the basic frameworks that support the PDS approach of school–university partnerships, you might be ready to seek out potential partners or to formalize some of the current relationships you have with either schools or universities depending on your position. I recommend beginning with one partnership at a time. In this chapter, we will discuss creating relationships, how to go about formalizing relationships between schools and universities and why it is important., examples of stages and agreements to foster school–university partnerships, and governance. Because each partnership is unique, you may have to adapt some of this information to benefit your own partnership situation(s). Then each PDS can determine how to carry out the 9 Essentials according to their focus, needs, strengths, and other factors (Brindley et al., 2008).

Why Partner?

Partnerships between schools and universities, especially institutions preparing teachers, have been labeled a desirable means of educational reform (Lieberman, 1991). The push to reform schools, improve teaching, and undergo professional development has led to almost the necessity of these partnerships for both the schools and the universities; partly to comply with accrediting agencies, state examiners, and the perspectives of potential funders. It is the goal of most teacher preparation programs to build and maintain PDS relationships because they are endorsed by scholars and afford both institutions the opportunity to leverage their combined resources (Sosin & Parnham, 1998).

Advocacy of the PDS approach for teacher preparation implies a different mission for the PDS than the traditional schools. In the traditional school, the main priority is to serve its students and their parents, which may result in only some incidental reform (Sosin & Parnham, 1998). In the definition of a PDS (Teitel, 1997a), the goal defined first is to improve pre-service teacher preparation. The second goal is to grow the professional development of both teachers and university faculty. The third goal is to provide a quality education to diverse students, and the final goal is to foster continued inquiry into ways to advance practice (Levine & Churins, 1999, p. 181). As a PDS grows, these goals can play out in many ways.

Why PDS?

Levine (1997) maintains that there are specific conditions for developing PDSs. There must be a commitment by partners to a joint vision of the PDS mission. They must be working together on the goals of a collaborative learning community, and each partner must have institutional commitment specifically related to the resources necessary to sustain the PDS. With this in mind, the PDS perspective holds to the idea that the school is a learning community, and when teachers learn and develop, student learning is also supported (Sosin and Parham, 1998). Communication and collaboration are key to interactions between schools and universities because schools are more than just a building where student teachers are assigned; schools are considered partners in teacher preparation (Brindley et al., 2008).

At this point, you might be thinking that PDS sounds great, but does this approach really impact student learning and all the other areas of focus for PDS programs? Much of the impact research on PDS over the years has been studied using qualitative methods. One can find numerous descriptive case studies on these unique partnerships. Quantitative methods have been used to a lesser extent. Boyle-Baise (2008) presented an overview of the results of some PDS research studies. Here are some of the highlights of the findings over time.

A two-year study was conducted by Ridley et al. (2005) that compared PDS prepared student teachers to student teachers who came from a campus-based program in a number of areas, such as planning lessons, effective instruction, reflectivity, and overall content retention of professional knowledge related to teaching. No statistically significant findings resulted from this research, but Ridley et al. reported that PDS prepared student teachers scored consistently higher than student teachers who came from a campus-based preparation program in all areas. However, during their initial year of teaching it was found that teachers from a PDS preparation program scored significantly higher in the areas of classroom management, maintaining the interests of students during instruction, and feedback than teachers who graduated from a campus-based teacher preparation program. Other research studies supported these findings (Houston et al., 1999; Stallings, 1991; Wait, 2000). These were impressive findings in favor of a PDS preparation program, but work must continue in these areas and other facets of a PDS program (Boyle-Baise & McIntyre, 2008).

Boyle-Baise and McIntyre (2008) described other areas of research where PDS-related factors and preparation were more successful. Houston et al. (1999) reported that across a three-year span, student achievement in reading, mathematics, and writing on the Texas Assessment of Academic Skills (TAAS) increased in PDS schools as opposed to non-PDS schools. Also, a larger proportion of PDS students passed the Examination for the Certification of Educators in Texas (ExCET) tests than did counterparts in traditional teacher preparation programs. PDS students were significantly more on task than their non-PDS peers. Finally, PDS students were more likely to be placed in small-group instruction and less frequently placed in whole-group activities than were students in the non-PDS classes.

Klinger et al. (2004) found that students' standardized test scores increased in PDS schools. Classroom management was more effective in a PDS school (Neubert & Binko, 1998). Conaway and Mitchell (2004) found that those involved in a year-long placement at a PDS school had more positive techniques when it came to classroom management. "The programs delivered through the PDSs resulted in improved preparation of teacher candidates when compared to non-PDS programs" (Boyle-Baise & McIntyre, 2008, p. 323).

These positive results related to PDSs are extremely encouraging, but it should still be known that managing the functioning of a PDS, a PDS cooperative, or PDS consortium can be tough. "A smaller subset of the field, those involved in actually trying 'to do' a PDS, agree on two additional realities: (a) They require an extraordinary amount of time, labor, and angst; and (b) when they 'work,' they improve the efforts of experienced K–12 educators, experienced college-based teacher educators, and credential candidates" (Snyder, 1999. p. 137).

The positive impacts and adhering to the supporting and guiding structures of PDS is well worth the collaborative efforts and hard work of so many who care deeply about the academic achievement of P–12 learners and the preparation of quality future teachers.

Teitel (2003) laid out his beliefs regarding PDS partnerships.

1. They should be transformative with the renewal of schools and teacher preparation programs, using the framework of PDS.

2. Equity is important. The Holmes Group stated that PDSs must play a role in confronting societal inequalities.

3. PDSs should be mutually beneficial as reciprocity is key.

4. Data and information play an important role in all aspects of PDS relationships.

5. Leadership is crucial, and anyone can be a leader.

6. PDSs face similar tasks and challenges despite a variety of contexts. There is a focus on P–12 learning, and data from various assessments are used to shape future plans and initiatives. (pp. xxi–xxii)

I started this chapter with "Why Partner?" because, initially, that's what many stakeholders want to know. They question how much time, money, manpower, and expertise, to name a few factors, the school must provide to make the relationship work. Schools often want to know what's in it for them. It is likely clear that the university's initial reason for reaching out about a partnership is so teacher candidates have clinically rich experiences as they move through their teacher preparation program, but PDS is so much more than that; however, sometimes it is difficult to explain to school administrators and potential mentor teachers whose available meeting times are few and far between.

When we meet with potential school partners, the potential course instructor and the PDS director visit the school with information about our PDS Consortium. We always try to bring Buffalo State PDS swag with us as a little gift to remember us by. Sometimes we have a handout, sometimes, depending on available technology, we have a slide presentation, sometimes we use our PDS website to explain the concept of PDS to a potential school partner, and sometimes we utilize a combination of the three.

At Buffalo State, we have found that inviting potential school partners to our events, such as our annual PDS Conference, PDS meetings, or professional development sessions, allows them a firsthand look at what PDS is and how it functions as a mutually beneficial network. They also have the opportunity to hear presentations on the initiatives of various PDS partnerships, as they all differ in their own way based on the strengths and needs of each partner, though they are built on the same frameworks described in Chapter 1.

Some benefits we at Buffalo State describe to potential school partners are the consortium's action research mini-grants to help support projects that involve our teacher candidates; a small stipend that the liaison committee decides on how to spend to further support the partnership; professional development opportunities; the opportunity to plan projects, initiatives, events, or interventions with a partner; and the overall ability to leverage resources, such as money, space, expertise, and manpower, to name a few. We also try to clarify our specific expectations for the partnership. What one institution has to offer may differ from that of other institutions, but we always ask potential partners for a clear vision of their expectations for the school–university partnership.

Additionally, we discuss our own research to demonstrate the positive impact of PDS on various stakeholders in the consortium. Along with several journal articles, Buffalo State has produced two co-edited texts— *Doing PDS: Stories and Strategies from Successful Clinically Rich Practice* (2018) and *The Impact of PDS Partnerships in Challenging Times* (2020).

Financial Resources

Initially, many PDSs that begin with external money are grant funded. These beginning PDSs depend on committed educators from the school and university who donate their time. In some instances, course releases or small stipends are provided for the individuals involved. Sometimes these partnerships are given a pool of money for operating expenses. This money might be from external funding or from money contributed by both the school and the university. Sometimes, particularly in larger, systemic PDS efforts, significant funding is provided from the beginning. When starting a PDS, funding will likely be needed for staff, technology, space, training, possible site visits and reading materials. The exact amount of money to begin a PDS depends on the size, scale, context, and focus of the endeavor. Of the total annual cost, some of it might be in-kind and some shared between the school and university (Clark, 1999).

Sometimes PDS costs or funding do not fit neatly into a school or university budget. When all is said and done, PDS can be expensive. In times of budget issues, PDS could be first on the chopping block to save money. This why it is imperative that both school and university partners be able to explicitly explain how the goals of the PDS align with the mission and goals of the partners. At times, PDSs must think outside the box and to innovatively and carefully leverage all resources in order to achieve their goals (Nolan Jr., 2007).

It can be difficult to gather financial support for the development of a PDS. Darling-Hammond (2005) stated: "Despite substantial moral support, the PDS movement has been launched with remarkably little funding" (p. 23). Even with this lack of funding, many PDS relationships continue today. Initially, when PDS was young, private funding provided a great deal of support to begin PDS partnerships. Much of this funding is gone, and the chance of institutional support is limited. PDS partners must now be extremely creative and innovative to sustain this clinically rich approach (Darling-Hammond, 2005).

Back in the early 1990s, Buffalo State saw the value of the PDS approach of school–university partnerships for the teacher preparation program. Today, funding has been limited to sustain the early progress made with the PDS approach. The Elementary Education and Reading department was granted a line for a full-time faculty member by the university. Instead of carrying out a search and hiring a new colleague, the department negotiated that the money that would be used to pay a new faculty member be used to sustain the burgeoning PDS consortium. I smile every time I recall that scenario. My colleagues (now retired) were brilliant, and the buy-in for PDS at the time was evident.

Since money appears to be tight at many schools and universities, it is best to call on an important aspect of the PDS relationship, leveraging resources, before stressing about the money to meet your shared goals. Maybe the university has a faculty member with expertise in a specific area of need for the school. Through the Buffalo State PDS agreements, professional development hours are included as part of the agreement. Then, maybe money earmarked for the need the faculty member is filling can be used for professional development for the PDS consortium. Or the honorarium for a speaker could be split between the two organizations. Sometimes creativity is required. Be sure to consider all the resources at your disposable to fulfill the partnership goals.

A few years ago, in an advisory board meeting, school partners told university faculty that the teacher candidates graduating from Buffalo State needed to know more about trauma-informed practices when student teaching, applying for, and beginning teaching positions. At that time, we had not made a line in our budget for anything related to this initiative. We had to stop and consider possible resources to tap into as part of the PDS consortium to meet this need. One of the PDS partners was already partaking in a great deal of professional development on the topic of trauma informed practices. They offered to host a PDS meeting at their school, and all consortium members were invited to hear the person who was guiding the school through their professional development speak. It was an enormous success. The talk was so informative, and all it took was a school inviting PDS consortium members to professional development that was already happening and budgeted for at one of our partner schools. Our work did not end there, of course. A faculty member at Buffalo State helped us to partner with a nearby agency who had the rights to show a film on trauma. This event took place on campus, which made it more accessible for teacher candidates. A resilience taskforce was formed on campus to better organize the effort. A faculty member who joined the taskforce shared that she had expertise in the areas of trauma and resilience, and the group began to discuss how the content, with her expertise, could be worked into a course that every teacher candidate was required to take. Along with other ongoing initiatives, the university was able to secure grants from a campus grant allocation committee. This helped to bring two speakers to campus, and the events were made available to all PDS stakeholders at no charge. This is just one example of how the Buffalo State PDS consortium worked to fill a need that was (and still is) important to teacher candidates, university faculty, and school partners. With more informed teachers, P–12 students likely benefited from the initiative as well.

All PDSs likely have a different way of funding the partnership and budgeting the money. As noted earlier, Buffalo State's PDS consortium has a yearly budget similar to that of a salary of a faculty member at the university. As the PDS director, I help to develop the yearly budget because the money comes solely from the university, and there are some restrictions on how it can be spent. However, most of the funds go to the school partners as part of the university agreements we enter with them each semester, and then the liaison team at each partner school decides on how to spend the stipend. The Buffalo State PDS consortium has developed standard agreements to provide consistency and fairness across partnerships (Ferrara, 2014).

However, if you are following the earlier suggestion to start small, you may begin with one partner. If this is the case, your institution and the partner can negotiate the PDS agreement to best meet the needs of both organizations (Ferrara, 2014).

Clark (1998) describes four ways that funding can be organized through effective PDS partnerships: (1) eliminating older programs in order to adopt something new, (2) an agreement to share funding, (3) the procurement of external funding, and (4) entrepreneurialism, which is a combination of the aforementioned approaches.

Here is another example from a different PDS network. Ferrara (2014) stated: "When the first PDS was created at my college, the school district and the college donated equal amounts. However, when the college decided to build a network of PDSs, the school districts paid a yearly fee to be included in the network. The fee is used to support all PDS initiatives based on the goals of the partnership, whereas the college pays the salary of the university liaison connected to the school" (Ferrara, 2014, p. 41). Again, it is likely that every partnership and/or network in some way differs from another. No one way is the best way.

Benefits to Schools

So, how is becoming a PDS beneficial to a school? There's no one answer, as each school and university have different strengths and needs. But in this section we will look at general benefits to partners of a PDS.

Schools can benefit from being partners with a university because it is more in the wheelhouse of the university faculty to secure grants that can be used to carry out projects with a school partner(s). It is a requirement of the university faculty to complete research projects, so they can help the PDS school partner while carrying out their teaching, service, and scholarship.

Partnerships between the school and a teacher preparation program at a university can result in close relationships between university faculty and teachers in the PDS. As trust is built, these relationships can lead to informal professional development among the university faculty and the teachers. As they work together side by side with teacher candidates in the schools, they exchange information. Through mentorship of teacher candidates, teachers might also benefit from receiving tuition vouchers to take courses for free at the university. The accumulation of these courses can sometimes help them earn additional degrees and/or certifications, and possibly move them to a higher step on the pay scale, allowing them to increase their salaries (Sosin and Parnham, 1998).

Ties to a university can also afford teachers opportunities to teach courses at the university as adjunct professors, broadening their knowledge base and strengthening relationships with the university while sharing their practical knowledge base and experience, along with making extra money (Sosin & Parnham, 1998).

Clark (1999) has discussed some of the benefits of PDS relationships for school partners, writing that "schools gain prestige from connections with universities and, often instructional and curricular resources from such collaborations" (pp. 79–80). Forming collaborative relationships can be a feather in a school administrator's cap. Data from joint research between the school and university can be used to provide evidence for the success of various initiatives or used to show a need in the school building.

PDS relationships can produce reduced student–adult ratios. Teacher candidates can be in classrooms to provide individual and small-group instruction that may not be feasible with only one adult in the classroom. This is an example of a tangible asset resulting from a PDS partnership. Basile (2010) described examples of tangible assets, such as "[R]educed student–adult ratios, professional development for clinical teachers, additional leadership within the school, additional adults in the school to lead enrichment activities, and changing systems that are inclusive of new resources" (p. 3).

On the contrary, intangible assets are not as clear or easy to evaluate as tangible assets. They may not provide immediate benefits to a school because intangible assets frequently develop across time. Basile (2010) stated: "Intangible assets are difficult to see and difficult to assess, but they include such things as the impact of all professional development, the extent of the relationships that build over time, changes in leadership, and the increase in student effort" (p. 3). All this leads to the idea of intellectual capital.

Intellectual capital is what people know and bring to an organization (such as a PDS relationship) that leads to enhanced values to others in the partnership. The PDS managing intellectual capital is crucial because there are multiple resources, systems, and kinds of knowledge to consider, which could impact the success of the partnership, and possibly student learning (Basile, 2009). Basile stressed the importance of "taking stock of these intangible assets that contribute to the school's intellectual capital is imperative if we are to better understand what happens in a PDS and why these assets are so important to the success of the teacher candidate and the students in the school" (p. 3). PDS benefits other stakeholders as well.

Benefits for Teacher Educators

Collaboration between teacher educators and school personnel in the PDS can be beneficial for the teacher educators in many ways as far as research opportunities and having knowledge of and/or being part of a school culture (Sosin & Parnham, 1998). Teacher educators can have opportunities to work with P–12 teachers and their students due to PDS partnerships. "These opportunities keep faculty grounded in real school challenges while increasing their opportunities for research and reflection" (Ferrara, 2014, p. 23). In addition, teacher educators in PDSs have more control over the quality of the clinically rich experiences of their teacher candidates (Ferrara, 2014). Clark (1999) has written that "universities improve their public image through outreach activities that connect with schools. Research and development funds from government and private philanthropy often are tied to conditions of partnership with schools" (p. 80).

Snyder (1999) described the benefits of universities getting involved with PDS. Supporting PDS indicated that universities were responding to demands to enhance the quality of teachers, as well as addressing teacher shortages. Universities may also benefit from some funding opportunities associated with their involvement with PDS. Another benefit was "a budding intellectual understanding of, and ethical commitment to, the importance of quality teacher education as a fundamental function of the academy" (Snyder, 1999, p. 137).

Barriers Instead of Benefits

Pritchard and Ancess (1999) parsed out research on possible barriers that may impact effective school–university partnerships.

1. Bolman and Deal (1993) described structural, human, political, and symbolic problems.

2. Whitford and Metcalf-Turner (1999) discussed barriers related to equity, sustainability, and comprehensiveness.

3. Lieberman and Miller (1992), Sirotnick (1991), Brookfield (1995), and Metcalf-Turner (1999) examined cultural differences between the school and university settings, such as time constraints and different reward systems.

Sirotnick (1991) developed a list of school–university partnership roadblocks. He pointed out the differences between the school and university cultures, such as norms related to time and space. Difficulties with consistent leadership and commitment from partners can be troublesome. Resources can sometimes cause problems for school–university partnerships. The understanding that there are no quick fixes and trouble living with ambiguity can lead to problems. Authentic collaboration and shared leadership can also be trying. Pritchard and Ancess (1999) stressed how valuable research to overcome frequent roadblocks would be for both PDSs and school instruction.

Approaches to PDS

This a very broad heading. When I think of approaches to PDS, different things come to mind. An approach could relate to a perspective or stance taken to carry out the PDS effort. Approaches could be ways to differentiate PDS program offerings. Approach could also refer to different models or configurations of PDSs. Keep this in mind as we check out a few of these types of approaches to PDS.

Professional development schools play a part in educational reform called professionalism (Sykes, 1997). Goodlad (1990) envisioned the effort for professionalism taking place in school–university partnerships. He explained the importance of renewal of schools and professional education to work together to bring about change in the system of education as a whole. Goodlad saw things like standards and other PDS guidelines as change agents (Sykes, 1997) to bring together schools and universities to bring changes in certain aspects of each organization. He viewed the necessity for a balance between the internal and external dimensions of change such as accountability demands (Neapolitan & Levine, 2011; Sykes, 1997).

PDS principles and guidelines can be used in two ways. Three approaches examined by Neapolitan and Levine used the internal development process approach for the achievement of shared goals and outcomes. Some see this approach as helpful in providing direction and stimulation for the PDS effort. From this perspective, it is seen as a bottom-up endeavor that is organic and adaptable. A second way that PDS principles and guidelines can be used is the external development process, which focuses on the rigor of the reform efforts with strong external standards (Sykes, 1997).

Neapolitan and Levine (2011) examined PDS approaches by groups that had PDS guidelines that were most widely practiced in the field of education. These approaches viewed the PDS effort as "a crucial institution supporting the preparation of educators, the conduct of applied inquiry and, the improvement of schooling" (Sykes, 1997, p. 159). Neapolitan and Levine selected the PDS approaches based on the organizations who have aided the development of PDSs around the world. Historically, these approaches have engaged in and supported PDS effort through endeavors such as obtaining research grants, collaborative research, funding scholarships, creating research centers, holding conferences, creating research centers and scholarship programs, engaging in research, and publication that promoted PDS. Neapolitan and Levine (2011) grouped the approaches they sought to examine by the view each held to as far as what is required for the PDS effort—either the need for direction and stimulation to promote innovation or the necessity to maintain fidelity to rigorous standards. Sykes (1997) writes that "these opposing views operate within different but overlapping spheres of action, each projecting a vision of reform" (p. 163). Neapolitan and Levine's approach choices may sound familiar. These approaches were discussed previously as frameworks to support PDS and as part of PDS history:

1. The Holmes Partnership

2. The National Network for Educational Renewal (NNER)

3. The National Association for Professional Development Schools (NAPDS)

4. The National Council for Accreditation of Teacher Education (NCATE)

Neapolitan and Levine (2011) grouped three of the approaches of the Holmes Partnership, the NNER, and NAPDS entities in the first sphere of action, which consisted of "the need to direct and stimulate innovation with the focus of action on support and sharing of craft knowledge" (p. 310). The networks cited under this category tend to be voluntary and funded by memberships. In this sphere, educational reform was categorized as a bottom-up endeavor that was controlled internally (Neapolitan & Levine, 2011; Sykes, 1997).

In the second sphere of action, Neapolitan and Levine (2011) grouped the NCATE standards and those put in place by the state of Maryland at the time. Sphere 2 was "the need to sustain fidelity to difficult ideals with the focus of action on professionalization of teaching through standard setting and accountability" (p. 310). Organizations in this sphere were those that joined professional-related associations to government groups that have the authority to put out standards for accreditation and licensure purposes (Neapolitan & Levine, 2011; Sykes, 1997).

These spheres and the organizations Neapolitan and Levine (2011) grouped under them have different visions of reform but run within overlapping spheres of action. While the discussion of the aforementioned approaches pertains more to the bigger picture of the PDS effort, the next two approaches relate to more generic school–university partnership configurations working toward a PDS structure.

Ravid and Handler's (2001) review of literature found four models of school–university partnerships. In order to provide teacher training via a PDS, schools and universities may enter into formal or informal relationships. Overall, the PDS approach focuses primarily on the preparation of future teachers. The consultation model is a one-way dissemination of knowledge, resources, and professional expertise to teachers for the improvement of classroom practices. The second model of school–university partnerships is the one-on-one collaboration where university faculty and teachers engage in the piloting of curriculum or research to improve instruction. In this model, there is more of an even exchange between the teacher and university faculty member. In the third model, the partnership is comprised of close relationships between the teacher and university faculty member that often leads to mentorship by the university faculty member. The fourth model entails the school and university working on projects based on a shared PDS agenda. These models can also be viewed as a progression of school–university partnerships with aspirations of becoming a PDS as the relationships mature. Then again, some school–university partnerships will look like or look close to one of the first three models mentioned above. Partners carrying out one of the first three models of a school–university partnership may find that the model is meeting their particular needs at this time, and they can continue to work on moving closer to the NAPDS 9 Essentials.

Baker (2011) described other configurations of school–university partnerships within the context of a specific three-year grant. The categories single-tier, multi-tier, and complex-brokered are described in general.

The single-tier partnership configuration is the simplest kind of partnership. This entails professors working with teachers in a school. In this instance, professors are viewed to have some expertise that will help to make improvements in classrooms. It is similar to Ravid and Handler's (2001) consultation model. These types of partnerships succeed when teachers are willing and receptive to working with professors to make improvements in the classroom. The improvement of classroom instruction working with the teacher is the main focus of this kind of partnership. The professor's work does not include widespread school improvement. Although simple, these types of school–university partnerships can be long-lasting. They might have stemmed from previously existing relationships, such as the professor's former students who work at a nearby school.

The multi-tier partnership configuration consists of many stakeholders from a range of levels of authority and decision-making capabilities. The initial relationship between a professor and a teacher carries on, but others have become part of the partnership. In this configuration, the focus of the partnership is more complex than the classroom and may include the classroom, whole school, or possibly a network of schools. The work is likely related to an area of the curriculum across many grade levels. District leaders who are aware of the expectations of the schools in the district may play an active role in the partnership. When the district leaders become involved, school principals may have increased expectations and responsibilities related to the partnership. There should be a strong tie between schools' improvement plans and PDS. University faculty members often take on the role of program facilitator or coach in these types of partnerships. They spend a good deal of time in the school and may work with grade level or instructional teams or consult with school and district administrators (Baker, 2011).

In the single- and multi-tier partnership designs, the view is that the university folks have the expertise in the partnership, but the configuration is different in the third or complex-brokered partnership design. In this situation, based on a need, experts are brought in to share new knowledge and best practices for the university and school educators. University faculty may play a part in selecting the expert and different formats may be used to deliver the content of the outside expertise. The hired expert may arrive and do a series of sessions. In another design, the expert serves as a trainer through workshops and consultations across time to improve teacher quality. "Complex-brokered partnerships face serious problems in creating structures that assure sustainability and ongoing commitment from local educators" (Baker, 2011, p. 56). The lack of ongoing support may slow down or hinder teachers' development of whatever content or practice they were learning with the expert. Parker et al. (2016) described their approach to PDS at a more granular, programmatic level.

Parker et al. (2016) described a different kind of approach to PDS and called their initiative at George Mason University "Pathways to Partnership." This was a "Developmental framework for building PDS relationships" (Parker et al., 2016, p. 34). There was a need for variation and flexibility in PDS partnerships. With all this in mind, the researchers sought to expand the idea of what a PDS is while still working within the 9 Essentials. Their program was based on the PDS philosophy with the purposes of improving P–12 learning, teacher candidate learning, mentor teacher professional learning, as well as school–university inquiry. The foundation for their programmatic changes were the NAPDS 9 Essentials. They were guided by the need to provide earlier and more rigorous field experiences for teacher candidates while still listening to the needs of school partners in difficult financial times.

As Parker and colleagues were making decisions on how to differentiate their program offerings and provide for more flexibility, they were sure to listen to the needs of all the stakeholders. For instance, there were schools not adhering to the NAPDS 9 Essentials that still wanted to be called PDSs. They didn't want to or were unable to support inquiry as part of their partnership.

They found that schools preferred the full-year internship model over others. As well, they learned that the teachers found it very confusing when teacher candidates from different points in their program were placed at one school. It was difficult for them to keep track of the different requirements for teacher candidates and various levels. Based on this feedback and the overall need for differentiation and flexibility, they sought to broaden the idea of a PDS.

First, they designed two options to allow for flexibility for teacher candidates. The first option ended with a year-long internship with one primary and one intermediate experience. Teacher candidates who selected this option would be allowed to substitute-teach in the school and receive a small stipend. The second option culminated with a semester-long internship experience for 16 weeks in one grade level. Ultimately, these options provided flexibility for the schools as well.

Parker et al. (2016) then provided options for their school partners or multiple pathways to partnership. Schools were able to select the pathway that was best for them at that time. The options were school partner, clinical practice sites, and collaborative inquiry.

If school sites were new to PDS, if they needed a break from a more intense partnership involving collaborative inquiry, or if they endured a lot of administrative and/or teacher turnover, they might select the Partner Site option. With this option, the school hosts teacher candidates for their early fieldwork, which consist of observations, individual tutoring, or possibly small-group or whole-group instruction. These sites can access university faculty for professional development or take a graduate-level clinical faculty training course.

If partners choose the second pathway option (Clinical Practice Sites), they must agree to host five teacher candidates in their final year or semester with enough willing mentor teachers who took the clinical faculty training course offered at the university for the teacher candidates. Parker et al. (2016) chose to rotate the full year and 16-week internship placements, so some schools didn't always get the preferred full year internship teacher candidates. A university site facilitator visited the school every other week, and in the meantime the teacher candidates sent the university site facilitator videos of their instruction for feedback.

The third pathway was the Collaborative Inquiry option. If a school selects this option, they need to agree to host at least five teacher candidates who have selected the year-long internship option. These sites have full-time university faculty members at the school one day a week. They not only supervise interns but also support inquiry-based research projects related to the collaborative work of the PDS stakeholders. The consistency of the university faculty member in the school assists in building trusting relationships, which helps to foster shared professional development and research endeavors between the school and university.

All of the pathways to partnership have site facilitators, access to the clinical faculty course, and a consistent relationship with a university faculty member. Parker et al. (2016) reflected on the success of their efforts and discussed ways to improve the program in the future. They also found that their partners appreciated the flexibility of these pathways. In addition, the pathways kept the university faculty from spreading themselves too thin and helped them to be more aligned with the NAPDS 9 Essentials with the schools that came on board as Collaborative Inquiry sites. Their careful gathering of feedback from their stakeholders and creative planning allowed them to better meet the needs of their partners and to broaden what it means to be a PDS (Parker et al., 2016). The next two approaches discussed somewhat align with parts of the aforementioned pathways to partnership, but more generically in the discussion of possible approaches or configurations with aspirations of following the NAPDS 9 Essentials.

Not only are there many approaches to PDS, there are also varying ideas regarding the notion of an approach. The first approaches discussed in this section were related to key reports, essentials, and standards throughout PDS history with a more general examination of how they overlapped and were both necessary for the PDS effort (Goodlad, 1990). The next two approaches were related to specific configurations, whereas the approach discussed by Parker et al. was a program-related way of broadening what it means to be a PDS while attending to the needs of stakeholders.

Teacher Residency

Just like the field of education's call for clinically rich practice was based on the field of medicine, so is the idea of teacher residency. In medicine, the residency is part of a doctor's training. During their residency, they put into practice what they learned in school, working with patients under the supervision of experienced doctors. Teacher residencies afford similar opportunities for teacher candidates to practice what they have learned at the university in authentic classroom settings with a great deal of mentorship. Teacher candidates work with expert teachers who model best practices with students for the teacher candidates (Guha et al., 2016).

Guha et al. (2016) explained that the teacher residencies of today were based on practices of the 1960s and 1970s. They derived from government funding provided to prestigious institutions of higher education to develop Master of Arts in Teaching programs to address a teacher shortage. These were post-graduate programs that took a full year to complete. These teacher candidates were placed in classrooms for a one-year student-teaching internship with expert mentor teachers while simultaneously taking courses at the university. At the onset of these programs, the government provided funding to support the cost of the teacher education program for teacher candidates. Although much of this initial funding has faded away, similar residency programs are in operation. These early programs laid the groundwork for an updated residency model where there are tighter connections between the school (or district) and the university, increased mentorship, and financial opportunities.

The specific *urban* teacher residency programs started in 2001 to recruit and retain quality teachers for the Chicago public schools. Boston and Denver created residency programs in 2003. The following year, the Chicago, Boston, and Denver residency programs formed a partnership that eventually became known as the National Center for Teacher Residencies (NCTR) and continually added additional programs to the group (Chu & Wang, 2022; Guha et al., 2016).

The teacher residency model differs from alternative certification options and more traditional teacher education programs. Most residency programs begin in a similar way as a PDS partnership. The model begins with a relationship between a university and a school or district with hiring needs. Teacher residencies provide for a lengthier placement in a school (usually a year) and affords teacher residents opportunities to observe and work with an experienced mentor teacher. The residency is often structured using a co-teaching model where the resident and mentor teacher share the responsibilities of instructing, assessing, and classroom management (Chu & Wang, 2022).

The amount of time residents spend in a school surpasses the time spent in the field of most of the traditional teacher education programs. Traditional education programs and alternative preparation programs tend to provide less field hours and less mentorship than teacher residencies (Guha et al., 2016).

Overall, teacher residencies

1. create a vehicle to recruit teachers for high-need fields and locations,

2. offer recruits strong content and clinical preparation specifically for the kinds of schools and communities in which they will teach,

3. connect new teachers to early career mentoring that will keep them in the profession,

4. provide financial incentives that keep teachers in the districts that have invested in them, and

5. offer teacher candidates a curriculum tightly integrated with their clinical practice, which creates a more powerful learning experience. The interconnectedness of theory to practice reinforces research-based best practices for teacher residents (Guha et al., 2016, p. 2).

Residency programs typically concentrate on places and subject areas where there are teacher shortages. The idea is that the residents will be prepared in the particular places and subject areas of shortage and then, ideally, stay there to teach after they are certified. "When used in this deliberative manner, teacher residencies can address a crucial recruitment need (Chu & Wang, 2022) while also building the capacity of the districts to provide high-quality instruction to the students they serve" (Guha et al., 2016, p. 2).

Many residency programs offer financial incentives to attract quality teacher candidates. For a commitment to stay in the district affiliated with the residency for approximately three to five years, residents might receive living stipends, tuition paid for, or student loans forgiven. Between 2008 and 2014, Teacher Quality Partnership Grants Program, an outgrowth of the Higher Education Opportunity Act, was the main source of funding for residency programs. Rural residency programs came about, in addition to the Urban Teacher Residency (UTR) model (Chu & Wang, 2022; Guha et al., 2016; Villarreal & Henning, 2020).

Henning (2018) described a unique version of a residency program at Monmouth University. The program is considered to be a paid internship. This residency program had similar goals as other residency programs, such as to enhance teacher candidates' knowledge and practice, to assist them in becoming fluent in their practice, and make the teacher candidates more comfortable with the school setting and the work of teaching. The residency program included an increase in the length of clinical experiences, the use of co-teaching, and assessing the impact of teacher candidates on student learning with the primary goal of improving the achievement of P–12 learners. The common goal of improving student learning helped to bring the Monmouth University Partnership together. They examined all their initiatives to decide if it would ultimately increase student learning.

The single goal of increasing P–12 learning led to greater buy-in, more collaboration, and a sense of shared responsibility for not only student learning but teacher preparation as well.

The teacher candidates' increased time in the schools helped them become able to build stronger relationships with the children, become more confident in the practice of teaching, and utilize increasingly complex teaching strategies to improve student learning. However, the Monmouth residency program did not have any external funding. Teacher candidates participated in multi-year apprenticeships to allow for as much experience in schools as possible. Then instead of working outside of their teacher preparation program, they are compensated by the schools.

Along with course work and field hours, the Monmouth teacher candidates spend time working in the schools whenever they are on break—including summer programs. This program is sustainable because the schools pay the residents as substitute teachers, and the residents can do the work of substitute teachers, paraprofessionals, and/or tutors at any part of the school, depending on the needs of the school, all with the support of a mentor. Henning (2018) explained that the more time teacher candidates spend in a school, the more they are valued by the school.

Research on teacher residency programs is limited. In general, residents reported having positive learning experiences that ultimately increased their knowledge and skills related to teaching and helped them to feel confident and prepared (Chu & Wang, 2022). Even less research has been conducted on the impact of teacher residency on student achievement. Some studies on teacher residency discussed that children with residents in their class improved or outperformed students who did not have a resident in their classrooms. For instance, students of residents and those who graduated from a residency program outperformed students who were taught by novice teachers in a 2015 study of the New Visions Hunter College Urban Teacher Residency (UTR) in New York City on state Regents exams. Another study was completed on the Memphis Teacher Residency Program. It was found that students of residency graduates had higher gains in student achievement than students who had other beginning teachers, and students of experienced teachers showed even larger gains on state exams (Guha et al., 2016).

Henning et al. (2018) suggested a technique for examining the impact of the resident on P–12 learning. Since teacher candidates are consistently in a school for a whole year, existing school data can be used to measure impact. They suggested that the resident and mentor teacher could craft student growth objectives at the beginning of the school year. Later in the school year, school assessment data can be utilized to compare the students' learning and the original growth objectives.

The attentiveness to the model, the integrity, and the implementation of the teacher residency are the keys to success. Residents and mentor teachers should be carefully selected to work in a strong school–university partnership. A tightly integrated curriculum based on a year-long clinical placement in classrooms and schools that model strong practice is a necessity for success of a teacher residency program. In addition, financial and mentoring support are crucial (Guha et al., 2016).

It is clear that high-quality teacher residency programs can have a favorable impact on the residents and their P–12 students. "Teacher residencies have focused on intensive clinical teacher preparation. It is possible that many PDSs either have or could have teacher residencies as the clinical preparation component of their design" (Burns et al., 2022, p. 39). As residency programs become more widespread in teacher education, it is likely that schools and universities will see the shared responsibilities for educating teacher candidates and P–12 learners. It is the hope of Henning et al. (2018) that teacher residency programs become the standard in teacher preparation.

Selecting a Partner

Clark (1998) developed ideas to consider when thinking about forming a PDS. He believed that in order for partnerships to be successful, "participants need to be thoroughly grounded in the context of their work" (p. 168). To reduce stakeholder mistrust, much discussion should occur regarding the mutually beneficial goals of the partnerships. Clark explained that, initially, a formal agreement developed by a few stakeholders and foisted on the larger group of stakeholders should be replaced by making sure that clear, extensive discussions take place to encourage the understanding of the partnership's purpose and function. Clark warned that burgeoning partnerships should be goal-oriented and not just forming a partnership for the sake of having a partnership. All partners are encouraged to carefully ponder the specific reasons for the partnership before embarking on a PDS relationship. This should also involve careful monitoring of the reasons to avoid an early failure of the partnership. After stakeholders comprehend the specific reasons for forming a PDS partnership, appropriate structures should be put in place to help carry out the goals of the partnership. This would include the membership and organizational frameworks of the PDS relationship, along with support by way of funding and governance procedures.

When it comes to professional development (PD), Clark espoused that the roles of the PDS participants be delineated ahead of time, particularly if the university faculty member is performing the PD sessions and it is understood that the topic of the PD is not necessarily held to being associated with views of the overall PDS. The faculty member from the university should be deemed a consultant so all participants know what to expect. This would be somewhat of a shift from the informal relationship between the university faculty, who usually informally works in the teachers' classrooms providing support for the teacher candidates. Additionally, Clark (1998) stated, "Getting the right people to participate to accomplish the purpose of the partnership is critical" (p. 168). In the same vein, it is crucial to select just the right leader to head up the partnership. "Ideally this person will have charismatic leadership qualities and be perceived as a friend (or at least a neutral) by all participants" (Clark, 1998, p. 168).

Boundary spanners are an important part of a PDS partnership. These folks help to keep communication flowing among all stakeholders in the group. Most of the partnership's members should be knowledgeable about the PDSs agenda to fulfill specific goals to avoid the failure of the partnership when important key members come and go. Clark (1998) has cautioned that "individuals engaged in partnership activities must be engaged in authentic ways" (p. 169). The partnership should continuously monitor that the group remains focused on the original goals in order to reaffirm the commitment of the group's stakeholders to the PDS relationship.

It's difficult to think of all these things before entering into a partnership. Some of them simply cannot be addressed at the early stages of partnership planning. It may seem minor to some, but one thing we tend to consider in our teacher education program at Buffalo State before entering into a partnership is the proximity of the partner school from campus. Remember that Essential 1 of the NAPDS 9 Essentials calls on PDS stakeholders to vehemently support antiracism endeavors, along with equitable and rightful teaching in an effort to address students' opportunity gaps (Zenkov et al., 2021). If the school is not near campus or is inaccessible by bus, this is both problematic for and unfair to students who do not have cars. We do have partnerships further away from campus, but we try to make sure that there are choices nearer to campus as far as the other sections of a course are concerned. Most students who attend Buffalo State University are the first generation in their family attending college and have one or more jobs while going to school. It feels neither equitable nor justified to put students in a position where they are forced to pay extraordinary amounts of money for ridesharing just to get to a school that is a requirement of their methods course or student teaching.

So, as you can see, there is much to consider when forming a PDS relationship, both on the side of the university and of the school. Clark's (1998) considerations delve into specific aspects of partnership that folks who are newer to the concept might not think to take into account. As well, each institution must consider various aspects of the partnership that might specifically impact in a negative way a group or groups of stakeholders.

From another perspective, Teitel (2003) has offered an alternative way to create a partnership. He begins with two tasks: investigation and initiation. As part of the investigation phase, Teitel recommends looking at your own organization, considering possible partners, and exploring the larger environment. Then, consider the benefits to your organization and decide if it is worthwhile to partner, or even worth further exploration and consideration. Teitel (2003) described the second phase as initiation. This involves locating partners that interest your organization, seem compatible, and worth your time. It is important to have a shared mutual interest. When these are determined, other challenges must be addressed.

Teitel (2003) divided challenges for developing a partnership into three domains: internal issues, issues in relationship to your partner, and larger contextual or environmental issues. For the first domain, examine challenges related to issues in your own organization. Prior to searching for partners, consider if your own organization would make a good partner. Determine if your organization is open to change and ready to innovate with others. Think about who and how many people in your organization would be supportive of a partnership, particularly the people with the most power. Finally, consider how your organization's culture, framework, perspective, and governance would match with those of a potential partner.

The second domain involves examining issues related to your potential partner. Think about what you already know about the organization. Determine if there is a positive or negative history with the potential partner. "Initially, it is imperative that universities, in their zest to build partnerships and PDSs, do not overlook the prior histories between schools and universities. Previous interactions and experiences will affect the way that the partnership is structured, the roles of the partners, and the nature of the relationship that is established. With that background information, partners can initiate the process of establishing partnerships more effectively by recognizing that some historical stances influence how and whether egalitarianism is achieved" (Lefever-Davis, 2007, p. 209).

Consider your various similarities and differences, and decide if trust can be developed between the two organizations to foster a collaborative relationship. If all the aforementioned responses seem positive, consider sealing the deal and formalizing the partnership. Teitel noted that some successful partnerships began with just an agreement by handshake. This may be OK initially, and then the two organizations can enter into a partnership after working together for some time. More discussion of agreements will come later in this chapter. Teitel (2003) stated: "Announcements and other ceremonies sometimes accompany these agreements. They can draw positive attention to the PDS as well as help define roles and organize structures, resource allocations, and decision-making processes" (p. 18). One further domain remains to be considered when examining challenges related to potential partnerships.

It is important to explore larger contextual or environmental issues. Visualize the larger context in which your PDS would be situated. "Looking at the larger environment helps you place your PDS development in a bigger context, something many PDS advocates miss" (Teitel, 2003, p. 15). Determine if there are barriers to partnering, and consider possible solutions for the obstacles. Consider the possibility of how interests can align and how allies can be made.

Again, I need to reiterate that building and maintaining a PDS relationship is not easy; the path can be mighty bumpy along the way (Sosin & Parnham, 1998). Sosin and Parnham found that three factors were essential for the realization of a PDS: insulation, information, and focus on positives. Insulation supports the capacity to rise above difficulties encountered. Information refers to the clarity involving issues related to beginning a PDS and if these issues are being consistently addressed by liaisons from both the school and university. Information must be disseminated accurately to foster stakeholder buy-in the PDS mission. It's usually best to focus on the positives in any situation. The same holds true for PDS relationships. Concentrate on the benefits of the PDS collaboration to various stakeholders, such as students, teacher candidates, mentor teachers, administrators, and university faculty, to name a few.

Another consideration is who from each of the partnering organizations gives permission to solidify the PDS relationship. At Buffalo State University, our agreements with schools need to be signed by the course instructor, the PDS director, the Chair of the Department, the Dean of the School of Education, and the university's financial officer. No one person at the institution can approve a PDS agreement. On the university end of the paperwork, we need only the signature of the school site principal (Gilbert et al., 2018). However, it is not always clear if the principal has the authority to enter into PDS agreements with the university. For instance, Sosin and Parnham (1999) wrote about their question of whether or not a principal from a school had the autonomy to form an affiliation with a university. They wrote: "If the process of formally creating a PDS is to go forward, the school district superintendent must agree to the affiliation. Selection of the teacher education program with which to affiliate may become a district decision rather than a school decision" (p. 18). We have run into these situations at Buffalo State. Strangely, even people in the same district had different responses to forming a partnership. There were principals who have immediately responded affirmatively and agreed to form a PDS with us; however, in the same district, there are principals who say that they have to ask permission from the district's supervisor of student teaching for a potential partnership centered around a methods course, not student teaching.

The topic above relates to another issue we have run into at Buffalo State. We have several institutions with teacher education programs in close proximity, so competition exists among the programs for school partners. Some schools want to have affiliations with many universities because of the benefits of partnership. However, this decision is typically made by an administrator, and the teachers expected to mentor the teacher candidates from various teacher preparation programs can become overwhelmed. We have also been in partnership with schools that had insufficient placements for our teacher candidates because they were taking candidates from a different university as well. Teitel (2003) explained that this can happen when there are more teacher education programs in an area than there are possible partner schools. He suggested that procedures be developed to provide fair opportunities for all the teacher preparation programs in the area. He also mentioned that this could go the other way, where there are more schools that want to partner than there are universities. Due to these types of complications, it is always good to try to put something in writing to formalize your relationship with a partner. Teitel (2003) agreed that PDS partnerships frequently can start off informally; however, it is important to eventually formalize the partnership so that the needs of both institutions are met.

At Buffalo State, there is a more formal process to work with the closest and largest school district nearest to campus. All partnerships must be approved by one person in the district. However, partnerships with other schools and districts typically begin due to personal connections, such as a faculty member having a former student at the school or an adjunct professor at the university who used to teach in the potential partner school. PDS relationships might begin because of grants or personal connections, or even an event might be the catalyst for collaboration (Teitel, 2003).

Another issue with having teacher education programs in close proximity can be a discrepancy in how teachers are reimbursed for their mentorship. Some institutions have been awarded large grants for residency programs and the like. These programs can afford to pay teachers a great deal of money for working with teacher candidates, while other programs have to reimburse the school (not each mentor teacher) or comply with a rate set by a governing body. However, programs that are running on grants are often not sustainable because that funding will eventually end.

Given these examples, it is evident why the frameworks and questions developed by Clark (1999), Teitel (2003), and others can be so helpful. It is important to address the possibility of different scenarios prior to entering into a PDS partnership with a school unable to sustain a mutually beneficial relationship.

Teitel (2003) listed questions to answer to determine the positive and negative characteristics of potential PDS partners. He recommended that institutions begin by brainstorming a list of prospective partners, and that they use such questions as those listed below to evaluate the potential organizations to narrow down who would make solid future partners.

1. Do you and the potential partner have matching or compatible philosophies?

2. Is there close enough proximity to the partner institution to make connections and not have to travel too far?

3. Has the history with this potential been positive or neutral?

4. Are there connections with people already in place or do you need to start from scratch?

5. Is there support from the institution to form a PDS?

6. Is there a foundation of trust built on competence, dependability, collegiality, positive motives for the partnership, and minimal or no issues with control? (p. 39).

Possible Barriers to Forming a PDS

Schools and universities tend to have distinct cultures with differences that can cause roadblocks to partnership. It is important for each institution to think about the differences and consider if the benefits of the partnership remain worthwhile. Schools and universities can vary in the way that employees are rewarded, how content is taught, how administrators run an institution, the control held by an institution, and how policies are made. There are also differences in how money is spent in schools as opposed to universities. Schools tend to focus on the educational programs they are buying and delivering to their learners in the most effective and efficient way possible (Trubowitz & Longo, 1997). On the other hand, universities possess multiple missions, which can lead to inefficiencies. Significant cultural differences between universities and schools are evident when it comes to examining the interactions between school teachers and university faculty members. These differences are apparent in interactions related to power struggles, lack of agreement on a shared vision, uncertainty about roles, lack of consistent communication, scheduling conflicts, the division of labor, and lack of support or recognition. Often, the success of a partnership boils down to treating one another with respect (Ravid & Handler, 2001).

There are usually barriers to anything worth pursuing, but when forming PDS partnerships it is important to have an understanding of possible obstacles ahead of time. Each institution having different priorities can be a barrier. "Interpretation of the PDS concept as prioritizing teacher education and professional development can be perceived negatively, whereas schools insist that the first and most important mission for the school is to educate the children, with staff development as a necessary but secondary goal" (Sosin & Parham, 1998, p. 16). Similar ideas for the mission of a PDS can provide for less barriers later in the partnership.

A lack of understanding or acceptance for the PDS approach can be another roadblock when it comes to partnering. The concept of PDS might be viewed as negatively impacting the school's mission of educating its children. Of course, universities are often viewed as ivory towers, not strong educational partners (Sosin & Parham, 1998). Barriers can arise when a perception occurs among teachers or schools that teacher educators or university professors lack an accurate understanding of what truly occurs in classrooms and schools. "Additional impediments to creating a PDS can include expressed lack of respect for teacher education, exemplified by teachers who became certified through emergency licensure and express low opinions of teacher education programs" (Sosin and Parham, 1998, p. 17).

Realistically, the selection of one school or more schools designated as PDSs takes up a larger proportion of energy and commitment of resources by the school of education than given to those schools not considered PDSs. In their comment on the Holmes Group's proposals for teacher education, Larabee and Pallas discussed the PDS concept and their own experiences. "Faculty in our own institution and others who have tried to establish a full-fledged PDS according to this (Holmes Group in Tomorrow 's Schools, 1990) model acknowledge this as a worthy endeavor that pays many dividends, but they note that it is very difficult to carry out. A small number of such institutions represents an enormous commitment of time, money, and staff for even the largest education schools" (Larabee & Pallas, 1996, p. 27b)

Essentially, the foundation of PDSs is the partnership. The early group of stakeholders forming the partnership can see the potential of a university and school coming together, knowing that extra effort and time will be required from both institutions to achieve shared goals. Here is a list of Teitel's (2003) reasons for why PDSs might begin:

- Perception of mutual interdependence: "We are in this together." Schools and universities (and sometimes community or other partners) can only be effective if we work more closely together.

- Internal cost–benefit analysis: "We can benefit from this in some way to meet our own organization's needs." Our partner(s) brings something to us that makes it worth the trouble.

- External perception cost–benefit analysis: "Collaboration makes us look good." This is worth doing because of how we are perceived.

- Incentive in the environment: "If we apply together, we can get this grant." An opportunity exists in the larger environment that makes it worth the trouble to collaborate.

- Personal connections: "I have an idea that might help both of our organizations." Opportunities develop out of formal or informal preexisting relationships (p. 9).

PDS Agreements

Consistent with the current research, I have thus far encouraged you to formalize your school–university partnerships in becoming a PDS. However, it is important to consider other viewpoints related to these formal agreements. Nolan et al. (2007) wrote of their institution's mature professional development partnership that functions without a formal agreement. They do point out that, formal agreement or not, their partnership is not without structures. "There are neither rigid reporting lines nor the super-ordinate structures one might find elsewhere. Its existence is recognized in the strategic plans of both the State College Area School District and Penn State's College of Education, but there is no organizational chart, no policy manual, nor any of the other trappings found in typical school or university organizations. The school–university partnership exists in a space between two rather venerable institutions and institutional cultures, influenced by both, but unlike either" (p. 105). Nolan et al. (2007) viewed their partnership as "a unique community with a culture of its own" (p. 105). They explained that their stakeholders have a bond that helps transform them to a more "we" mindset instead of a bunch of "I" mindsets. It is interesting to consider this example of a school–university partnership with no agreement, though, overall, consensus holds that an agreement is a good idea.

Teitel (2003) admitted that some partnerships, including some long-standing and flourishing partnerships, started, and continue to be run, based on informal "handshake" agreements. However, Brindley et al. (2008) hold that "PDS relationships are not informal 'handshake' agreements. Instead, they are carefully thought-out arrangements involving a multitude of issues, all of which need to be delineated in a written agreement" (p. 73). There are indeed partnerships with no formal agreements out there, but this tends not to be recommended.

Like numerous others, Teitel has advocated for partnerships to have at least a somewhat formal agreement. He suggested that partners take time to decide on what is included in the partnership agreement. Stakeholders can consider what the document looks like and who signs it. They can ask themselves questions to help determine what goes into the agreement. The questions can relate to shared beliefs, plans for money and resources, or the length of the agreement.

Some partnerships prefer not to make broad, long-term agreements, but instead to include a renewal date. After an agreed-upon date, partners can discuss and evaluate the collaboration and decide if they would like to continue the partnership. Ferrara (2014) has described PDS levels of growth in school transformation. The levels are beginning, developing, standard, and leading.

At Buffalo State, our agreements were constructed based on some of the NCATE PDS Standards (2001) rubric criteria to determine the level achieved by each partnership, such as beginning, developing, and at standard. At Buffalo State, our agreement levels begin at initial for the very first stages of partnership. The agreements are by semester as they align with specific courses taught in the teacher preparation programs. The levels indicate the nature of the partnership and the money given to schools aligns with the levels. Our partner schools are given a small stipend as a thank you for their level of partnership.

I was not around when the original agreements were drafted, but updates have been decided by our advisory council, called TEUPAC. The most recent update was a memorandum of understanding (MOU) pertaining to Buffalo State's perspective on equity and diversity. This was approved by Buffalo State's entire Teacher Education Unit (TEU) to explicitly make our stance known regarding this matter to our school partners.

The NCATE PDS Standards (2001) provided criteria and rubrics to evaluate PDS participation based on the five standards. The rubrics provided the criteria for the levels of beginning, developing, at standard, and leading. The general criteria for the beginning level are "beliefs, verbal commitments, plans, organization and initial work are consistent with the mission of PDS partnerships." PDS partnerships at the developing level "pursue the mission of a PDS partnership with partial institutional support." The at-standard level is where "the mission of the PDS partnerships is integrated into the partnering institutions. PDS work is expected and supported and reflects what is known about the best practices." The general criterion for the leading level indicates that advanced PDS work is sustaining and generative, leading to systematic changes in overall policy and practice in the partner institutions. There is also an impact on district, state, and national level policies. Each of the five NCATE PDS standards (2001) of learning community; accountability and quality assurance; collaboration; diversity and equity; and structures, resources, and roles of a PDS partnership are evaluated using the criteria in the rubrics for beginning, developing, at standard, and leading to determine levels.

Ferrara (2014) provided specific criteria or program components for each stage of development. In the **beginning** stage, the PDS initiatives present are a PDS liaison at the school, placements for student teachers, teacher candidate observations, and mentor teachers. The **developing** stage contains all four of the components at the beginning stage and courses at the school for teacher candidates and practicing teachers, teacher candidates provide tutoring or the P–12 learners at the school, and there is a PDS steering committee. The **standard** stage includes all the components from the developing stage as well as new hires are mentored by practicing teachers, and practicing teachers become adjunct faculty at the university. PDS stakeholders design and participate in projects, teacher candidates attend and present at conferences, PDS stakeholders provide input on policies and serve on school and university committees, and school and university stakeholders engage in collaborative research. Finally, along with the components of the other stages, the **leading** stage also includes PDS stakeholders publishing, and the PDS is considered a school with exemplary practices.

The Buffalo State PDS consortium uses criteria from the developmental guidelines to determine the level of each partnership based on the criteria on the rubrics for each of the five NCATE PDS Standards. The names of the levels have been adapted. The results indicate the overall participation level and determine the amount of money the school will receive for partnering with Buffalo State. The criteria are used to create the PDS agreements signed by administrators and faculty at Buffalo State and school administrators and liaisons for the partner schools. Each agreement is preceded by the Memorandum of Understanding (MOU).

Teitel (2003) noted the importance of formalizing the partnership with an agreement but added that some choose to develop the agreements right at the beginning of the relationship while other partnerships formalize things after they have had time to work together. He noted that "announcements and other ceremonies sometimes accompany these agreements. They can draw positive attention to the PDS as well as help define roles and organize structures, resource allocations, and decision-making processes" (p. 18). This is interesting to consider, and I guess it would have to depend on the level of trust between the school and the university, or perhaps the key players from each institution.

At Buffalo State we strive to set up partnerships early. We might need an extra section of a methods course the following semester, so we will look for and meet with a potential partner school the semester before. However, the PDS agreements are not signed until the actual semester the school is a partner. This can be a detriment. In some instances we have had to negotiate a partnership a semester before, and then when it came time for teacher candidates to go to the school, the administrator said they lacked placements for our teacher candidates because they were partnering with another university as well. Luckily, because we have so many great partners, connections, and a good reputation, we are usually able to find another partner school for the methods course. Lack of commitment can be a serious problem when forming relationships with another institution.

Partnerships can begin with teachers and their former professors from the university, but before formalizing the agreement, it is crucial to carefully consider who should be involved. Consider equity and diversity when weighing who should be part of the initial stages of the partnership. For instance, if a teacher welcomes a university faculty member into the school for observations, hosting methods courses or student teaching, it is important to get permission from the principal before committing to the partnership. As well, it is important for the faculty member to speak to their department chair and the person who oversees the development of new partnerships for your institution. This will avoid bad feelings later on, as well as the possibility of having to break up the relationship if administration does not approve.

Level of Commitment

You will probably find, or may have already found, that levels of commitment can differ in your PDS universe. Sometimes schools simply aren't into the partnership; other times, candidates at the schools are not seeing positive models of instruction. Issues can arise when a single university professor is not really connecting with the school. You might be thinking, "Geez, what if this happens and you have all signed an agreement?" At

Buffalo State, we have agreements with partners semester by semester. Then there is room to make necessary adjustments the following semester. Teitel (2003) observed that "finding the balance and matching levels of commitment can be a challenge. Open-ended partnerships need to keep in mind the need for an 'out' or a 'sunset' provision that can be applied to a relationship that isn't meeting the needs of the partner(s) but just limps along anyway" (p. 14).

Other situations may require an exit or break from an institution. I am coming from the university side of this situation, so I will give you a few examples from my experiences. There are instances where a faculty member knows their partners so well that they are able to identify that the school, specifically the teachers, need a break from the partnership. Maybe the teachers have to learn a new curriculum, or many of your usual mentor teachers have switched grade levels and are overwhelmed. Causes for these situations are countless. The university and/or school liaison should recognize that it is time for at least a break. The school can still be part of the consortium, but it has become clear that, currently, the relationship is no longer mutually beneficial.

At Buffalo State, we have experienced this situation. We want only positive and mutually beneficial relationships with all our partners. Some solutions have been to partner with a school every other semester to give them a break from mentoring teacher candidates for half of the school year in an attempt to avoid teacher burnout.

There was a new partnership where teacher candidates were not seeing best practices in the classroom, so the course instructor, department chair, and PDS director agreed that a change needed to be made. Because it was so early in the relationship with this school, there was not a high level of trust and familiarity between the university and the school, so the university was not yet in a position to have an open dialogue about ineffective practices. In order to do what is best for the teacher candidates, we did not enter into an agreement with this school the following semester. However, the school is still part of the Buffalo State PDS consortium and can benefit from professional development opportunities and PDS meetings at partner schools to learn about their programs.

We have also been in a very difficult position and had to end a relationship with a longtime school partner because the school was extremely far away for our teacher candidates. Over the years, the partnership had been incredibly strong, when more teacher candidates lived nearer to the school. As we have more and more students who are not local attending the university, it is more of a strain on them to get to the partner school, especially if they have no vehicle. It is no fun to end partnerships, but thankfully these situations are few and far between.

Here is an example of how one teacher preparation program developed their PDS program. After attending NAPDS 2011, Quinnipiac University's School of Education faculty used what they learned from the session to formalize the relationships they had with two schools. The following year, Quinnipiac's partnerships with two area schools became formalized through a Memorandum of Understanding (MOU) (Dichele, 2016).

One of Quinnipiac's partner schools was a charter school that from its inception sought to be a laboratory school that would offer highly innovative methods and programs for children who attended but also for those in the field of education who sought to collaborate. "Furthermore, there was a specific goal in the original charter that [the school] would become a place to train young teachers to be successful in complex, urban environments with mixed populations in terms of ethnicity and income, ability and achievement. The specific goal was to have a teacher and teaching intern in every grade, every year" (Dichele, 2016, p. 5).

Quinnipiac University's relationship with the charter school lent itself to a mutually beneficial partnership. For instance, the university and the charter school held workshops together so university faculty and the charter school teachers could stay up to date on changes in the field of education. This sparked Quinnipiac University's interest in learning from other area schools as well. After partnering with many schools, Quinnipiac found a public school that was as open and interested in gaining and sharing knowledge with a university as the charter school. At the center of both of Quinnipiac's school partnerships was student learning with a focus on social justice and equity. All three institutions were deeply dedicated to student achievement and how to carefully implement lasting improvement to both the PDS schools and the university teacher preparation program. To start, there was a clinical reading course at both of the PDS schools. Quinnipiac teacher candidates worked on reading with small groups of students at both charter schools. This was an example of a mutually beneficial relationship.

Classroom teachers from the schools train the teacher candidates, especially in ELL literacy methods. "Our Quinnipiac teacher candidates maintain data on their students, providing teachers with examples of student work and assessments. Students' reading levels improve, and teacher candidates are able to meld theory and practice in very specific and realistic ways" (Dichele, 2016, p. 7).

To assist with the successful partnerships, they had a paid liaison from each of the schools who handled classroom placements for teacher candidates and university collaboration. The liaisons dealt with any problems; they were able to see the connection between the school and university to provide opportunities for all stakeholders. The university also had coordinators and liaisons for both schools. At the university, this fit for the faculty members' service requirement for promotion and tenure. They also had a formal PDS committee that met on a monthly basis. The committee was comprised of the two school liaisons, the two university faculty liaisons, university faculty, and school administrators. They rotated, where the monthly meetings were held at a school and then the university, and so on. This led to shared workshops and professional development among the three institutions. Teachers at the PDS partner schools became adjunct faculty members at the university. They also developed a post-graduate mentoring program for first- and second-year teachers at the PDS partner schools, and the professors from the university were doing research about this initiative. This example demonstrates how much PDS partnerships can grow in a matter of five years' time (Dichele, 2016).

As previously mentioned, PDS work is not easy, and time is needed to build strong and trusting relationships with partners. Decisions must be made in the best interests of both the teacher candidates and the P–12 learners. I've included some difficult situations and Dichele's (2016) PDS evolution to provide you with some different examples of PDS relationships. One aspect of the PDS that can influence the success of the partnership is governance.

Governance plays an important role in successful PDS partnerships. NAPDS Essential 7 calls for governance structures to provide a strong framework for the relationship to function and grow. A sustainable foundation is critical for a successful PDS to guide the work of the school–university partnership. The governance structures allow for collaboration and reflection, with the inclusion of all stakeholder voices. Governance structures should afford stakeholders opportunities for shared decision making in various areas of the partnership, such as goals, evaluation of outcomes for constant improvement, and how resources will be leveraged. Participation in these relationships must be mutually beneficial for all stakeholder groups (NAPDS 9 Essentials, 2021).

Due to the complexity of bringing two institutions together to engage in simultaneous mutual renewal, with both the school and university trying to grow in the area of professional development, and to partake in both research and development while working to improve the education of P–12 learners and teacher candidates, the governance structures tend to face four critical tasks as well as four process challenges (Teitel, 1998).

Teitel (1998) discussed four critical tasks of governance. The first critical task of governance is to build bridges. Since schools and universities are such dissimilar organizations, the PDS governance guidelines must afford both institutions opportunities to voice differences in philosophy and goals as well as determine what is in the domain of the school, what is in the domain of the university, and with what activities do the school and university domains overlap.

The second critical task of governance is to support mutual renewal. When a partnership sets a synchronized agenda for mutual renewal there must be governance structures that not only link the school and the university but also provide detailed information regarding roles for stakeholders in the change processes of both the school and the university while the new shared structure is meshing well with the already existing structures of the school and the university, and the joint structure is growing more important in decision-making processes (Teitel, 1998).

Teitel's (1998) third critical task of governance is managing the day-to-day tasks. As part of this task, governance groups must handle the short-term needs of the partnership, especially in the areas of securing and allocated of time and money.

The fourth critical task of governance is assessing and planning for the long term. This part of governance deals with the long-term needs of the partnership while considering both the interests of school and the university, while securing consistent streams of revenue for the time and money necessary for the collaborative (Teitel, 1998).

Along with these four critical tasks, PDS partnerships can also face four process challenges while developing or maintaining governance structures. The first process challenge is working with the existing governance structures of both the school and university and helping to transform the structures to better meet the goals of the partnership. Governance must strive to address the differences of all the PDS stakeholders (Teitel, 1998).

The second process challenge is to strike a balance between spontaneity and structure. Teitel (1998) noted that "governance structures need to provide stability, legitimacy, and access to power and resources and, at the same time, be open to innovation and change" (p. 2).

Teitel's third process challenge is promoting both parity and equity within the partnership. Typically, the university has a reputation of trying to dominate the school–university partnership. During the establishment of PDS governance, inclusivity is crucial to help alleviate trust issues and to foster parity and reciprocity among stakeholders. As well, equity should be addressed, as it is rarely considered in other PDS structures.

The fourth and final process challenge is to connect people and institutions. Initial PDS relationships usually begin with personal connections among individuals from the school and the university. The challenge of the governance structures is to build on the existing personal bonds. As well, the governance structures should be inclusively broadening connections to broaden relationships. The structure should also carefully describe the roles of different jobs within the partnership so tasks are not ascribed to a specific person as that individual may not always be part of the collaborative. If these specifics are built into the governance structures, the partnership will go on even when key players leave (Teitel, 1998).

To makes things a little trickier, in determining how to address structures, resources, and roles, there are challenges that Teitel (2003) breaks down into four dilemmas. These dilemmas are understructuring vs. overstructuring, building bridges vs. developing roots, aligning and blending with the old vs. developing the new, and centralization vs. autonomy as they apply to structures, resources, and roles.

The first dilemma relates to the tension that exists between understructuring and overstructuring the partnership for effectiveness related to structures, resources, and roles. On one side of this dilemma is the worry of not instituting enough structure for the PDS. The worry is that without the appropriate amount of structure, the PDS might be on the periphery forever, with the possibility of being weakened due to personnel turnover and leadership changes. This would be a roadblock for renewal. On the other side of the dilemma is that there is too much structure, too many rules and regulations that were too rigid and hampered the creative aspects of the PDS. It is important to strike a balance between understructuring and overstructuring in the PDS when it comes to structure, resources, and roles.

Teitel's (2003) second dilemma is building bridges vs. developing roots. From one angle, it is important to build bridges between the school and the university. However, the development of roots is necessary for institutional renewal. Unfortunately, due to the difficulty of forming a partnership, the tendency is to stick to bridge building and to neglect developing roots that are needed for change.

The third dilemma relates to aligning and blending with the old vs. developing the new. It is important to blend the structures, resources, and roles when building a PDS. Teitel (2003) provided an example: "Teachers taking on new responsibilities and leadership roles may find reluctance, resistance, and even opposition from other teachers or building administrators. New decision-making structures and new revenue streams and resource allocation processes set up for the PDS have to coexist, align with, or replace older sources, structures, and processes" (p. 59).

The fourth dilemma concerns centralization vs. autonomy as they relate to structure, resources, and roles. It is important to find a good balance between centralization vs. autonomy. It is basically a tight–loose situation concerning the structures, resources, and roles in a PDS. As more became known about PDS, more were developed with a more systemic or tighter approach. However, since all PDSs are somewhat different, there should be some looseness or local autonomy in order to customize or tailor the structures, resources, and roles to fit with a particular PDS (Teitel, 2003).

Often, a PDS governance structure is comprised of three levels: liaisons, steering committees, and multi-site coordinating councils.

Liaisons

Teitel (2003) described how a common PDS governance structure is the use of liaisons—that is, person-to-person connections. There can be liaisons from the school side of the partnership. Ferrara (2014) pointed out that people with both instructional and classroom experience, along with problem-solving skills, good communication skills, and dependability, possess many of the qualities needed to be an effective liaison.

The school liaison is typically a teacher, or sometimes an administrator, who has an interest in professional development. The liaison helps to place teacher candidates in classrooms with mentor teachers at the school (Ferrara, 2014), and also helps to arrange talks or seminars for teacher candidates at the school. The school liaisons usually perform these tasks without extra money or release time.

Usually, the liaison from the university side is a faculty member who brings their methods students or student teachers to the PDS.

The university liaison typically spends one or two half-days at the PDS site each week during the semester. The university liaison may conduct research or facilitate or participate in professional development activities or study groups at the school (Teitel, 2003). Ferrara (2014) has noted that the liaison is the link between the school and university and helps to implement PDS initiatives.

The scope and authority of a liaison differs from PDS to PDS. The liaison typically makes low-stakes decisions related to the day-to-day tasks of the PDS, such as the use of their personal time spent on PDS and planning professional development. Some liaisons may have a small budget. Usually, principals from the PDS and chairs or deans make higher-stakes decisions brought to them by the liaison (Teitel, 1998).

Having a PDS liaison has some clear benefits. Liaisons can play a vital role in the school–university relationship. They work to involve stakeholders in their institution and translate for them the culture of the other partnering institution. The liaison usually has a powerful connection with the liaison from the partnering institution and serves as a key player in the governance structure of the PDS, which allows them to make quick decisions based on a good share of autonomy. The plans or decisions of the liaison can be catalysts for change that impact many stakeholders (Teitel, 1998).

However, Teitel (1998) has also outlined possible drawbacks to using a liaison. Although the liaison typically holds a key PDS position, the person does not have a great deal of power in their own institutions due to a lack of structural legitimacy for the role of liaison, which can be frustrating for the liaison who is working diligently to make the PDS partnership more effective. Initiatives that involve others are sometimes challenging for the liaison to implement. Some of the challenge dissipates if the liaison's work is woven into governance structures. However, the work of PDS is extremely time consuming and requires a great deal of effort. Such challenges are frequently piled on the liaison, leaving them overwhelmed by duty in all directions.

School or Site-Based Steering Committees

A PDS typically begins with a liaison and then moves into the use of a steering committee. In other instances, the steering committee is formed first as a way to get people involved and help with decision making. The existence of a steering committee is helpful because if a committee member leaves, other members remain to carry on the partnership. In contrast, if a great amount of work and responsibility is placed on one liaison, things could easily fall apart if they decide to leave the organization (Teitel, 2003).

Ferrara (2014) noted that a steering committee is usually comprised of various PDS stakeholders who help create a mission and action plan with the intention of attaining the goals of the partnership. The steering committee can vary in size. The committee can be as simple as the liaisons, a school administrator, and perhaps some school faculty members. At Buffalo State, we call this a liaison committee, but it functions basically in the same way. In a more developed PDS you might see additional representatives on the committee, such as more faculty members from the university, graduate students, parents, or representatives from community organizations on the PDS steering committee.

Along with contributing to the mission and goals of the PDS, another duty of the steering committee includes record keeping. "Record keeping is an important component of the process helping the steering committee stay focused on PDS tasks. Maintaining written documentation of progress during the beginning stages of implementation and afterward is critical because it serves as a reminder of both accomplishments and future goals" (Ferrara, 2014, p. 39). Steering committees may meet monthly, biweekly, or weekly to address all the details of the school–university partnership and long-range planning, such as professional development activities. From a more recent perspective, video-conferencing may alleviate some of the strain of these frequent meetings. At Buffalo State, our liaison committee typically meets about once a month or once or twice a semester. "In more developed PDSs that are embracing a simultaneous renewal agenda, committees have responsibility for the broader school or university improvement agenda-focusing, for instance, on curriculum and instruction at both institutions or pursuing a joint action research agenda" (Teitel, 1998, p. 7). Partnerships at this level at my institution usually only focus on one or two initiatives that benefit a variety of stakeholders. Some of the areas of focus or projects are included in this book. Many were funded by our consortium's action research mini-grants.

Multi-Site Coordinating Councils

Another layer of PDS governance could be a multi-site coordinating council. These collaborative groups can include multiple universities and/

or multiple schools or districts. Teitel (1998) stated that a university will link up with several schools in the area. This is the type of collaborative with which I'm most familiar. Our version of a multi-site coordinating council is our advisory board, which includes PDS student representatives, university faculty members, mentor teachers, liaisons, and school or district administrators. At these meetings, information about PDS activities and initiatives are shared. Many times, university faculty members are most eager to get feedback from the partner school representatives on the needs of the schools, what PDS could assist with, and how the entire consortium might benefit from the work of one school or district.

Other collaboratives may call multi-site coordinating councils PDS planning councils or possibly steering committees. These governing bodies usually have the opportunity to send at least one person from each PDS site to gather with the university folks and possibly community members to focus on policies and issues. The multi-site coordinating councils tend to attract attendees with a bit more power than do steering committees. The attendees might be superintendents or principals from a district or school. From the university side of the partnership, the multi-site coordinating councils may be attended by university deans, chairs, and faculty members. The committees tend not to meet as frequently as the steering committees and liaisons that hold more local autonomy. This group may make decisions about money and other resources that can be leveraged as part of a mutually beneficial PDS or multiple PDSs. Important issues such as equity and parity may also be addressed at this council level.

The advisory board at Buffalo State meets three to four times a year. At my institution, we have found that by using video-conferencing for these meetings, we have more attendees. It is often difficult for school administrators to leave the school for a meeting on campus. With video-conferencing, school administrators are still where they need to be but are able to participate on the PDS advisory board. Additionally, video-conferencing has worked well for mentor teachers and/or teacher liaisons who would have to leave the school to come to campus for a meeting when there is a shortage of substitute teachers in our area. About three or four times during the academic year, we do hold meetings at partner schools and invite all stakeholders; however, having many consortium members descending upon a school can be tricky for the school due to space issues, technology, money, and time. When we do have PDS meetings at schools, the partner school administrators and faculty are very proud to show off school initiatives, particularly projects with the Buffalo State PDS consortium.

Transformative Approaches to PDS Governance

This type of governing structure occurs only as part of a systemic initiative. The liaison, steering committee, and multi-site coordinating councils usually maintain the existing university and school governance structures and try to fit in PDS structures wherever possible. A transformative approach calls for a sizable redesign of existing school and university governance structures to foster a higher level of collaboration and simultaneous renewal. With the transformative approach, some type of "Professional Education Council" is usually formed. This council might be comprised of university faculty responsible for teacher education, teacher candidates, department chairs, and representatives from partner schools. The council would likely have an oversight role in teacher preparation at the university and school levels (Teitel, 1998, p. 13).

This type of approach to PDS governance can bring many more stakeholders into the decision-making process regarding teacher preparation; however, roadblocks can occur. This approach may cause some inner turmoil in the partner institutions due to undefined job roles, run-ins with unions, disturbances in communication, and worries about evaluation, promotion, and tenure (Teitel, 1998).

Decision Making

As a PDS is just starting out, it is important to talk through which decisions that group should address jointly. One way to begin is for the group to work on something collaboratively that involves lower-stakes decisions. An example involving lower-stakes decisions provided by Teitel (2003) was having PDS governance decide in which classrooms teacher candidates will be placed. The group should begin with lower-level decisions and work their way up to matters that have higher-stakes. Teitel suggested the use of a "ladder of decision making," which is "establishing a hierarchy of types of decisions that need to be made in the partnership and identifying who is making them" (p. 65).

Effectiveness of Governance Structures

Teitel (1998) shied away from recommending one governance structure over another due to the differences in each PDS. One structure that's effective in one PDS setting may be ineffective in another. Effectiveness of governance structures can vary based on many characteristics of the PDS, including the stage. As the PDS evolves, governance structures must evolve with it.

Teitel (1998) has offered some guidance related to planning, for example, "It is useful to think of PDS governance in terms of a start point and a direction: PDSs need to be fluid in their structures, but consistent in the visions and goals and directions toward which they seek to move" (p. 15). Kindzierski et al. (2021) found this to be the case in their research related to the bending but not breaking of PDS structures during challenging times. Teitel added the importance of increasing membership and participation in the PDS network. Concurrently, there should be a focus on bringing the PDS stakeholders from the university and schools together to make connections and to foster collaboration as a way of altering the cultures of both institutions. This assists with relationship building and the sustainability of the partnership(s).

It is extremely important for the PDS collaborative to work toward receiving recognition or awards to help legitimize the partnership inside and outside of the PDS network. This will assist the partnership toward making the PDS work as part of existing structures of the institutions, or at least moving in that direction. High-level involvement, or at least a presence on the committees of the partner institution, can also help with increasing PDS power and higher levels of decision-making abilities and the move toward simultaneous renewal (Teitel, 1998).

Starting Up

Teitel (2003) recommended that governance bodies of burgeoning PDSs develop long-term plans for facilitating the renewal process and monitoring the progress of the collaborative while addressing long-term needs and interests of stakeholders. Initially, PDS governance should include securing funding for the sustainability of the PDS. Teitel admitted that it might not be at the top of the list for those starting up a PDS, but he explained the importance of planning ahead. He advised those beginning a PDS to collect baseline data to gauge the progress and impact of the partnership. He advocated for long-term planning around the goals to indicate the direction and focus of the collaborative to move forward and provide a way to keep members on track and cognizant of why the partnership was formed. Similarly, to foster participation and confidence in the PDS, El Amin (1999) encouraged that choice be part of PDS governance: "Choice allows all partners to make personal investments that they might not otherwise make. Choices that affect the whole are made through the democratic process. Representatives on the administrative board consult with their constituents to solicit their opinions before voting as well as to seek their input in raising new issues" (p. 6).

As noted earlier, there is no one effective governance structure that works for every PDS. Nolan Jr. et al. (2007) described how their PDS put structures in place for day-to-day operations, but since they considered their collaborative to be a community, they viewed themselves as held together by dispositions and norm, whereas organizations depend on structures and rules. According to Nolan Jr. et al., we all "attempt to adhere to a set of common values that include equal participation, teacher leadership, inquiry, and professional respect." Although Teitel (2003) warned PDS leadership against relying too much on the norms and values of community, Nolan Jr. et al. saw their PDS as a community comprised of volunteers, so they decided they didn't want to treat their stakeholders as an organization or institution would. "We are held together by relationships, common tasks, mutual respect, and a shared set of values. We believe that our approach to governance, resources, and roles should reflect this reality" (Nolan Jr. et al., 2007, pp. 103–104). It's beneficial to examine alternative views. Since all PDSs are different, maybe this group's deviation from the norm really works for their PDS.

PDS Stages

According to Teitel (2003), "there are several stage theories available to use for PDS development" (p. 47). For example, Teitel discussed the four I's of investigation, initiation, implementation, and institutionalization, whereas Dixon and Ishler (1992) discussed the six stages as formatting, conceptualization, development, implementation, evaluation, and termination/reformation (Walmsley et al., 2009).

Walmsley et al. (2009) also pointed out many of the stages used to explain various levels of development in a PDS. The NCATE PDS standards (2001) described four stages: beginning, developing, at standard, and leading. The Michigan Partnership also delineated four stages: initiation/exploration, design, pilot, and stabilization/refinement. After examining these aforementioned models, Walmsley et al. determined that a professional development model should address more details and aspects of the PDS. They set out to provide more specific explanations for the progress of a PDS, with stages that included exploration, formalization, action, institutionalization, critical growth, and sustainability. They explained that reflection and evaluation are crucial parts of each stage. The **exploration** stage involves dialogue among university faculty and school administrators. There is discussion about what PDS is and the potential mutually beneficial opportunities that could arise from a school–university partnership. During this stage, possible challenges are discussed, along with possible benefits, so that each stakeholder can make an informed decision about entering a partnership. They must gauge whether the school and the university have similar educational goals and beliefs. Differences and similarities in both the school and university communities, such as culture, must be pondered to ensure the potential for a successful partnership moving forward. The university faculty and mentor teachers must view themselves as co-learners, acknowledging all they can learn from one another, with neither party having a sense of superiority over the other. This will foster long-term commitment and engagement from both. It should also be decided who from both the school and the university will take part in PDS communication and implementation, and who will usher the relationship into the next stage. It is possible that the school and the university are not an appropriate match, and the relationship could possibly end at the exploration stage.

In the **formalization** stage, each party must draw from colleagues and administrators to discuss the terms of the PDS relationship. The school principal would discuss the potential details of the partnership with both the teachers in the school and the superintendent and/or school board, while university faculty and administrators must talk about possible roles and commitments in the partnership. To move forward with a successful relationship, all parties should agree on the formal partnership. Either the school or university can initiate an agreement or contract with the other party. The agreement should lay out the agreed-upon terms that detail responses to potential financial or legal issues. Parties from both the school and university then sign the formal document, which specifically lays out the roles and responsibilities of both the school and the university. However, the verbiage on the specific activities of the partnership should be kept rather broad so that the relationship can grow and evolve throughout the school–university union. After the agreement is signed by the two parties, it is important to set up a committee that will have scheduled meetings to carry out the goals of the partnership. There are usually a few stakeholders from the university and a few stakeholders from the school, and members of the committee can change or rotate. As noted above, these committees are sometimes called steering committees, or liaison committees. Regardless of the name, this group is an important aspect of the partnership to foster communication, build trust, make PDS-related decisions, and evaluate the partnership. Walmsley et al. (2009) suggests having an evaluator familiar with both the school and university examine the goals and the outcomes of the partnership and provide feedback.

Action is when activities take place with both the school and university stakeholders. These activities help to build relationships, and the strength of the relationship can be the difference between a successful and impactful PDS as opposed to one that fizzles. To foster a healthy and respectful partnership, university and school faculty must be willing to work together and with teacher candidates on projects and initiatives that are mutually beneficial. Respect and trust grow over time and solidify the partnership until it seems natural for faculty and teacher candidates to be in the school and school folks feel comfortable on the university campus. Having a liaison from both the school and university who work together with a steering committee also helps to ensure a strong relationship. As the partnership strengthens, university faculty will feel comfortable bringing teacher candidates to observe, serve, and co-teach at the school. The steering committee might set up opportunities for the teacher candidates to work on various projects that help with their preparation but also benefit the students at the PDS. The committee can also seek funding to support the projects by co-writing grant proposals. The action stage can take time, but if the partnership remains beneficial for both the school and university, the partnership could move to the institutionalization stage. Walmsley et al. (2009) provided an example of an action plan in a landscape format and an overall goal at the top. Beneath the goal are five columns: planned outcomes, planned activities, people involved, timeline, and how to measure. The steering committee can in the columns and maintain this work as a detailed record of their action plan.

Institutionalization occurs due to the strong relationships and action that took place in previous stages. At this stage, school and university partners may share funding to support the PDS as well as time for the liaisons from both institutions to maintain a strong relationship. Partners are likely in the institutionalization stage if administrators from both the school and university agree to provide more release time or pay to the liaisons to maintain and strengthen the PDS relationship. At this stage, the steering committee may development an action plan for the year. The committee could collect data on the action plan items. The data may be aggregated and analyzed by an evaluator and shared among PDS stakeholders to make future decisions about the partnership. At this stage, stakeholder roles can change, and they may become more of a benefit to other stakeholders. For instance, mentor teachers can take on more of the responsibility for the preparation of teachers. Mentor teachers may become adjunct professors at the university. P–12 learners may benefit from having teacher candidates at the school. An extra person helping out or teaching in the classroom along with their regular classroom teacher can allow for more individualized and small-group instruction. The key to the institutionalization stage is collection of data for administrators that justifies PDS work and propels the partnership into higher stages.

The **critical growth** stage is when PDS stakeholders take active roles in data collection, evaluation, reflection, and investigation to assess if the partnership remains beneficial to both the school and university. This is the "what's next" stage. Stakeholders may decide to revise the yearly action plan to involve the PDS in more mutually beneficial projects. The steering committee may be interested in engaging in research pertaining to the strengths and/or needs of the partnership. At the critical growth stage, PDS partners partake in increased data collection and reflection to examine the impact of the partnership and how to move forward in a way that is beneficial to all stakeholders. Standards and structures related to PDS can be revisited to help renew the partnership and provide ideas for action plans. Evaluation and reflection are key concepts during critical growth that help to catapult the partnership into the sustainability stage.

In the **sustainability** stage, the PDS partnership has grown and flourished over years. In that time or thereafter, the PDS may have withstood and/or have undergone changes in university or school leadership. Remaining stakeholders may have to make a case for the partnership to continue. A way to help sustain the PDS relationship is to provide new leaders with evidence of the success of the PDS. This could be action plans or data illustrating the success of the partnership for P–12 learners and teacher candidates. At this stage, funding and recognition for the PDS partnership are crucial. School–university partnerships may undergo funding changes, or the roles of some stakeholders may have changed over time, with people growing into leadership roles and/or new people coming on board, either from the school or the university. At the sustainability stage, partnerships may be plagued with challenges such as program or grade restructuring, schedule conflicts, and the pressures of accreditation.

Walmsley et al. (2009) explain that there are challenges at each of these stages, pointing out the importance of reflection and evaluation no matter what the stage—even at the final stage of sustainability. They admit that each PDS partnership is unique and may face any number of challenges along the way, yet they offer a structure that can be utilized to build a brand new PDS partnership. "Once a strong partnership is established, most involved see it as a necessity for the best education of preservice teachers and schoolchildren, as well as for the professional growth of university and school faculty" (Walmsley et al., 2009, p. 77).

The Michigan Partnership created four stages (Torres, 1992). The first stage is **initiation/exploration**, which is the "getting to know you" phase of PDS. Partners begin to work together, educate, and learn from each other, and come to a consensus on the problems they need to tackle. The second stage is **design**. In the design phase, initial approaches and theories about the problems they decided to tackle are developed. **Pilot** is the third stage. At this phase, approaches that PDS participants designed are tried out. The approaches are then assessed and revised alongside the theories to which they are aligned. Finally, the fourth stage is **stabilization/ refinement**. The capacity built by PDS participants is utilized to continuously refine what they are doing across a long time span. These stages can be used by your PDS steering or liaison committee to determine and discuss the current stage of your partnership.

Wilson, Heckman, and Clark studied 14 school–university partnerships that existed from three to five years across the country, and with this data they created the following developmental stages.

1. **Getting Organized**—In this initial stage, organizers consider who will be part of the partnership and the purpose of the partnership. They may develop rules or systems of governance and verify available resources. The duration of this stage is determined by the eagerness of the organizers

to agree on a goal that addresses joint dissatisfaction of some current condition. When the organizers come to the realization that it is their responsibility to change the status quo, they are then likely able to move on to the next stage in the process.

2. **Early Success**—Participants in a partnership recognize the common interests and concerns among group members. Excitement is shared in meetings and discussions about shared issues, as well as encouragement that they are heading down the right path.

3. **Waiting for Results**—After the excitement wanes, this is a time period where participants attempt to accomplish goals. At this stage, some who are not patient with the process will abandon the partnership. Others will examine the structure of the partnership, reassess the goals, and possibly assume or assign new roles.

4. **Major Success and Expansions**—As the partnership begins to achieve results, participants and participation may increase. A large group of stakeholders working on a specific reform can result in increased common understanding and dedication to overcoming an issue. Also at this stage, the partnership tends to receive more recognition, funding, resources, or membership, which adds to the overall reach of the partnership.

5. **Mature Partnership**—The investigators' examination of three- to five-year partnerships rarely bore witness to a partnership at the level. Along with skillfully accomplishing its own goals, the partnership provides leadership to other partnership endeavors with similar goals. Critical inquiry abounds to examine partnership progress, and members are involved in making significant changes. The symbiotic relationship at this stage affords new long-term commitments to resources, lines of inquiry, continued learning, and the piloting of possible solutions or alternatives.

6. **The Death of the Partnership**—At this stage, the partnership deteriorates or ends, typically due to a cease in funding or the departure or role change of a key organizer

or key partners. In other situations, the members of the partnership may choose to take the collaboration in a new direction, or may have lost sight of the original goals of the partnership (Clark, 1999).

When you have decided to move forward on a possible partnership, there are two initial stages. **The first stage is investigation.** Teitel (2003) described three potential challenges to be considered. You should examine any internal issues your school or university may have at the time. You should also determine any possible issues that occur with your institution and a potential partner. Finally, check out the bigger picture to determine if there are larger issues outside of the partnership to consider. If these appear nonexistent or minimal, you may decide that the partnership is worthwhile and can be mutually beneficial. Examining internal issues, as well as issues existing between partners, and considering the impact of any external factors can be executed at any of these stages in order to assess the viability of the partnership. You can then move to the **second stage of initiation: the start-up.** At this point, you must verify that the school and the university are a good match, determining that the interests, missions, and goals of the two entities are compatible.

Initially, it is important to develop trust (Ferguson, 1999). Each partner must determine if the other organization is dependable and back up their promises based on trustworthy motives with a collegial manner. Ferguson developed five steps to guide and evaluate the formation of new partnerships related to trust. He proffered the areas of competence, motives, dependability, collegiality, and control. Ferguson (1999) suggested that the overall first step in partnership formation is development of trust—organizations want to know whether potential partners have the competence and dependability to deliver on what they promise, whether their motives can be trusted, and whether they can be counted on to act collegially (Teitel, 2003).

The **third stage is implementation**, which is built on the foundation of trust. This is when the school and university begin performing activities together based on their agreement. The school–university partnership has now laid the groundwork for deep collaboration and communication. At this stage, partners must determine decision-making processes, plan together, and potentially leverage their resources to implement events, meetings, or professional development workshops. The PDS agreement can always be revisited to ensure the implementation of activities is aligned with the agreed-upon plan between the two institutions, and that they are beneficial for both groups as part of the renewal process. Also, neither the school nor the university wants to feel stuck in a relationship that is no longer working.

At the implementation stage, partnerships found at the higher levels on the rubric are making large-scale updates or changes to existing policies and practices significant to the partners based on their trusting and collaborative relationship. The collaboration at this stage focuses on shared responsibility for student learning, which is the overall goal of PDS. University faculty care deeply about the impact PDS has on P–12 learners, and school faculty members take on some of the responsibility for the preparation of preservice teachers. This alignment in joint common goals strengthens the coherence of the partnership and better aligns teaching practices.

PDS members must recognize and utilize the various skill sets of each stakeholder in order to positively impact student learning at the implementation stage. As well, jointly planned and executed activities can afford university faculty, teacher candidates, mentor teachers, and PK–12 learners and their families opportunities to work with people with backgrounds different from their own. Such involvement may positively impact all stakeholders, providing knowledge and experiences with diverse groups of individuals (Teitel, 2003).

No matter which developmental model you select to examine the stage of your PDS, the model will provide you with a general sense of the likely progression of your organization, what might occur at each stage, and possibilities on what to expect next. These developmental levels can help you understand what to expect and what your organization may need to do to progress. The stages can also assist you when you are setting goals and making plans related to future initiatives.

Reflection Time

Pause

Deliberate

Share

This chapter provided a great deal of advice on how to grow a PDS, what steps and stages are involved, and what to expect in the big picture. What spoke to you? Are you ready to initiate a partnership? What kinds of things do you need from a partner as part of a mutually beneficial relationship? What can you do to strengthen an already existing partnership or PDS? Can the NAPDS 9 Essentials help you think about this?

Spotlight on PDS Beginnings

I hope you are beginning to understand all that goes into a successful PDS. Throughout this book, I provide many examples from the SUNY Buffalo State PDS to illustrate concepts related to PDS in general.

To illustrate what can occur at the early stages of building a PDS, below is an interview with Sarah Solley, Chair and Assistant Professor in the Elementary Education department at SUNY Potsdam. I asked the questions. Her responses are in italics.

What does PDS mean to you?

Collaboration . . .

What are your first steps as you begin your PDS journey?

Our Center for School Partnerships and Teacher Certification have recently created advisory boards consisting of past graduates, university faculty/staff, and local district teachers and administrators. These advisory boards are meant to discuss current trends in education, identify gaps in our teacher preparation program, and develop collaborative projects, among others purposes.

What challenges do you face?

Being a university in the North Country, all our local districts are spread far apart. Many students face transportation issues to host sites (more recently, the rising cost of gas has become an issue) since most sites are 40 minutes or more away.

How are the NAPDS 9 Essentials informing your initial decisions about PDS?

Right now, we are focusing on strengthening our clinical preparation while providing our area districts with the much-needed support as they navigate teacher, staff, and bus driver shortages.

Sarah shared their initial steps into the PDS world. In the beginning, they focused on clinical preparation (Essential 2) and shared governance structures (Essential 7). They also used aspects of other Essentials to address stakeholder needs. If you are working in a teacher preparation program, it is a great idea to begin slowly with one or two school partners. If you are a school partner, it is important to provide authentic experiences in schools for teacher candidates while voicing your needs and interests as part of the PDS governance structures.

Chapter 3

PDS Stakeholders and Roles

So, you have read about the history of school–university partnerships, particularly professional development schools. You know about the frameworks that support the partnerships and some of the key players in the world of PDS. We have discussed ways to start up a school–university partnership and formalize the relationships with agreements. We also took a look at possible developmental stages PDS partnerships may undergo. While these are important aspects of PDS, it is really the people and relationships that hold these partnerships together. In this chapter we will discuss PDS stakeholders, such as P–12 learners, teacher candidates, university faculty or supervisors, school administrators, and mentor teachers. You will learn of the roles and responsibilities of these stakeholders in PDSs and the potential impact of their participation.

Roles

When a school–university partnership aspires to become a professional development school, it is important to adhere to the NAPDS 9 Essentials as much as possible. This will likely happen gradually. As your partnership begins examining the 9 Essentials, it should become clear that changes will need to occur within the partnership. For example, as the partnership takes on new organizational and governance structures or completes different tasks and activities, the need for new roles will likely emerge and possibly create some challenges.

During the start-up stages of a PDS, there might be changes in how roles in the partnership are defined. With new leadership roles, conflicts could arise. Support and time for preparation should be provided for people taking on new roles and/or adapting in their former roles. At the beginning of this PDS work, things tend to be a bit flexible as PDS stakeholders begin learning about and adhering to the NAPDS 9 Essentials.

Initially, if PDS is a new endeavor, it is unlikely there will be specific job descriptions. However, institutions that have multiple partnerships and are beginning with a new partner may have procedures and role descriptions in place from previous experience. When first forming a PDS, it is also difficult to create specific job descriptions when most of the work going into the partnership is voluntary. When getting a PDS off the ground, the work generally entails folks pitching in and working collaboratively, making it difficult to assign specific roles. As the partnership gets off the ground, although there are no specific job descriptions, new and/or adapted roles begin to emerge. New PDS-related responsibilities will slowly take shape for various stakeholders while they are still expected to fulfill the regular duties of their original, paying job (Teitel, 2003).

Interestingly, Nolan Jr. et al. (2007) explain that in their partnership, they do not use the term *roles*. They surmised that the creation of the roles could be problematic for the partnership. They thought it might lead to more fixed structures and relationships that were not dynamic. For instance, "It can also place inappropriate demands on particular individuals simply due to the organizational role that they occupy" (Nolan Jr. et al., 2007, p. 103). Instead, they chose to use the term *functions*. These functions came about based on what was needed to begin and maintain their partnership. They found that their partnership had more of a focus on community as opposed to adherence to very specific roles. They were then able to make changes to any role or to create new roles (function) as needed or as the relationship progressed. They did not want to be forever stuck with roles that did not meet the changing needs of the partnership as it grew and developed. As well, they determined that when a role is developed it makes it feel like all tasks should be completed by the person in that role instead of by the group. This method also helped to bring in more PDS stakeholders and afforded multiple people in the partnership the ability to make use of talents because it did not appear that the work had to be completed by someone holding a particular role in the organization (Nolan Jr. et al., 2007).

Whichever way you decide to begin, some groups of stakeholders will likely have far different needs or expectations for the partnership. I will describe some of these general groups below and how being in a PDS partnership can impact them. To maintain the burgeoning relationship, it is important to be aware of the desires of the various PDS stakeholders and provide opportunities for them to voice their needs and perhaps provide insights and feedback on the functioning of the PDS collaboration.

Mentor Teachers/Cooperating Teachers

Teachers play a crucial role in the success of a school–university partnership. Their leadership and capacity are essential for partnership work. Teachers can take on new roles when they mentor and supervise teacher candidates. Mentor teachers might collaborate with university faculty to assist with redesigning course content in a teacher preparation program. Teachers might also teach college courses, partake in research, or become involved with new kinds of staff development. These teachers open up their classes for observation and discussion. The PDS approach to school–university partnerships can add a layer of complexity to partner schools. Being a PDS can foster new excitement for professional development opportunities and allow mentor teachers to have more classroom assistance from teacher candidates (Bowen & Adkinson, 1996; Ferrara, 2014).

Glickman and Bey (1990) reported that mentor teachers have the most influence on the quality of a teacher candidate's student-teaching experience. The cooperating teacher mentors can also control what the student teachers learn as part of their student-teaching experiences.

One reason mentor teachers take on a student teacher is to lighten their workload by having more assistance in the classroom. Mentor teachers can ask teacher candidates to perform tasks the mentor teacher least desires to do. Some mentor teachers are paid for their role; others may receive a tuition waiver from the university. Mentor teachers might also accept teacher candidates in their classrooms to be connected to the university or to impress an administrator (Weiss and Weiss, 2001). Cobb (2000) found a few more reasons why mentor teachers might agree to work with teacher candidates in a PDS. Some mentor teachers enjoyed the materials and technology provided by the university for participating in PDS. Other mentor teachers said PDS participation gave them both personal and professional gratification as well as pride in the profession.

Research results detail both benefits and drawbacks to being a mentor teacher. Schneider et al. (1996) found that mentor teachers experienced a feeling of renewal because they had the chance to have discussions with colleagues, breaking from the more traditional feeling of isolation. Bullough et al. (1997) determined that mentor teachers become more reflective of their instruction when working with teacher candidates. Mentor teachers in a PDS tended to be more apt to try new instructional techniques and examine different content and approaches (Houston Consortium, 1996). Mentor teachers enjoyed being stimulated intellectually and felt energized when they experienced new ideas. They also liked the opportunities to be part of school-based research and interacting with PDS stakeholders (Trachtman, 1996). Along with less isolation (Ariav & Clinard, 1996), mentor teachers found themselves feeling less powerless (Crow, 1996; Neufeld & McGowan, 1993). Mentor teachers also thought their classroom practices improved (Crow, 1996), stating they had a stronger feeling of professionalism and felt more empowered (Morris & Nunnery, 1993). They felt a sense of empowerment when university faculty included them in partnership planning in which they had equal say in making decisions. University faculty viewed the mentor teachers as experts and gave them a great deal of respect (Rodger and Tiffany, 1997).

Some drawbacks were noted. Mentor teachers were concerned about the amount of time spent with teacher candidates, on top of all their other duties. Mentor teachers found it difficult to work with teacher candidates who were at risk of failing or who doubted themselves (Schneider, Seidman, and Cannone, 1996). As mentor teachers in a PDS provided feedback, helping teacher candidates to connect theory to best practices as part of their overall preparation, they saw themselves more as teacher educators than mentors (Teitel, 1997). Mentor teachers experienced growth as they took on these new roles (Wiseman & Cooner, 1996).

With the PDS approach, mentor teachers and school leaders often share responsibility for teacher preparation. As a PDS partnership develops, collaboration among stakeholders can lead to new roles and responsibilities, such as teacher leadership (Rieckhoff & Larsen, 2012).

Teacher Leadership

Teacher leadership can be defined as "the process by which teachers, individually or collectively, influence their colleagues, principals, and other members of the school community" (York-Barr & Duke, 2004, pp. 287–288). Another definition of teacher leadership is "a strategic, process-oriented stance motivated by deep concern for students and activated through formal, informal, and hybrid leadership roles that span the boundaries of school, university, and community" (Hunzicker, 2018 p. 24). Many teachers in the field of education reach a point in their career where they want more out of their job. If the role of administrator is not a desirable option, many teachers wonder what will make their job more fulfilling. Being a teacher leader might do the trick!

Teacher leadership can reactivate a teaching career and still allow quality teachers to work with students. A PDS partnership could offer more opportunities for leadership development. Most teacher leaders or aspiring teacher leaders are wonderful teachers who prioritize the students' best interests in all endeavors (Silva et al., 2000). This reputation can boost teacher leaders' credibility with their colleagues (Carver, 2016), which assists them to further impact teaching and learning outside of their classrooms. Teachers value peers who have demonstrated their excellence in teaching. When teacher leaders have an easier time gaining the respect of their colleagues, they may acquire leadership positions more informally with their peers based on previous relationships (Spillane et al., 2003). In PDS partnerships, teachers have ample opportunities to take on leadership roles by providing professional development, instructional coaching, and more (Hunzicker, 2019). However, a teacher assuming new PDS leadership roles can also experience negativity from colleagues.

Book (1996) described how in some PDS partnerships, teachers have taken on more of a leadership role, which could potentially lead to a strain between that teacher and their colleagues. More collaborative decision making could help to remedy this tension. As well, the principal could help with the adjustment to new roles in a PDS by helping to build community, fostering leadership in various areas of the partnership, as well as supporting the process of change. Good leaders lead with purpose and encouragement from a position that supports power with, not over, people. This distributed leadership stance is at the heart of PDS and can be transformative. When administrators support teacher leadership it has been found that both teachers and students benefit, and these benefits are enhanced when the teacher leadership takes place in a PDS partnership because of the focus on professional learning (Hunzicker, 2019). PDS has elevated teacher leadership to a new level. Teacher leadership positions in a PDS can be newly created or come from traditional roles and responsibilities. These could include running meetings, supporting teacher candidates in a PDS, and aiding in the development of curriculum. As well, teachers might co-teach courses with university faculty members, take part in research, and monitor teacher candidates. They might also publish and present research. All these activities allow teachers to have a voice and grow their leadership abilities, but when teachers gain knowledge and skills from these endeavors, these can be considered professional development (Darling-Hammond, 1994a; Desimone, 2011; Nolan Jr. et al., 2007). Hunzicker (2012) found that when professional development rooted in their job is collaborative that teacher leadership skills will likely develop as well. PDS school–university partnerships support teacher leadership by providing teachers with the time, resources, and authority to cooperatively recognize problems, come up with solutions, and work through specific initiatives and efforts related to their students, curricula, and more (Rutter & Leon, 2014). Larsen and Reickhoff (2014) examined PDS principals who practiced distributed leadership. They delegated leadership responsibilities to teachers and found that such distribution empowered seasoned teachers to partake in decision making. This also created interdependence between teacher leaders and principals. There was an increase in teacher participation in professional development, efforts to reform, and PDS activities. Carpenter and Sherretz (2012) noted that when PDS teachers are allowed to initiate teaching- and learning-related improvements, the results can be a higher caliber of teaching, an increase in student achievement, and higher-quality schools. These teacher leaders may serve as mentors or cooperating teachers for teacher candidates in a PDS.

Teacher Education Programs

Of the many kinds of teacher preparation programs, here we will focus on the professional development school. Mantle-Bromley (2001) described key features of PDS-based teacher education programs that help produce more well-prepared teachers. First, it was found that having clinical placements throughout the teacher education program (instead of just student teaching) helped to prepare teacher candidates. The PDS approach helps to make better connections between theory and practice. In PDS-based teacher education programs, teacher candidates receive support and supervision from mentor teachers and university supervisors. PDSs are comprised of various kinds of stakeholders who can provide support to scaffold teacher candidates. The final feature of PDS that helps to better prepare teacher candidates is the notion that PDS-based programs are collaborative in design and implementation.

Teacher Education programs have the important responsibility of preparing new teachers who will eventually impact PreK–12 learners and possibly become leaders in schools and districts. Teacher quality has significant consequences for P–12 learners; therefore, the quality of the teachers' preparation matters (Snyder, 1999). "The quality of teachers is an essential factor the academic achievement of students. Policy makers focus on teachers because research indicates that raising teacher quality is significantly aligned with increasing student learning. Although there is a clear connection with teacher quality and student achievement, the variables associated with teacher quality vary. Some policy makers focus on strong knowledge of content, others focus on selectivity in terms of academic achievement, and still others claim that adherence to rigorous standards is essential" (Whitford & Barnett, 2016, p. 457).

Teitel (2003) stated, "The report of the National Commission on Teaching and America's Future (1996) made a compelling case that good teaching matters and is the essential key to improved student learning. One of the commission's major recommendations calls for reinventing teacher preparation and professional development, with a central element being the recommendation for yearlong internships in PDSs" (p. 5). Involvement in a professional development school affords teacher educators the ability to ensure that what they are teaching in the university teacher education program reflects what is actually occurring in schools. Teacher educators spend a great deal of time in classrooms interacting with P–12 learners, teachers, and teacher candidates. These classroom experiences are important as teacher educators help teacher candidates connect theory and practice (El-Amin et al., 1999). "For teacher education, PDSs provide an opportunity to create a venue for literal praxis, the development of teaching skill and practice in context. PDSs provide an opportunity to bridge the gap between the abstract and the authentic in the preparation and development of teachers and other educators" (Teitel, 2003, p. 3).

University Faculty/Supervisors

This section relates primarily to the university representative at a PDS. Burns et al. (2016) explained that as opposed to seasoned faculty members, new faculty, adjuncts, and/or retired teachers tend to be the university representatives at PDS sites. Given the emphasis on scholarship at major research universities, faculty at these institutions may be more concerned than their teaching university colleagues about the theoretical underpinnings of the educational process and how research contributes to an understanding of it (Trubowitz & Longo 1997). This orientation toward scholarship may be at odds with addressing real-life problems of schools. As a result of these socialization patterns, research university faculty may be less likely than teaching university faculty to initiate collaborative partnerships with schools. This assertion is supported by Holland's (2005) work suggesting that engagement is more likely to be present at institutions that emphasize teaching and learning more than research.

"In the case of PDSs, for instance, many college-based educators do some 'good' in the world as well as pay their bills through Professional Development Schools research grants and consulting with schools and districts. The nature and location of that work changes drastically in a PDS approach. Not the least significant change is that such consulting is often construed as the 'college's contribution' to the PDS. Thus, the 'changer' is not only being asked to alter his or her work but also to abandon income" (Snyder, 1999, pp. 138–139). Working at a PDS can help university faculty gain a better understanding of school challenges and needs. Opportunities for research are ample (Ferrara, 2014). A major enticement for university faculty pursuing promotion and tenure are the opportunities for research and publication in a PDS relationship (Dixon & Ishler, 1992). With that, let's explore some research on the specific roles of supervisor, student teaching supervisor, and university supervisor.

Supervisors

Typically, teacher candidates are supervised by faculty, adjunct faculty, or a student-teaching supervisor from the university's teacher education program. Despite the importance of the student-teaching supervisor in teacher education programs, Burns et al. (2016) have pointed out that, unfortunately, student teaching supervision jobs are usually assigned to newer or adjunct faculty, retired teachers, or even graduate students. They found that precious little supervision was conducted by more seasoned research faculty members in a teacher education program. This is concerning due to the lack of understanding of the teacher preparation program's mission and the ability to tie theories learned in education courses on campus with the practices being observed or utilized in a school setting by supervisors who are not permanent faculty members in the teacher preparation program.

The number of times candidates meet with supervisors, the number of times the supervisor comes to the school, and the amount of scaffolding and feedback teacher candidates receive from the supervisor will vary depending on how many student teachers the supervisor is assigned, the distance between the schools (if not all at one site), the amount of compensation, the number of required hours of the supervisor, and possible school or mentor teacher restrictions.

The type of supervision and feedback can also vary, even among student-teaching supervisors at the same institution. Video-recording lessons and receiving feedback electronically has also been used more frequently. Some student teachers may find that their program has a mix of in-person and online observations and feedback. The structure of the student experiences may differ based on the types and length of placements. Some student teachers may be placed in a full academic year internship for certification in one school and/or grade level. Other student-teaching placements may be a semester long at one school and/or grade level. Another student-teaching structure may involve student teachers going to two different schools at two different grade levels for half a semester each (Parker et al., 2016). These varied placements could be to meet certification requirements or to provide student teachers with more diverse experiences. For instance, at Buffalo State, student teachers have the option to student-teach locally and then complete their second placement at an American school abroad.

More recently, school–university partnerships have attempted to develop programs, such as residencies, that help meet the schools' needs for substitute teachers while providing a range of experiences for student teachers, and possibly some extra money (Henning, 2018; Henning et al., 2018).

Some student teacher programs also require orientation and seminar sessions as part of student-teaching requirements (Gimbert & Nolan, 2003; Weiss & Weiss, 2001). These sessions may be informational, such as providing requirements for certification, testing, or graduate school. Seminars may focus on issues that are site-specific to groups of student teachers and that address specific questions or issues the student teachers have. As well, there may be projects, possibly some sort of culminating assignment, like a portfolio and/or reflections about the student teachers' experiences

(Weiss & Weiss, 2001). Again, each experience will differ depending on university requirements, state mandates, school environments, mentor teachers, and the student-teaching supervisor. Student-teaching experiences can also vary due to natural disasters or world events that may influence the continuity or quality of the experience.

The means by which student teachers are assessed and evaluated can also vary. Some requirements for passing student teaching and/or getting certified are state mandated, and others via teacher preparation programs. Most recently, many states are using variations of teacher performance assessments to gather evidence of the student teacher's early abilities in the areas of planning, instruction, and usually assessment. Again, it is evident that a great deal of alternatives exist in the student-teaching experience, which is not surprising, but as you will read, many differences in these culminating experiences have varied throughout history (McIntyre & McIntyre, 2020).

McIntyre and McIntyre (2020) have provided a detailed history of clinical practice and supervision in the United States. Understanding what issues, decisions, and events led to where we are today with student teaching can aid us in making informed decisions about current programs and supervision. McIntyre and McIntyre cite Samuel R. Hall in 1823 as beginning the first training school for teachers in the United States. Hall published a popular book on his lectures related to school teaching and began the American Institute of Instruction. However, even years after Hall's contributions, the state of teacher education was chaotic.

In 1870, a controversial proposal was made at the Annual Meeting of the American Normal School Association to specify teacher preparation program admission criteria, as well as a two-year program in a normal school. This proposal provided how much time should be spent on different types and topics of instruction. However, it was met with a great deal of opposition (Edelfelt & Raths, 1998). Also, at that time, supervision did not look like it does today. It mostly entailed superintendents moving around, persuading teachers to use instructional practices they deemed to be important (Marzano et al. 2011).

At the beginning of the 20th century, agreement was rare on what student-teaching experiences should entail. It was found that prospective teachers did not receive appropriate guidance on what courses they should take to best inform a future teaching career, and that little consistency existed across universities as far as requirements for student teaching. At that time, the length of student teaching varied from six to forty weeks (Henderson, 1918).

When the recommendations of a National Society of College Teachers of Education (NSCTE) taskforce on student teaching were ignored by NSCTE, several members of the task force met in 1920 and formed the National Association of Supervisors of Student Teaching (NASST). Later, the NASST became the Association of Teacher Educators (ATE), which exists today. At the first meeting of the NASST, the president presented in an address 23 issues related to what is now called clinical practice. These recommendations included detailed suggestions related to student teaching. In addition, a course prior to student teaching was proposed to provide more classroom experience before student teaching. Some of the same issues discussed at the first annual meeting of the NASST remain issues today (Bennie, 1978).

Another step closer to PDS were the laboratory schools affiliated with universities in the early to mid–20th century. You may recall that one of the first laboratory schools was started by John Dewey and his wife. Laboratory schools provided an environment for preservice teachers to train. They were also known for conducting educational research and the development and use of innovative practices (Bennie, 1978).

In the 1930s, researchers went back and forth on the student-teaching aspect of teacher preparation. For instance, some research found that many programs did not include both academic and professional training for preservice teachers. Many of these programs failed to provide any type of field experience for teacher candidates prior to student teaching (Hughes, 1933). Discussion occurred about the separateness of the university and school and the gap between what teacher candidates learned on campus and what they learned in the schools while student teaching (Peik, 1937). Stratemeyer (1937) called for more differentiated field experiences depending on the level of the preservice teacher. This radical idea, at the time, took years to catch on. As the decade ended, there remained a lack of cohesion between what was taught on campus and the student-teaching component of most teacher education programs. This lack of alignment between the university and the school content can still be found somewhat in the present day (McIntyre & McIntyre, 2020).

In 1945, a report on the state of clinical practice in teacher education was commissioned by the American Association of Teachers Colleges. The report that came out in 1948 was not only accurate about the current state of education, but it also contained recommendations that impacted the future of teacher education. Technically, the report was called *School and Community Laboratory Experiences*, but it became known as the Flowers Report, named after the chair of the commission. The Flowers

Report contained recommended principles of laboratory experiences and outlined programmatic guidelines for these experiences. Major points included the importance of the integration of field experiences with the teacher preparation program. The report also recommended a more individualized teacher preparation program where field experiences and the length of student teaching depended on the readiness of individual teacher candidates based on continuous assessment. It also stated that the teacher education program should have control of field experiences, with course instructors involved in field experiences and selection of skillful cooperating teachers (McIntyre & McIntyre, 2020). This groundbreaking report made an important impact on student teaching for years to come (Bennie, 1978).

In 1961, Lindsey wrote of the need for national standards related to clinical practice. She advocated for clarity regarding competences and what types of field experiences would help to develop the competencies. She then spelled out what competencies look like in preservice teachers. She opined about the importance of teacher educators being strong role models for preservice teachers, so they continued this professionalism after they graduated from the program. As well, in 1961, *the Building Good Relationships: A Major Role of the College Supervisor* was published, providing guidelines for college supervisors on relationships with teacher candidates, schools, and mentor teachers (McIntyre & McIntyre, 2020).

Lindsey's proposed standards for clinical practice programs and experiences developed quite slowly. In 1970, the Association for Student Teaching issued guidelines for teacher education programs. These guidelines echoed the recommendations set forth by the Flowers Report, including the proposed individualization of clinical practice with the teacher candidate helping to plan the individualized program. In addition, the report emphasized the importance of preservice teachers engaging in critical analysis and reflection regarding their field experiences and student teaching and advocated for school–university partnerships, ongoing evaluation of teacher education programs' field experiences, and more. Although the report highlighted the importance of resources around recommended clinical practice programs, since the 1970s, funds to support these experiences have dwindled (McIntyre & McIntyre, 2020), which continues today.

In the latter half of the 20th century, focus on supervision in clinical practice increased. Initially, many supervisors were gathering more quantitative data during observations. Goldhammer provided five stages for clinical supervision in 1969, which included conferring between the supervisor and teacher candidate before and after the actual teaching observation. Although several publications during that time provided guidelines and support for supervisors, no supervisory standards related to clinical practice caught on. Also, during this time the laboratory schools began to close, and this led to the development of teacher centers. Teacher centers had governmental, school, and university teacher education program support. This positive movement brought schools and universities closer together by embracing theory and practice and fostering collaboration to benefit preservice and in-service teachers (McIntyre & McIntyre, 2020). Teacher centers were closely related to professional development school partnerships—which brings us back to PDS. This history of supervision truly does provide the background and basis for current-day supervision in professional development schools.

Traditionally, a triad of participants are involved in each individual student-teaching situation. The triad consists of the student teacher (or intern), the mentor teacher, and the university supervisor (Gimbert & Nolan, 2003). In a PDS, these traditional relationships may look a bit different. Student teaching in a PDS relates back to Gore's (1991) description that the triad needed to be democratized. Although Ganser (1996) indicated that there is usually some sort of power struggle in the triad over the teacher candidate between the mentor teacher and the university supervisor, the experience of Gimbert and Nolan's (2003) PDS intern indicated they experienced "mutual respect and professional camaraderie" as aspects of these relationships (p. 364).

The formation of a PDS can provide a tighter connection between schools and teacher education programs, especially relating to student-teaching experiences. The role of supervisor has become increasingly more integrated with the overall teacher preparation program (Clift & Brady, 2009). In their research, Gimbert and Nolan (2003) found that a supervisor in a PDS went through various stages of supervision across an academic year. Some of these stages included "knowledge and focus on individual children; the role of goal setting and evaluation; and the flexible structure of the internship that supported an individual intern's process of learning to teach" (p. 353). These have been shown to be key experiences for student teachers.

"Evidence that the student teaching experience has a more powerful effect than university coursework on prospective teachers makes this even more important to university educators" (Teitel, 2003, p. 4). Burns et al. (2016) found that the research they analyzed yielded specific supervisor tasks, such as providing explicit assistance, engaging in individualized support, fostering a sense of collaboration and community, providing curriculum support, and modeling and supporting innovative research. Overall, these supervisor tasks helped to foster learning for preservice teachers.

Burns et al. (2016) determined that due to an increase in collaboration in school–university partnerships, the tasks of supervision have grown and become more complex. This has elevated the importance of the supervisor in the teacher education program and suggested a reconceptualization of the job. Not only does the increased sophistication of the position of supervisor call for more involved support, but there may also be a need for more advanced and innovative supervision, possibly in combination with varied technological tools. As well, they suggested that this increased complexity of the supervisor role may lead to the need for more than one person taking on the different supervisory roles. "PST supervisors in an era of increased clinical education and school–university collaboration require a shift in functions from supervisors of learning to liaisons for learning" (p. 68). Due to recent shifts, Burns et al. (2016) called for the use of more consistent terms and a logical conceptual framework that expresses the intricacies of supervising preservice teachers with more clinically rich experiences and PDS partnerships.

Gone are the days of supervisors just popping in for a couple of teaching observations. Ideally, due to the school–university partnership, programs are moving away from more traditional programs where little contact occurred between the supervisor and the mentor teacher (Clift & Brady, 2009) to communicate and clarify expectations and foster the development of the teacher candidate. In this way, student teachers are not trying to please both the mentor teacher and the supervisor, whose expectations may vary (Weiss & Weiss, 2001).

Supervisors must work to build relationships through an understanding of the classroom, school, and community contexts while fostering coherence between teacher candidates' clinical experiences and their coursework on campus by helping to make connections between theory and practice (Burns et al., 2016). One way to make these connections is through reflection (Freese, 1999).

It is important for supervisors to foster reflection of clinical experiences (Burns et al., 2016; Gimbert & Nolan, 2003; Weiss & Weiss, 2001). "Traditional models of student teaching supervision are not usually oriented toward fostering student teacher reflectivity, collaboration, and decision-making" (p. 17). In a PDS, reflectivity is grounded in a cooperative learning environment that engages all stakeholders. As well, in this reflective teaching situation, teachers and supervisors are learning from children, teacher candidates, and their colleagues (Gimbert and Nolan, 2003; Weiss & Weiss, 2001). Understanding how children have learned from previous experiences leads to better teaching and learning. Reflection can be used to puzzle through many classroom experiences, particularly during student teaching through cognitive inquiry. Reflection can be used to analyze and more deeply understand experiences. However, there is little chance of fostering this in teacher candidates in supervisory approaches that promote reflectivity unless the school and university partners provide support of reflection as a regular practice (Weiss & Weiss, 2001).

Teacher Candidates

Teacher candidates are stakeholders in a PDS. "Teacher candidate" is an overarching term for the university students involved in a teacher preparation program. They might also be called PDS vs. non-PDS graduates, or preservice or novice teachers. Below, you will also see more specific terms, such as student teachers or interns who tend to be in a PDS for student teaching, their final experiences in the teacher preparation program. Most of the time, placements are made for the teacher candidates at the university level in PDSs or other paths if they are in a more traditional program. School partners may have a say in the selection of teacher candidates for their building and the matching of teacher candidates, and mentor teachers can be conducted by school partners, the university supervisor, or sometimes even the candidate themselves. Some programs afford the students more choices regarding their final practice teaching experiences (Parker et al., 2016).

Teacher preparation in a PDS differs from a more traditional program in several ways. PDS programs strive to create coherence between the theory teacher candidates learn on campus and the practices used in schools. Clinical experiences in a PDS affords teacher candidates with opportunities to observe in classrooms, practice planning and teaching, engage in debriefing and reflection as well as discuss questions and obtain new knowledge in seminars and by working with teachers. In this way, teacher candidates obtain a plethora of insights and skills as opposed to a specific set of rote behaviors that will likely be deemed inadequate

(Darling-Hammond, 1994; Pritchard & Ancess, 1999). "The interactions between schools and SCDEs mandate communication and collaborative effort, as schools are no longer "places" where student teachers are assigned, but rather are partners in the many aspects of candidate preparation" (Brindley et al., 2008, p. 71).

As the PDS approach to teacher education and school–university partnerships has become more widespread, awareness has increased regarding how much time, resources, and energy is needed for a successful collaboration, so more evidence is needed concerning the impact of PDS on various stakeholders, such as teacher candidates. Researchers have used both quantitative and qualitative methods to examine the features of PDSs in an effort to determine both their importance and strength (Castle & Reilly, 2011).

Many studies demonstrate positive differences for teacher candidates who went through a PDS-related teacher education program, but more must be known about what features or structures impacted the positive results. Castle and Reilly (2011) reviewed comparison studies that examined teacher preparation with varied features and structures. The outcomes of these studies fell into the six categories of "self-confidence/efficacy, instructional practice/competence, thinking processes, inquiry and professionalism, perceptions of preparation, and employment/retention" (p. 344). The structural features of PDS that led to the aforementioned outcomes were time in the program and the length of the field experiences (earlier and longer), more involvement from school partners, more frequent and consistent supervision, and feedback. There were a mix of assessment strategies and more experiences with diverse and real learning situations along with scaffolding and opportunities for reflection (Castle & Reilly, 2011).

For instance, Sandholtz and Dadlez (2000) discerned a significant gain in teacher efficacy based on the self-reported data of teacher candidates after spending a year of teacher preparation with the PDS approach. Similarly, an examination of elementary science teachers in a PDS-based methods course in science resulted in a significant increase in the participants' personal science teaching efficacy (Flores, 2015). Teacher candidates prepared in a PDS-based teacher education program felt well prepared and confident about teaching (Blocker & Mantle-Bromley, 1997; Book, 1996).

In the area of satisfaction with their teacher education program, those based in a PDS were significantly more satisfied with the teacher preparation they received. The PDS-based teachers rated the areas of program content, practical skills obtained, instruction, and assessment, as well as their study schedule and the school's contribution to the preparation program as significantly more positive than those not in a PDS-based teacher education program. It was also found that teacher candidate perception of their mentor teachers' teaching skills were rated significantly higher by their teacher candidates than the mentor teachers of mentor teachers who were not in a PDS (Helms-Lorenz et al., 2018). From the mentor and in-service teacher perspectives, it was perceived that graduates from PDS prepared programs had higher levels of preparedness as opposed to those not prepared in a PDS program. The in-service teachers even perceived the PDS prepared teachers to be better prepared with more confidence and greater quality than they were when they first started their teaching careers. It appeared that school administrators concurred with the teachers' perceptions of the PDS-trained teachers by hiring them (Cobb, 2000).

The positive impact of PDS-related experiences continues. Castle et al. (2006) examined student-teaching evaluation forms as well as portfolio assessments and determined that teachers who went through a PDS program had more experience and were of higher quality in the areas of planning, instruction, assessment, management, reflection, and overall professionalism. Ridley et al. (2005) studied both PDS-prepared and campus-prepared teacher candidates in the final year of their program and their first year of teaching. They examined the areas of lesson planning, effectiveness in teaching, reflectivity, and retention of professional teaching knowledge. In the final year of their teacher preparation programs, Ridley et al. found that although the PDS-prepared teacher candidates' scores were higher in those areas, there were no statistically significant differences between the two. However, in the first year of teaching results, they found that the PDS-prepared teachers scored significantly higher than those teachers in the campus-prepared group in the area of effectiveness in teaching. In a separate study, it also appeared that teachers who graduated from PDS-based teacher education programs had significantly higher retention rates three to six years after graduating. Fleener and Dahm (2007) concluded that retention numbers could increase with substantial opportunities to practice teaching and make theory to practice connections. PDS benefits teacher candidates as they are able to gain experience working in classrooms with a variety of students and teachers at the PDS site (Ferrara, 2014).

These are but a few examples of the positive impact of PDS on teacher candidates. It is important for researchers to continue to study the impact of PDS on various aspects of preservice and in-service teaching and retention using a variety of methodologies to persist in the pursuit of preparing high-quality teachers for P–12 learners.

P–12 Learners

When it comes to the primary priority of PDS, opinions conflict. For instance, the very first of the 9 Essentials hearkens back to the four PDS pillars of the Holmes partnership (2007), with the first pillar being the improvement of P–12 student learning. However, Goodlad emphasized that the culture and practice of local schools should be the main priority for educational change and held that other priorities would follow over time (Durden, 2005). In the traditional school, the main priority is to serve its students and their parents, which may only result in some incidental reform (Sosin & Parnham, 1998). In the definition of a PDS (Teitel, 1997a), the goal defined first is to improve pre-service teacher preparation. Providing a quality education for P–12 learners comes in at goal three. Finally, the mission of the National Association for School–university Partnerships (NASUP) states "to improve student learning" before other priorities (https://nasup.org/). Despite these somewhat mixed messages, P–12 learning is definitely a critical goal of PDS.

It is interesting to think about the impact of PDS on P–12 learners. The students at a PDS can benefit from individualized or small group tutoring provided by teacher candidates or university faculty. Due to the university connection, students can benefit from strategies passed on by the university faculty and by possibly benefit from programming at the university. The stakeholders from the university, teacher candidates, and faculty can provide PreK–12 students with supportive role models (Ferrara, 2014). These are things that do transpire as part of PDS relationships; however, how is the impact of the aforementioned PDS activities with P–12 learners determined?

It is difficult to isolate or to determine if something related to PDS really impacts the children in partner schools (Fisher et al., 2004). Achievement scores have traditionally defined impact for P–12 learners. Del Prado Hill et al. (2020) challenged this notion through an analysis of case studies about their PDS consortium's impact on various stakeholders. Across the 19 case studies from various PDS initiatives, P–12 learners were impacted in the following ways: identified practices to support the learning of all children in a classroom, providing extra support and encouragement for content, provided extra opportunities to practice English, made sure there was consistent instruction for the students when classroom teachers were absent, gave children the opportunity to learn about college and careers, provided early identification of developmental delays which leads to immediate referrals for relevant services if needed, provided extra resources, the children were able to have interactions with people with different perspectives and experiences, provided enrichment and after school opportunities, and fostered the development of leadership skills and confidence in P–12 learners. These positive impact areas emerged from a variety of types of data gathering and analyses across the case studies. As data are collected and examined, a determination of what counts as impact, how impact data is gathered, defined, measured, and analyzed for all PDS stakeholders should be addressed. Kimball et al. (1995) cautioned that we must question what is meant by student success. Increases in standardized test scores is not necessarily the goal of PDS (Trachtman, 1996). Instead, meaningful teaching for understanding so that all students can be successful is a purpose of the PDS movement (Darling-Hammond, 1994; Holmes, 1990; Levine,1992).

This shift in the understanding of student success will require new methods of assessment of student learning. Regardless, findings demonstrate an increase in student achievement test scores in PDSs. For instance, as part of a methods course, teacher candidates were required to buddy read with a group of elementary school students. After the first semester of this program, all the classroom teachers wanted to be part of this initiative. Before the buddy reading program, the students had a 69% passing rate on the state achievement tests in the area of writing. After year one of the buddy reading program, the passing rate increased to 82%, and after the second year, the passing rate was up to 92% (Wiseman & Cooner, 1996). Similarly, Houston et al. (1995) found significant increases in students' math and reading scores on state achievement tests within two years of the PDS implementation. Houston et al. associated these results to the one-on-one and small tutoring provided by the teacher candidates to fulfill part of their methods course assignments. Although these studies were not designed to indicate that PDS might have caused these improved results, there were clear indicators of relationships (correlations) between variables. These might have been lower student–adult ratios, a close alignment of the curriculum with test objectives, or possibly, collaboration between the teachers in the school and university faculty to puzzle through issues related to the classroom or instruction. Improved results related to PDS were also found in the areas of persistence rate (Judge et al., 1995) and higher or improving at an accelerated rate academic scores compared to state average scores (Webb-Dempsey, 1997). These are just a few examples of studies examining the impact of PDS on P–12 learners.

Overall, the data illustrates the ways in which PDS has impacted PreK–12 learners positively. However, it is understandable that potential PDS stakeholders would want to have research findings that demonstrate positive results in a similar context with similar demographics, level, school subject, or other targeted areas. Further PDS-related research findings are discussed in Chapter 5.

School Administrators

When considering the PDS approach to school–university partnerships, it is important to include school administrators as stakeholders. One of the top reasons to include school administrators is that they are usually the people who make the decisions about starting PDS relationships with universities (Gilbert et al., 2018). In this section, we will first take a look at educational leadership preparation programs. Just as this book has covered a lot about PDS and teacher preparation, PDS should also be part of leadership preparation. Programs that prepare educational leaders should foster the development of school–university partnerships. These partnerships between educational leadership preparation programs and schools or school districts can offer continuous opportunities to develop leaders and/or support high-quality leadership (Young et al., 2005). As well, educational leadership programs can be improved with collaborative work among universities, current school administrators, professional organizations for administrators, and possibly government policymakers (Young et al., 2002).

University faculty in teacher education programs should work with the educational leadership faculty to discuss increasing school–university partnerships using related research to make programmatic decisions. It is a possibility that an educational leadership team of faculty can learn from the successes and missteps of the teacher education program at their institution who might have been involved in school–university partnerships for some time. For instance, it is not productive to form partnerships that are not sustainable. University faculty are also required to, along with their teaching, do service and partake in scholarly activities. Prior to entering into a time-intensive partnership with a school or school district, university faculty members should determine if the service and scholarly endeavors they plan to partake in, keeps them on the path to tenure and promotion. To create and maintain partnerships for leader preparation, open communication and collaboration are crucial. Potential partners should explore the steps to partnership, such as appropriate resources and what they would need from partners to be collaborative and result in effective partnerships for all stakeholders (Breault & Breault, 2010). If the PDS approach is here to stay, it is crucial that leadership programs in higher education understand the importance of preparing future leaders to foster communities of professional learning in their future schools. In order to accomplish this, programs might need to make structural changes in order to prepare future school leaders for envisioning their schools as places where everyone learns (Tilford, 2010).

Let's move from how PDS can relate to educational leader preparation to the benefits of PDS for in-service administrators. PDS can help school administrators transform their schools into rich learning communities. School–university partnerships offer assistance for school initiatives that can positively impact P–12 learners and their teachers. Having university faculty in a PDS school can help foster a higher level and interest of professionalism and the potential for participating in scholarly activities (Ferrara, 2014). Unfortunately, efforts to reform schools have placed heightened responsibilities on the school administrators to focus their energy on goals to improve programs and gather evidence related to student learning leaving less time for school transformation or renewal (Larsen & Rieckhoff, 2014).

The main priority of administrators (as well as teachers) should be to positively impact student learning. As instructional leaders, they play quite a big part in student achievement. Positive relationships have been found between instructional leadership and the involvement and innovativeness of teachers (Sheppard, 1996). It is widely known that across all factors related to school, classroom instruction has the greatest impact on student learning; however, school leadership is the second highest factor to contribute to student learning (Leithwood et al., 2004). Student achievement tends to be higher in schools where the principal practices shared leadership with both teachers and the community (Wahlstrom & Louis, 2010).

Kleine-Kracht (1993) described how a school administrator's influence on P–12 learning can occur through both direct and indirect leadership actions. Actions of direct instructional leadership typically occur when the principal directly interacts with teacher and other school staff members in reference to their classroom, their instruction, curricula, and most importantly the P–12 learners' academic performance. These interactions are usually quite specific and might be in the form of curriculum planning, classroom observations, or more informal types of exchanges with teachers (Kleine-Kracht, 1993; Larsen & Rieckhoff 2014), whereas indirect leadership is related to the whole school, not just one teacher, such as dealing with the school environment, physical and cultural classroom contexts, and overall instruction. The effectiveness of these types of initiatives depends on leadership and the principal's capacity to foster positive relationships throughout the school (Larsen & Rieckhoff, 2014; Wheatley, 1992) while working with a university partner to create an atmosphere of professional learning in the school for all stakeholders (Foster et al., 2000).

When Tilford (2010) studied principal leadership, the analysis yielded six assertions that depicted how principals made sense of their PDS roles:

Assertion 1: When principals willingly embrace the PDS work by seeing connections between the PDS goals and their other leadership work, these connections allow the PDS work to become "a part of" rather than "apart from" the beliefs, experiences, and goals that underlie their current leadership.

Assertion 2: The lived experiences valued by principals throughout their career are closely tied to the leadership style they promote as PDS principals.

Assertion 3: Being open and willing to change is important for principals if the PDS work is going to be integrated into the culture of the school.

Assertion 4: Principals can enter at multiple career points and with a variety of school conditions by adopting either a developing, integrating, or culminating stance on the PDS work.

Assertion 5: When PDSs engage in inquiry into student learning, inquiry serves as a "tipping point" that increases principal commitment to the partnership. "Simply stated, teacher inquiry is defined as a systematic, intentional study of one's own practice."

Assertion 6: Principals are motivated to participate in PDS work for multiple reasons. Each of the three principals had somewhat different goals for participating in the partnership with the university. The vision each principal has was connected to his or her beliefs about leadership and the role of the principal. These goals were also influenced by the contexts of their schools including the readiness of their staff (pp. 63–71).

These assertions can be helpful for stakeholders who need to select or train appropriate nominees for leadership roles in PDS. Motivation and experience are good determiners of people who are best qualified to serve as principals in a PDS. PDS principals should consider the school to be a place where everyone learns and be open to accepting a shared responsibility for teacher preparation. The principal should have a desire to welcome university faculty into the school to assist the current teachers in the school to boost P–12 learning for an integration of school and university to prepare teachers and positively impact P–12 student learning. A crucial part of PDS is an openness to change via inquiry (Dana & Yendol-Silva, 2003; Tilford, 2010). Principal leadership is also a key to a strong PDS partnership (Tilford, 2010).

However, not all administrators beginning a school–university partnership have the same experiences which may impact a principal's perspectives on PDS (Tilford, 2010). Characteristics of a school, such as the size, the intricacies, and the faculty and staff of a school, along with the number of teacher candidates and university faculty, can impact the role of the principal in a PDS partnership (Bowen & Adkinson, 1996). I am not trying to paint a picture that partnership and leadership are a match made in heaven, or by any means as easy. In Bowen and Adkinson's (1996) examination of principals' duties and interactions as PDS administrators, the participants expressed areas of concern that the researchers broke into categories. The groups of principal concerns included the following: how the administrators spent their time and defined their roles and responsibilities as part of a PDS; difficulties they experienced, and how to communicate expectations between the university and the teachers at the school; managing the overall issues related to having teacher candidates and university faculty in the school; teacher candidate assignment to mentor teachers; and issues with scheduling. The principals had to help frame and develop relationships with the university and use the partnership as a way to provide professional development for the teachers in the school. The principal participants were also concerned about the impact of PDS on P–12 learners.

Most school administrators who become involved in a school–university partnership are hoping for a positive influence on P–12 student learning and teacher professional development. However, some principals felt it was their duty to support teacher education programs. Beyond the impact of PDS on their schools, some principals were committed to supporting the preparation of future teachers (Gilbert et al., 2018).

Administrators Forming Partnerships

It is important for PDS stakeholders to decide on an overall grand mission for the partnership to strive for or tackle in order for the stakeholders to establish and sustain effective partnerships sustained (Edwards, 1995; LePage et al.2001; Mantle-Bromley 2001; McGee, 2001). The formation of an overall grand mission between the school and university could be challenging due to tensions with areas such as theory and practice between the two organizations (Levine, 2005). However, Larsen and Rieckhoff's (2014) research yielded positive reactions from principals regarding their relationships with university faculty. One participant shared, "Knowing that I could pick up the phone and reach one of these people, meant so much. I could ask their advice or just talk with them about my frustrations" (p. 320). The principals were excited about their conversations with university faculty about research, professional development and more. Their findings are reinforced by Breault and Breault's (2010) review results that showed the importance of these relationships in school–university partnerships. They found that partnership stakeholders were able to better access intellectual and professional benefits when they were participating in meaningful and valuable ways.

These relationships blossom through communication. LePage (2001) found that an increase in communication in a PDS relationship allowed stakeholders to more clearly recognize their roles and responsibilities within the partnership as well as the overall mission and goals of the group. Through communication, the roles and responsibilities of stakeholders are negotiated in order to prevent tensions and one or more stakeholder groups being silenced. This type of collaborative effort can lead to a PDS achieving goals, and possibly lead to transformative change (Breault & Breault, 2010).

Williams (1996) described how school change can occur in the three phases of initiation, implementation, and institutionalization (continuation). The goal is to bring simultaneous reform to both schools and teacher education programs in a way that cuts across any institutional boundaries to positively impact P–12 learners and the preparation of teacher candidates. Williams described the implementation phase of his PDS as a change in teacher education programs at universities being solely responsible for teacher preparation—the preparation of teachers is linked to both school reform and university reform. Joyce (1983) described stronger forces in effect in most educational institutions to maintain the status quo as opposed to forces related to innovation or improvement. To take on the more powerful forces of doing what has always been done, those in favor of an innovation must develop informal structures to promote and maintain momentum of the idea until it is realized as part of the overall institution or permanent. If the ad hoc structures supporting the innovation are weakened, likely the implementation of that innovation will fail due to schools being complex and averse to change (Fullan, 1991; Sarason, 1990). In order to overcome the forces that maintain the status quo, Joyce (1983) suggested that a procedure be developed "in which organizational stability actually depends on the continuous process of school restructuring" (p. 79). Doesn't this sound familiar? This continuous process of change or restructuring is closely related to the idea of simultaneous renewal (Goodlad, 1994). The notion of simultaneous renewal was at the core of Goodlad's ideas about school–university partnerships. Returning to the phases of change, the final phase is institutionalization; however, Fullan (1991) explained the importance of addressing the organization's concerns regarding institutionalization during the implementation phase and along every developmental step to create a plan for institutionalization. Of course, the school principal would be very much involved in the phases of change.

The phases of change can be complicated enough; remember that doing PDS is not easy (Snyder, 1999). But school administrators often find themselves with many more tasks on their plate besides the work of PDS, and there may be varying levels of support for innovation in the school–university partnership with the goal of institutionalization. For instance, it was found that it was difficult for principals to meet the coordination and management demands of PDS that are, in part, tasks that stave off resistance to innovation and ultimately institutionalization, even when there was an assistant principal in the school (Bowen & Adkinson, 1996).

Let's dig a little deeper in the third phase of change: institutionalization. As previously noted, this is one of the ultimate goals of the PDS approach to school–university partnerships. Preparing teacher candidates in clinically rich settings continuously grows. As the PDS preparation approach becomes the model of most teacher education programs, part of the school reform is for the principals of partner schools to commit to open up the school to preservice teachers and serve as clinical setting to prepare them to be teachers over an extended period of time. When this occurs over time, this model of teacher preparation becomes institutionalized. This means the partner school has accepted their role in the preparation of future teachers, and having them in the school is an everyday occurrence or part of the operations of the school.

Miles and Huberman's (1983) research model helped to determine why some partner schools were able to more easily reach the phase of institutionalization with innovations related to PDS. Bowen and Adkinson (1996) determined that school principals played a key role in the effective implementation and eventually institutionalization of PDS-related innovations. In the school's environment, the school administrator can put some pressure on the teachers in the PDS to utilize whatever PDS-related innovation is being implemented while providing support for the teachers to help them with the innovation utilization. As well, the principal can help with institutionalization of the innovation by altering the organizational structure of the school to better accommodate the use of the PDS-related innovation. Bowen and Adkinson predicted that the more a principal provides supports to better the PDS and stave off any obstacles blocking institutionalization, the more chance there was that the PDS will be institutionalized. For any of this work to occur, the principals in Gilbert et al.'s (2018) research discussed the importance of trust. Gilbert et al. found that "principals articulated that this trust laid the foundation for the work done within the program, and all aspects of the work together had to be woven within this fabric of trust" (p. 79). In sum, the PDS approach provides a beneficial model for school reform. It affords partners ways of collaborating and leveraging resources that allow for the PDS to develop over time (Darling-Hammond, 2010; Teitel, 2008). Finally, within this context, the principals' responsibilities position them as change agents in the overall reform efforts.

Leadership may be the most important aspect of the job of a school administrator, particularly as part of a school–university partnership. The PDS context also affords opportunities for shared leadership so more people are part of the decision-making process because it is an environment that provides supports for leadership to develop. When PDS principals foster shared leadership, this can lead to two hallmarks of PDS both collaboration and teacher-driven research where teachers are a critical element as they serve as both active and equal partners (Cobb, 2000; Connor & Killmer, 2001; Larsen & Rieckhoff, 2014). Rice's (2002) research demonstrated that the principal played an important role in PDS due to supporting teachers to collaborate and fostering shared leadership. The research also suggested that there was an evolution of the role of a PDS principal. Initially, the administrator concentrates on issues related to management and organization. While later, the PDS principal tended to focus more on new approaches to leadership and schoolwide changes (Bowen, Adkison, & Dunlap, 1995; Gutierrez et al., 2007). It was also found that effective PDS principals believed in advocating for teachers and supporting collaboration (Foster et al., 2000), while Stroble and Luka (1999) described how principals teach other people how to make effective decisions.

The PDS approach to school–university partnerships affords stakeholders leadership roles in the network. This method of school reform affords leaders many supports as they work to fill the goals of the partnership. The PDS approach is impactful at fostering the development of leaders. The PDS approach allows the school and university leaders the opportunity to work together on common goals related to school reform. This collaboration allows school leaders the opportunity to focus on school improvement objectives and provide pointed professional development to support eventual schoolwide changes as well as growth in leadership abilities (Rieckhoff & Larsen, 2012).

Rieckhoff and Larsen (2012) examined key areas from PDS principal perspectives. These areas included the development of leadership abilities, the attainment of school improvement goals, focused planning for professional development, and progressive growth in school change.

To address these areas and the growing complexity of the role of principal in a PDS, such as coordinating partnership-related resources, effective leadership is vital (Gutierrez et al., 2007). Leithwood et al. (2004), described the effect of school leadership on P–12 learners. They found that leadership effects account for one-quarter of the total effects of school, which justifies the importance of improving school leadership. P–12 learning achievement was higher in school buildings where the administrators shared the leadership responsibilities with the teachers and the surrounding community (Wahlstrom & Louis, 2010).

Stroble and Luka (1999) examined the shifts in leadership that can occur in a PDS partnership. They described how school leaders who were transformational were able to foster decision-making skills in other stakeholders, such as mentor teachers. This illustrated the critical role of the school administrator as part of a successful school–university partnership (Rieckhoff & Larsen, 2012).

Several variables influence change in a PDS where principals are viewed as change agents for reform to occur (Bullough et al. 1997). Bass (1985) detailed four behaviors of leaders who were transformational. Bass labeled these behaviors "idealized influence, inspirational motivation, intellectual stimulation, and individualized consideration." Transformational leaders are strong role models with a vision and mission, have high expectations of those who follow by inspiration based on motivational sharing of a vision, promote creativity and innovation to followers for problem-solving, and foster a support where the needs of the followers are heard. In addition, Fullan (2002) describes five characteristics of a change leader. These characteristics are moral purpose, a deep understanding of the change process, capability to enhance relationships, knowledge development and sharing, and the ability to make things more coherent. These attributes are utilized by change leaders through people and teams to make transformational changes to an organization (Fullan, 2001).

PDS principals manage the partnership, help to prepare teachers in their school buildings, support teacher research to improve practice, and keep the focus of all the tasks of the partnership focus on improving P–12 learning (Bier et al. 2008). The PDS approach is important for school reform because it provides for supports for collaboration and leverages resources that promote partnership growth over time (Teitel, 2008).

Equity

Having access to a quality teacher can be viewed as a fundamental right. This is a core PDS understanding. PDS research should strive to understand and communicate the importance of this fundamental right in order to obtain a deeper understanding of why professional development schools that aim to educate educators should be funded in the same ways that medical hospitals are funded to train those in the field of medicine (Snyder, 1999).

There are have been discussions regarding the achievement gap that exists in schools among students of varying races and class backgrounds. PDS school–university partnerships have been a proposed option for the achievement of more equitable outcomes related to student learning. This is a key element in the idea of PDSs; however, even with good intentions, the commitment of PDS to increase equity in society, Vallie et al. (1997)

noted how this goal had been rarely achieved despite being included in many of the PDS planning reports and statements released by national organizations. Murrell (1998) suggested that if PDSs were not including parents and community members that even though there was a strong connection between the school and a university, the PDS approach could actually contribute to things being less equitable if parents and community members were excluded.

Murrell and Borunda (1998) pointed out the seemingly frequent lack of ties from PDSs to community, neighborhood, and overall social reform efforts; however, they do cite a positive example of a partnership (Wheelock College and Trotter School) that addressed equity issues related to academic diversity by redefining diversity to include both academic and cultural differences (Pritchard & Ancess, 1999).

Equity plays an important role in PDS school–university partnerships. In these relationships, all interactions and decisions should be based on the premise of equality. The idea of equality cuts against hierarchical relationships, allowing for collaboration built on both trust and mutual respect (El-Amin et al., 1999). In PDS relationships, resource sharing is not necessarily equal for both the school and university partners. Resources must be shared but also based on what each partner is able to contribute to the collaboration. In turn, in PDS relationships, stakeholders should be formally recognized and rewarded for whatever contributions they were able to bring to the environment (Brindley et al., 2008).

As equality can be deemed the most fundamental shared PDS value, partnerships should be facilitated equally so that competitive relationships and utilization of resources does not occur. These types of cultures can allow for space-related, financial, and human resources to be hoarded for the benefit of one partner. However, when nonhierarchical school–university partnerships are fostered, this makes for a safer environment where participants are not afraid to voice creative ideas and take risks (El-Amin et al., 1999).

Reflection Time

Pause

Deliberate

Share

What is your role in your partnership, or what would you like it to be? What is the status of your responsibilities? Consider if the roles and responsibilities in your partnership are clear and equally divided.

Spotlight on PDS Student Representatives

In Chapter 3, we discussed the various stakeholders involved in PDS and their roles and responsibilities, along with some findings related to school–university partnerships. Separately, teacher candidates and leadership in the realm of PDS were covered; however, research on leadership opportunities for teacher candidates is sparse. The quality preparation of teacher candidates is among the main goals of professional development schools. The role of teacher candidates in a PDS tends to focus on the planning and implementation of appropriate lessons, learning about classroom management, assessment, and reflection—and all the other important dispositions they will need in order to be teachers. There is evidence of teacher candidates participating in inquiry and research projects as part of their role in a PDS, and teacher candidates can witness their mentor teacher modeling leadership in the school building and as part of the PDS, but overall, there are not abundant opportunities to develop leadership skills for teacher candidates in a PDS.

The SUNY Buffalo State (BSU) Professional Development Schools (PDS) consortium views teacher candidates as an extremely important stakeholder in PDS partnerships. Early on, the Buffalo State PDS developed a PDS student representative program. This affords teacher candidates the opportunity to develop leadership skills embedded in close relationships with partner schools (Ware et al., 2017). This program allows teacher candidates to apply for the voluntary position of PDS student representative (rep). The PDS director and current graduate assistant and student representatives review the applications during the spring semester and decide who to bring in for interviews. The application and interview materials are included.

Part of the interview has representatives consider possible research projects related to PDS. Possible topics are discussed between the director and student reps. Based on the research topic, the reps are assigned mentors for their research projects. After meeting with their mentor, the reps begin their project over the summer break. When they return in the fall semester, they continue with their research project and take on the duties of a PDS student representative.

The PDS reps spend up to four hours a week in the PDS office. This space is dedicated to PDS teacher candidates. They are welcome to study, relax, eat, and fulfill their PDS duties in the office throughout the academic year. A graduate assistant (GA) also works in the PDS office. They are there to assist the student representatives, who are typically undergraduates in one of the teacher education programs. Because the GA is a student who is part of the PDS leadership team, they are up to date on PDS initiatives and the roles of student reps. The GA determines what work is needed to support PDS endeavors and assigns tasks for each week.

There are very busy times for the Buffalo State PDS. For instance, in the beginning of the fall semester, the reps help to spread the word about PDS and activities. Reps often visit education classes and spend a few minutes explaining PDS and inviting their peers to partake in PDS activities. They also create bulletin boards in various buildings on campus where teacher candidates have their classes with information about PDS. PDS takes part in a Teacher Tailgate event and a free conference for all stakeholders early in the fall semester.

The PDS student representatives help to advertise the events, prepare materials, and help with set-up and attendee check-in. The Teacher Tail-gate is an event for teacher candidates in any program at the university to learn about the opportunities available to help them get more involved and to foster their interest in teaching. Clubs, programs, and campus offices set up tables to inform teacher candidates, and food is always provided. The student reps are there to talk to students and assist with the event's implementation.

The SUNY Buffalo State PDS also holds an annual PDS conference. The conference is free for all consortium stakeholders. Again, they assist with all aspects of the events and encourage teacher candidates to attend. There are usually concurrent sessions, and two keynote speakers. There is also an opportunity to do poster presentations. Many representatives who completed their research in the previous academic year present during this part of the conference.

While assisting with these events, the PDS student reps also continue to work on their research projects with guidance from their mentors, the GA, and the PDS director. During the slower weeks, they can work on their research during their PDS office hours. In the fall, the reps also complete proposals for student poster presentations or electronic presentations at the National Association for School–University Partnerships (NASUP) conference. If their proposal is accepted, the reps then work to obtain research and travel awards from campus programs to fund their trip to the national conference. Along with the presentations, these awards can be added to the reps' resumes. These types of experiences help to set them apart from other applicants for teaching positions.

At the national conference, the GA and student representatives present their posters and often participate in concurrent sessions with faculty members. Many of the GAs and student representatives have won awards for their presentations and participation at the NAPDS conference. They attend sessions and reflect on what they learned. All the while, they are representing Buffalo State on a national level. As NASUP members, they can participate in meetings and vote when necessary.

Not only do the PDS reps act as ambassadors for the Buffalo State PDS at the national conference, but they also represent their peers at Buffalo State. PDS reps are members of the advisory council and convey the needs and wishes of the campus teacher candidates. They are present when school partners discuss the needs of the schools and what the teacher candidates coming into the schools at various levels should need to be well prepared to do. If necessary, the PDS will provide professional development for the teacher candidates, as well as for the rest of the stakeholders, on these topics.

The GA and student representatives also assist with the PDS newsletter each semester. The newsletter highlights the accomplishments of PDS consortium members, advertises upcoming events, spotlights school partners, and describes other newsworthy PDS-related events. The newsletter is sent to all members of the PDS consortium. As well, many of the student representatives continue to present their research at local events, and sometimes even publish their research findings with a teacher education faculty member.

As the reps complete their volunteer hours in the PDS office, they often communicate with teacher education faculty and network with school partners at PDS events, such as the PDS meetings we have at partner schools throughout the academic year. The reps often help to set up these meetings, make PDS announcements, and introduce speakers. Since the reps are well known for their many accomplishments by the education faculty, they are often asked to take part in events unrelated to PDS, or to help with special projects, and frequently they win scholarships and awards for all their hard work and dedication to the Buffalo State PDS.

Throughout their year of service to PDS, the student reps are mentored by the GA and PDS director. They are supported in all aspects of their position. Weber and Klein (2020) detailed structures of support for GAs and PDS student representatives, and many of them are used to support and encourage the student reps. Not only do the student reps build leadership and communication skills (oral and written), they also practice time management and appropriate dispositions as work to fulfill their dreams of becoming teachers. (See Appendix B for PDS representative forms.)

Chapter 4

Branching Out

Previous chapters have discussed what it means to be a PDS, how to formalize a partnership, and what possible roles and responsibilities might be involved. I want to stress again that every PDS relationship is different due to the needs, strengths, and interests of each partner institution and the stakeholders that comprise the collaborative. Aside from adhering to the flexible NAPDS 9 Essentials (Kindzierski, Garas-York, & del Prado Hill, 2021) your PDS school–university partnership can be whatever your stakeholders want it to be. A PDS is a dynamic relationship that grows with its stakeholders and its surroundings. The ways that the PDSs I work with adhere to the NAPDS 9 Essentials will look different from the ways other PDSs follow the NAPDS 9 Essentials. As well, the ways that PDSs adhere to the NAPDS 9 Essentials will not look the same for each collaboration across the years. As situations change, so must the PDSs. Not only do these changes help to address current needs or trends in education, they also help in renewal and to keep up with the growth of stakeholders. This chapter concerns ways that PDSs have or could branch out to tailor the PDS to its stakeholders or to provide new and exciting opportunities that can emerge from a partnership.

This chapter (including the Spotlight section) presents ideas on how PDSs might stretch to better understand professional identities and beliefs, to engage in new methods of instruction, such as co-teaching, to participate in professional development, and to engage in research. This list is certainly not an exhaustive list of ways PDSs can help fulfill the goals of school–university partnerships and the overall simultaneous renewal of schools and teacher education programs to produce quality teachers for the improvement of P–12 student learning.

Professional Identity and Beliefs

Participation in a PDS can impact the confidence and self-efficacy of both future teachers and in-service teachers. Teachers can gain a better idea of what it is like to be an instructor, and how to strive for higher levels of preparedness and professionalism. The following studies provide evidence of these positive findings of PDS-prepared teacher candidates.

Helms-Lorenz et al. (2018) examined the outcomes of a PDS secondary teacher education program. They compared teachers in non-PDSs and teachers in PDSs over three years. They found that PDS teachers conveyed higher levels of teacher efficacy each of the three years. The PDS teachers also rated their teacher preparation and their learning opportunities significantly more positively than did the non-PDS teachers.

Newman et al. (1998) also studied the views of teacher candidates pre- and post-PDS prior to student teaching regarding stages of concern about teaching, teacher efficacy, understanding and implementation of integrated curriculum, and implementation of technology in instruction. They also examined PDS and more traditionally trained teacher candidates on their levels of preparedness. They found that the teacher candidates from the PDS preparation felt and were better prepared to begin their teaching careers. Their analysis determined that the teacher candidates who were PDS prepared were more efficacious and had reached a level of comfort to an extent that teacher candidates could consider concerns beyond their own personal survival in the program.

In addition, Walling and Lewis (2000) studied differences between PDS and more traditionally prepared teacher candidates. They concluded that the PDS-prepared participants developed an awareness of the various issues educators face, while at the same time increased the degree to which they cared about children and teaching. The same participants also shifted their goals regarding teaching from more of a job orientation to that of a career orientation, while emphasizing knowledge and skill development. However, the teacher candidates who were prepared in more traditional teacher education programs appeared to be less focused on the issues teachers must face and less motivated regarding their concern for children. As far as their personal motives, the traditionally prepared teacher candidates maintain more of a job orientation. These results led to the conclusion that PDS-prepared teacher candidates appeared to possess a better developed sense of professional identity after completing their teacher education programs, when compared to teacher candidates who completed a traditional teacher preparation program. Overall, Walling and Lewis (2000) determined that their data provided some evidence that the experiences of those teacher candidates in PDS programs may foster a more mature level of professionalism based on their beliefs and attitudes as opposed to those candidates who completed a more traditional teacher preparation program.

Finally, Fountain (1997) determined that PDS experiences positively impacted the confidence levels of PDS teacher candidates teaching in urban schools. They felt this was a worthwhile experience and led to large numbers of the participants applying for jobs in urban schools. These findings speak volumes about the positive experiences and beliefs of PDS prepared teacher candidates. These future teachers may be more likely to participate in other PDS projects or initiatives later in their careers due to these helpful early experiences and the insight and confidence that have been nurtured.

Co-Teaching

Co-teaching in a PDS partnership is another way that stakeholders are afforded ways to branch out and try different and innovative techniques in classrooms with the benefit of having more than one teacher in the classroom in an effort to provide more quality instruction for P–12 learners.

Initially, co-teaching was a technique used in classrooms where some students with disabilities were included with general education students. Co-teaching was aimed to support students with learning disabilities (Peery, 2017), but it has also been found to be beneficial for teachers (Badiali & Titus, 2010; Peery, 2017; Rexroat-Frazier, 2017) and preservice teachers (Hurd & Weilbacher, 2017; Peery, 2017). There are seven main models of co-teaching used. They are one teach–one observe, parallel teaching, one teach–one assist, station teaching, supplemental teaching, alternative or differentiated teaching, and team teaching (Ackerman, 2017; Harter & Jacobi, 2018).

Co-teaching is an especially effective technique in a school–university partnership because it helps to increase preservice teacher engagement in the partner school. Co-teaching can allow teacher candidates to maximize their time and effectiveness in the field when they can jump right in and work side by side with their mentor teacher using co-teaching. Co-teaching allows for the preservice teachers to actively participate and collaborate with seasoned teachers while applying what they have learned in their teacher preparation courses, and this can allow for more positive field experiences (Mann et al., 2020).

When co-teaching is used in a classroom, the teacher candidate is elevated to the position of teacher alongside a more knowledgeable other. In this way, teacher candidates can have different experiences working with diverse groups of learners (Gerlach, 2017; Sachs et al., 2011; Yopp et al., 2014). By working as a co-teacher during field experiences, the chance that the teacher candidate will be unprepared in future teaching endeavors is reduced (Ackerman, 2017; Hurd & Weilbacher, 2017; Ross et al., 2011).

When co-teaching models are used, mentor teachers can also benefit (Mann et al., 2020). Co-teaching can help reduce the teacher–student ratio because another potential teacher is in the classroom, which allows each of them to spend more quality time with individuals and small groups of students (Ackerman, 2017; Gerlach, 2017). As well, the mentor teacher and teacher candidate can each focus on different aspects of the classroom tasks (Rexroat-Frazier, 2017; Stumpf, 2015). In this way, they are both able to effectively contribute to the learning environment, particularly in the areas of management and instruction (Grubesky, 2014; Harter & Jacobi, 2018; Mann et al., 2020).

Mentor teachers and teacher candidates can both gain experience working with the different co-teaching models, which can positively influence overall instruction. Having two people working together to implement new instructional models yields an environment of reciprocal professional development that can benefit multiple PDS stakeholders (Mann et al., 2020). Along with an environment of reciprocal professional development, other forms of professional development are afforded by PDS partnerships.

Professional Development

Professional development is another way to continue to grow in the field of education. Professional development is a large part of the PDS approach to school–university partnerships. The name "professional development school" is tricky because it often leads people to believe that the organization is only about professional development, which as you know by this time is not the case. However, a PDS approach to a school–university partnership has structures that can assist with providing appropriate professional development for multiple stakeholders. For instance, administrators in attendance at a PDS advisory council meeting might express that teacher candidates need to have knowledge pertaining to a certain strategy or concept prior to entering field placements. Mentor teachers in attendance would likely agree. Together, multiple stakeholders in attendance at the meeting might make initial plans to ensure that teacher candidates are prepared to work with P–12 learners. PDS can work with schools or community organizations to leverage resources to obtain professional development in the designated concept or strategy needed for all stakeholders.

This is a practice of the Buffalo State PDS consortium. For many years, PDS provided professional development (PD) for all stakeholders based on their needs. This PD took place as part of an annual PDS conference, at local PDS partner school meetings, or at special events on campus. In recent years, more of this PD has been completed online synchronously, recorded, and then been made available for asynchronous viewing moving forward. These sessions are available on the PDS website for stakeholders to access at any time.

Professional development is necessary in order to support efforts for school improvement. The active involvement of stakeholders can help foster a sense of ownership, bring people together, and increase cooperation for the improvement initiative. The success of school improvement efforts is tied to educator professional development (Joyce & Showers, 1988; Murphy, 1990). Guskey and Huberman (1995) described the function of professional development as part of the process of change: "Knowledge systems are simultaneously the objects of change and factors that support or constrain the change process" (p. 38). In addition to receiving knowledge as part of professional development, teachers should also share knowledge related to teaching and learning (Nolan & Francis, 1992).

As part of a PDS partnership, multiple stakeholders can benefit from professional development that is either tailored to a specific partnership or appropriate for an entire PDS network. El-Amin (1999) noted that elementary mentor teachers revealed that professional development is one of the main reasons they participated in a partnership. They explained that they are better able to identify and meet the needs of their P–12 learners due to instructional approaches learned from working closely with preservice teachers and university faculty on the required unit plans and through participation in other professional development opportunities. Teachers also shared that they counted their mentorship of preservice teachers as a large contributor to their professional growth.

Taylan et al. (2022) examined professional development for teacher educators. It has been found that PD is beneficial for teachers as part of a school–university partnership (Sandholtz, 2002), but little has been examined about professional development of teacher educators in a PDS partnership. First, Taylan et al. (2022) noted that one of the main concerns of teacher educators was connecting theory and practice, or what the teacher educators were learning in courses on campus with their clinical experiences. In the triangle of mentor teachers, teacher candidates, and teacher educators, along with the other two groups, teacher educators can also benefit from professional development, specifically PD that helps to make connections between theory and practice (Smedley, 2001) and assists teacher educators with remaining up to date with the current practices used in partner schools (Bartholomew & Sandholtz, 2009). Teacher educators who had the opportunity to work with P–12 learners found this very beneficial and viewed such work as professional development (Taylan et al., 2022). These interactions and experiences could potentially be beneficial to the preservice teachers working with teacher educators involved in professional development as part of a school–university partnership. Taylan et al. (2022) saw PD for teacher educators as a means through which they can better integrate theory and practice for teacher candidates. In addition, because most teacher educators think about themselves and teachers and researchers, Taylan et al. proposed that the inclusion of research and research-based practices in P–12 learning environments would enhance the experiences. Their research stemmed from an initiative to improve student learning and teacher education by narrowing the gap between theory and practice as part of teacher educator practices. This required teacher educators to renew their P–12 teaching experiences in schools by teaching in a P–12 setting for one year as part of their research. In Taylan et al.'s study, teacher educators were fifth-grade math teachers. Aside from teacher educator professional development, this project was also found to positively impact student achievement in math. The teacher educators reflected, conducted research, and planned instruction that engaged P–12 learners and the teacher educators.

Teacher educators appeared to believe that in addition to preparing teacher candidates, research was part of their teacher educator identity (Swennen et al., 2010). Taylan et al. (2022) found that teacher educator professional development was different in this situation because they were not working with mentor teachers, but they worked as 5th-grade math teachers for the duration of one year.

Taylan et al. (2022) determined that having a teacher educator actually teaching math classes and meeting with other teachers about planning and student results may have made the teachers in the school less resistant to trying research-based strategies than if the teacher educator came into the partner school and recommended the research-based strategies. The sharing of these strategies with teachers and the information teachers provided about the students and the school context strengthened the school–university partnership. Teacher educators also noted that the collaborative reflection and planning along with conducting research were beneficial parts of their professional development. This learning had the potential to allow teacher educators to be better models moving forward when working with teacher candidates.

INQUIRY

The research of Taylan et al. (2022) shed some light on the school–university partnership tensions related to theory and practice, or what teacher candidates learn on campus and how it applies to what they are observing and implementing in their field experiences in PDS partner schools. Field experiences with the cooperation of the mentor teacher and teacher educator are good settings in which to make connect theory and practice (Stoddard, 1993). However, Bullough et al. (1997) found that at least the views of practicing teachers in a school–university partnership remained virtually unchanged despite working closely with teacher educators and teacher candidates. They viewed theory as unrelated and having limited worth as opposed to authentic classroom experiences. Another way to help bridge the chasm between theory and practice is through inquiry or research involving multiple groups of stakeholders.

Shaefer (1967) described a school as a hub of inquiry, indicating the expectation that teachers should be conducting inquiry on a regular basis to help assess teacher practices and student learning processes. Teitel (2004) noted that more updated action research in schools related to school settings, school improvement, and the development of teachers is necessary due to inquiry being a central piece of PDS. "A central tenant of PDS work involves linking the work of teacher preparation to the goal of school improvement" (Yendol-Hoppey et al., 2008, p. 24).

Yendol-Hoppey et al. (2008) defined teacher research or inquiry as "the systematic, intentional study made by teachers of their own classroom practice" (p. 24). Teacher inquiry can begin by teachers developing a question related to school improvement. They then begin to collect data, analyze the data, share their results, and using the findings, take action. This type of professional activity geared toward school improvement and "the process of integrating teacher inquiry into the fabric of PDS work can cultivate a favorable disposition in prospective and practicing teachers toward participation in school improvement while developing professional knowledge related to the area of inquiry" (p. 24). Involving multiple stakeholders to share the responsibility for school improvement makes PDS part of the school improvement plan and models this type of collaborative responsibility for teacher candidates. As well, there is a perception that teacher education programs create tasks for teacher candidates to complete that are not valued by or aligned with what is going on in the partner school. The shared responsibility for school improvement brings all stakeholders together to support the specific needs of the PDS. Prospective teacher assignments should be part of the shared responsibility and PDS work, with a focus on the real needs of the partner school (Yendol-Hoppey et al. (2008).

Nolan Jr. et al. (2007) described how inquiry has been a longstanding core feature of their PDS partnership. They described three ways that teacher candidates and their mentors engaged in inquiry. One way was through shared inquiry, where the mentor teacher and teacher candidate defined and completed one single inquiry together. Another way mentor teachers engaged in inquiry with teacher candidates was parallel inquiry, which entails the mentor teacher and teacher candidate conducting two parallel teacher research projects and supporting each other as they conduct their own research. A third way mentor teachers and teacher candidates inquired together is through inquiry support, which entails the teacher candidate taking full responsibility for the inquiry, with help from the mentor teacher by supporting topic selection, project design, data gathering, and data analysis. "PDSs can create a collaborative arrangement with their university partners, through a variety of inquiry orientations and impact levels, ranging from two or three participants to a whole-school initiative" (Yendol-Hoppey et al., 2008, p. 35). It is important that the work of PDS follows from school improvement plans, which should guide the inquiry. Of course, this could change over time.

These types of inquiry afford teacher candidates and mentor teachers a great deal of flexibility; however, Silva (2000) found that mentor teachers were often worried about the amount of time inquiry work would take (Button et al., 1996). As well, some mentor teachers were not confident about engaging in inquiry. Finally, Silva (2000) found that mentor teachers were concerned about how and where the inquiry work would be shared, with specific worry around the possibility of having to write a paper. Interestingly, the area of inquiry as it relates to PDS has been given only limited attention (Berry et al., 1998; Pritchard and Ancess, 1999; Teitel, 2004).

If you have had any teaching experience or have even stepped foot in a classroom, it is easy to understand why teachers might worry about the time and energy it would take to also conduct research along with all the other tasks involved in being a teacher or especially a mentor teacher. I was open to and involved in research projects when I was a classroom teacher, but if that was also a requirement of being a mentor teacher, I'm not sure I would have accepted a student teacher, although I had been teaching for several years. Based on my experiences as a classroom teacher, research assistant, and researcher, I think there are many reasons why the idea of inquiry and research are daunting for mentor teachers.

As previously mentioned, time and energy are likely at the top of the list for reasons of concern. Mentor teachers may worry that the time spent on research might impede on precious time with P–12 learners one on one, in small groups or whole groups, or even their personal time outside of school. Mentor teachers may be concerned about their anonymity and that of their students as part of research. When my class and I were participants in a major research project, it was difficult to get administrative permission, collect all the consent forms from students and parents, and make time for data collection aside from all the other things going on in the classroom. Mentor teachers might be hesitant to engage in research due to a lack of understanding about what research entails. There are different ways of framing the research that may make participation seem more or less enticing depending on individual mentor teachers.

When inquiry is framed as collaborative and when engaging in research as part of a PDS can help provide teachers with new strategies and practices or ways to improve student learning, it may seem more appealing to some mentor teachers (Teitel, 2003). Mentor teachers may also feel comfortable learning about inquiry by observing the work of teacher candidates (Silva, 2000).

Nolan Jr. et al. (2007) provided characteristics of teachers with an adaptive inquiry orientation as it pertained to teaching. Adaptive inquirers viewed teaching as complex and raised critical questions about schooling. These teachers partook in inquiry to make sense of problems of practice by collecting data and using evidence from its analysis to assess the impact of their instructional practices on students. They analytically examined underlying beliefs and assumptions regarding all aspects of schooling. Adaptive inquirers participated in professional development that allowed them to access resources to assist them in researching problems of practice more effectively. They viewed themselves as active members of communities of practice and that knowledge is distributed across them. They also looked for ways to connect their inquiries with what they knew about the larger community. These teachers were committed to enacting practices that aligned with what they believed and had evidence pertaining to the impact on learners even if they flew in the face of what was the norm. Finally, they showed a willingness to take what they had learned and enact alternative ways of teaching that they believed would benefit learners.

In a burgeoning PDS, these characteristics are most likely aspirational, but it is important to understand the qualities of these adaptive inquirers as inquiry is such a central part of PDS and can be utilized as the partnership grows and develops. Again, this is another way to branch out and meet the needs of stakeholders.

There are also PDS stakeholders interested in engaging in research on a larger scale, with the hope of presenting or publishing at national conferences or publishing in journals or writing grant proposals. These activities take them beyond their own PDS and are viewed as ongoing professional development (El-Amin, 1999). Neapolitan and Tunks (2009) described a structure for more involved research that was tied to the NCATE PDS Standards (2001) and in alignment with the various stages of participation as well as the American Educational Research Association (AERA) research methodologies. The stages were beginning, developing, at standard, and leading. "Although the approach described herein cannot possibly capture the contextual variances of every partnership, the framework does offer a systematic and developmental approach to research framed by the grounded theory of the NCATE's PDS Standards (2001)" (Neapolitan & Tunks, 2009, p. 5). They found that in a search through PDS articles between 1988 and 2006 that 68% of the articles were comprised of non-research methods, such as descriptions of various PDS programs, literature reviews, and reports and ideas about PDS. The remaining research articles examined PDS using qualitative methods. These were mostly case studies. No experimental studies were found. They surmised that the trend of more descriptive publications stemmed from a lack of time to develop the trust needed for schools to allow for the random selection required for experimental studies that could examine PDS's effect on student achievement. They called for more rigorous research methods that could determine the effect of PDS on student achievement as well as teacher preparation. Neapolitan and Tunks (2009) stated that "the intention for creating the framework is to empower PDS workers at all levels to conduct appropriate research, therefore providing local, state, and national organizations with the accountability required" (p. 6). The researchers married NCATE's PDS Standards (2001) with research methods recommended by AERA. "The framework conveys a guide for PDS researchers to examine their partnerships' developmental levels and current research practices with an eye toward systemized, methodologically based research agendas" (Neapolitan & Tunks, 2009, p. 6).

As stated, Neapolitan and Tunks (2009) used the wording of each stage of the NCATE PDS Standards to determine their PDS research recommendations. For the first developmental stage, beginning, they recommended the four research methods of philosophic, case study, survey, and historical based verbs from the criteria from the beginning stage rubric, such as planning, articulating, exploring, and envisioning. Using the aforementioned methods, researchers can study the burgeoning relationships at this early stage of PDS development. They found that the tools of observation and document analysis can provide information about the relationships and collaboration involved at an early stage without hindering the growth of the partnership. They also recommended surveys as a tool but only if they were anonymous. These methods and tools are appropriate because levels of trust have not been established yet.

At the developing stage, PDS partners have come to an agreement on the mission of collaboration and the meaningful connection of teacher candidates and mentor teachers. At this stage, the work of PDS has yet to trigger any policy or practice changes. The NCATE PDS Standards rubrics at the developing level has stakeholders making recommendations about action research or the formal sharing of practices through observation. Partnerships at the developing stage will also influence university personnel to make instructional practice changes in their courses. At this stage, the increased amount of collaboration appears more defined and fosters a higher amount of trust among partners that can open up more opportunities for research. Neapolitan and Tunks (2009) found appropriate research methods at the developmental stage included the same methods from the beginning stage but at a deeper level due to increased trust among stakeholders. As well, they added ethnography and quasi-experimental research. The authors also called attention to the increased empowerment of the mentor teachers and viewed them as gatekeepers across the stages, given that they are the only ones who interact with both the teacher candidates and the P–12 learners in the schools. The increased empowerment of mentor teachers increases the potential for action research with university faculty and mentor teachers. At the developing stage, school partners are less likely to allow research that calls for random selection. Quasi-experimental research affords the next best option. Neapolitan and Tunks (2009) caution researchers to design their methods carefully when doing quasi-experimental research due to halo effects and other possible interferences. The halo effect is when someone's positive judgment of one of a person's attributes biases, perhaps with no basis, their feelings about another of the person's attributes. The halo effect can have negative consequences, such as clouding judgment and leading people to make decisions that could be deemed unfair or inappropriate.

Partnerships that have attained the at-standard stage have both the university and school fully integrating the PDS mission. There is no question regarding the expectation of PDS work reflective of best practices. The PDS work at the at-standard stage exhibits effectiveness that typically yields positive results for teacher candidates and P–12 learners. Partnerships at this stage demonstrate changes in their policies and their practices based on their PDS work to provide meaningful support to stakeholders. At the at-standard stage, the partners' ideas about PDS have meshed, and there exists a heightened awareness of the impact PDS has on the gains of learners. Neapolitan and Tunks (2009) stated: "Finally, at this stage, policy change to support the PDS calls for a clear research objective" (p. 8). They recommend all research methods at this stage. They suggested using qualitative methods to dig deeper into the results of quasi-experimental and experimental studies. "Policymakers who have supported or who intend to support PDS programs expect hard numeric results signifying the effect of the PDS program on student achievement" (Neapolitan & Tunks, 2009, p. 8).

Neapolitan and Tunks (2009) described the leading stage as "advanced PDS work that is sustaining and generative, leading to systematic changes in policy and practice in partner institutions, as well as impact on policy at the district, state, and national levels" (p. 8). A PDS at the leading stage has an impact not only on their own partners but on the larger community in the field of education. Partners at the leading level help to support PDS programs in the lower levels of development. Neapolitan and Tunks (2009) noted that "owing to the far-reaching aspect required of this level of development, research implications suggest less control over variability than that at the previous level, namely because of the immensity of the expectations to foster policy changes in broader educational settings"

(p. 9). As far as their research agendas are concerned, the authors viewed the leading stage as the partnership starting over, but instead the research takes place outside of the original institutions in regional or national settings. Neapolitan and Tunks recommended the four research methods from the beginning stage (case study, survey, historical, and philosophic): "These original four methods represent the PDS's regenerating itself in new settings, essentially creating a beginning or initial formation. When a program is developing at a distance from the original, other forms of research (including ethnography and the experimental designs) fall short because of the need for collaboration and trust to obtain personal and sensitive data, unattainable from the vantage point of expanding the PDS beyond the borders of the original program" (p. 9). The PDS program at the leading level works to communicate with and promote PDS programs at other levels because the findings of the leading PDS help to steer policy change.

Engaging in research is likely the most flexible way for a PDS to branch out. While PDS inquiry may start on a small scale related to school improvement in one school, research has the potential to accommodate the need for study and/or the desire to study for most PDS stakeholders.

Reflection Time

Pause

Deliberate

Share

What are other ways stakeholders can branch out or build on initial PDS partnerships to better meet their needs?

Spotlight on
International Professional Development Schools (IPDS)

Recent migration patterns and technology stress the need to think globally (Florian, 2017). The movement of people across the globe keeps changing the demographic makeup of countries. The result of this shift is present in the growing number of schools and their diverse populations of students. This evidence can provide a need for change in the teaching workforce and teacher education programs through a lens of equity and social justice (Florian, 2017).

PDS is in a position to provide teacher candidates, teacher educators, and mentor teachers authentic cross-cultural experiences. One goal of the PDS approach calls for teachers advocating against inequity and providing learners with instruction that is inclusive while informing and empowering all their students. Teacher education programs that hold to the PDS approach to school–university partnerships also focus on affording teacher candidates experiences in partner schools with diverse student populations, along with providing class work pertaining to issues of equity and diversity while including multicultural education (Taylor & Sobel, 2010).

Because the demographics of schools are changing, teacher education programs must change as well to provide for quality education for all students (Futrell, 2008; Villegas, 2008). A teacher candidate should assume that their future classroom will be filled with a diverse group of students, and teacher education programs must prepare them for the differences and inequities they will observe (Florian, 2017). Teacher candidates should be poised to embrace that students in their future classrooms will all learn in different ways and be prepared to teach effectively in these settings.

Educators must engage in cross-cultural experiences to assist in better understanding themselves and people around them who are different (Merryfield, 1995). Meeting the needs of all learners is essential to ensure equity and assist all children to achieve and be successful in an increasingly challenging world.

It is clear that teacher candidates must be prepared to work in schools with diverse groups of students, yet teacher preparation programs have had an overwhelming increase in the scope of curricula to be covered in their programs, with almost no increase in the length of the classes. Teacher educators should stress to teacher candidates the expectation that they will meet learners who are different in a range of ways and how that can and should be embraced.

The ideal way to implement cross-cultural learning is to become knowledgeable about and spend time in a community that is different from one's own cultural background. Teacher candidates should be encouraged to carefully observe and practice active listening in the community. Such experiences are what teachers need if they are to develop culturally and contextually relevant pedagogy for students whose backgrounds are different from their own. It is the hope that teachers who work with students with different backgrounds from themselves will be able to recognize students' assets and utilize that knowledge to better understand students' behaviors and any difficulties students bring to school and situate them sociopolitically instead of beginning from a deficit perspective (Sleeter, 2008).

Teacher preparation programs can help shift the mindset of teacher candidates. "If the idea that all children will vary and differences are to be expected as an ordinary aspect of human development is accepted, then all teachers, not just some, should be prepared in ways that support this view. This is an important element of a reform agenda for teacher education that is fundamental to developing new approaches to diversity in teacher education that do not position it as a problem" (Florian, 2017, p. 12). These approaches should occur within school structures that require teachers to also act as change agents to foster inclusion and equity.

It is important to prepare teachers who hold consistently high expectations for their students and include multicultural principles and approaches as part of teacher education programs. Engaging in global experiences as part of the PDS teacher preparation approach can afford educators with firsthand, authentic experiences to identify possible biases and redesign previously used principles and approaches (Tidwell & Thompson, 2008).

Culturally relevant pedagogy is a way to examine biases, stereotypes, and prejudice while concurrently appreciating and celebrating one's own culture and that of others (Myers & Jenkins, 2020). It is helpful to culturally support high achievement for all students by using effective instruction in a learner-centered environment where the assets the students bring to school are recognized, nurtured, and used to foster student achievement (Richards et al. 2007). When considering cultural competence, Milner (2010) put the focus on teachers instead of students. He explained that educators should develop cultural competence to effectively educate all students. Milner called for teachers to foster meaningful relationships with their students by understanding the many aspects of their identities. Culturally competent teachers perceive the culture of their students as assets that are valued as a critical component of their success. For teachers to become more globally minded, they should become familiar with educational standards from around the world and engage in training in international schools (Brown & Kysilka, 2002).

The PDS approach is uniquely poised to address a variety of challenges, including expanding globally (Kindzierski et al., 2021). The NAPDS 9 Essentials (NAPDS, 2021) can act as a guide for more effective practices and outcomes. PDS partnerships are made to develop dynamic relationships between higher education and partner schools, with the overall principle and conceptualization that teacher candidates profit from real-world experiences, increase growth in university/P–12 collaborative professional development, and offer value-added dimensions to partner school classrooms. PDS is a special kind of school–university partnership made to leverage university and school resources in a mutually beneficial partnership within the framework proposed by Darling-Hammond (1994) and Brindley et al. (2008). Human resources, time, space, expertise, and when possible, financial support are resources that can be leveraged by PDS partners with a focus on relationships informed by research and best practices (Ferrara et al., 2014; Garas-York et al., 2017; Teitel, 2004).

The foundation of PDS can be used at a global level as well (Merryfield, 1995). The National Association for Multicultural Education, studying 100 members, found that cultural immersion was among the main influences that inspired the respondents' commitment to multicultural education (Paccione, 2000). Culturally immersive experiences help teachers to move outside of their comfort zone and change their understanding of others (Boyle-Baise, 2008). Teacher candidates heightened their level of understanding of Latino, Spanish-speaking youth during a two-week field experience (Ference & Bell, 2004). Their work aligned with components for effective cultural immersion, such as cultural education before entering the field experience, living with host families, and engaging in community activities, along with consistent reflection related to race, culture, and power (Boyle-Baise, 2008).

There are many examples of how school–university partnerships can foster cultural competence through PDS structures (Ferrara et al. 2020). PDS can benefit stakeholders in second language teacher education (world language teachers and English as a second language teachers) by providing opportunities for teacher candidates to become observers and action researchers to study and reflect on skills, beliefs, and practices (Vélez-Rendón, 2002). Research has shown the value of interaction in culturally diverse settings to increase teacher candidates' understanding of diversity. International travel provides a unique opportunity for growth in intercultural understanding because it incorporates physical and psychological challenges that involve cognitive, affective, and behavioral domains (Cushner, 2007; Egeland, 2016; Santoro & Major, 2012). Teacher candidates were impacted by clinically rich international experiences due to the challenge of preconceptions about those with cultural differences, to expand understanding about possible methods for schools and classrooms, and to foster individual and professional growth (Pence & Macgillivray, 2006; Willard-Holt, 2001). Teacher education programs are encouraged to make this opportunity available to teacher candidates in order to increase the skills needed for them to enter 21st-century classrooms in an interconnected world (Cushner, 2007).

The SUNY Buffalo State International Professional Development Schools (IPDS) program provides education majors, student teachers and experienced educators the opportunity to explore teaching and learning across the globe through short-term, faculty-led travel. This program was established in 2012 and now includes 11 school–university partnerships in nine countries, led by over 18 university faculty members (with two more programs under development). The IPDS experience was developed to provide teacher candidates with structured and meaningful learning about education within cultures outside the United States to spark in teacher candidates both the need to know and the desire to learn more about cultural and ethnic groups that are likely to be present in their future classrooms.

Using PDS structures, the IPDS leadership sought to build capacity to extend its reach so that IPDS now includes PK–12 school partnerships in Santiago, Chile; Medellín, Colombia; Cabarete, Dominican Republic; San José, Costa Rica; the Dominican Republic; Nürtingen, Germany; Roatán, Honduras; Siena, Italy; Torremaggiore, Italy; Kigali, Rwanda; and Lusaka, Zambia. Additional collaborations are under construction in Oviedo, Spain, and Istanbul, Turkey. Each program started with one faculty member who had contacts in the target country. Each IPDS program has at least two faculty members who make up the leadership team for each partnership. These faculty teams work to maintain the partnership during the actual travel as well as pre- and post-travel through email, video conferencing, and social media.

Each program cycle includes recruitment of undergraduate and graduate students. In the application and interview process, the faculty team reviews the applications together and then interviews all potential candidates, using an IPDS-created set of questions to determine if it is likely that students will demonstrate appropriate dispositions while on the trip. A preparatory course is taught by the program faculty team to increase knowledge of the host country, prepare instructional materials for the classrooms of partner schools, build community among the travelers, start a research project, and support students as they apply for scholarships. Then the group travels to the host country for clinically rich field placements, service-learning projects, data gathering, reflection (through an online blog), interaction with the partner university, language learning exploration to build empathy and pedagogical skills, and touring of host country cultural and historical sites. Students also gain cultural knowledge by living with host families. When the IPDS participants return to campus, they share reflections and student research at the Buffalo State undergraduate and graduate student conferences as well as at the annual PDS conference. These students are then able to be IPDS ambassadors and tell new groups of interested students about their cross-cultural experiences and how it transformed their perspectives.

Designing and implementing the program took a great deal of time and effort, but the IPDS leadership recognized the important need to create more rigorous assessment strategies for program improvement, viability, and expansion to reach a greater number of students from all backgrounds and to extend the impact of the IPDS experience on campus.

As IPDS participants return from study-away experiences, many mention the transformation they have undergone (del Prado Hill, Chicola, & Horstman-Riphahn, 2020). However, as Quade (2002) notes, tools are needed to quantify and document growth when students say, " 'It changed my life' " (p. 121). Deardorff (2006) offered an important model of intercultural competence to articulate a process orientation of the knowledge, comprehension, and skills it is hoped participants will develop to identify internal and external target attitudes (or dispositions). Deardorff (2011) argued that the central question is whether participants were able to see from the perspectives of others. To determine if participants have developed this ability, programs should first prioritize goals related to intercultural competence and then state goals and measurable objectives. The important shift in focus from program evaluation to outcomes assessment is geared to a more learner-centered and authentic assessment. This assessment must move from standardized to a more customized assessment to fully determine the impact of international experiences (Deardorff, 2015).

In an attempt to avoid making simplistic assumptions about the inherent value of international education experiences, a comprehensive approach to evaluating both outcomes and program effectiveness is necessary. Evaluation and reflection are important aspects of PDS (NAPDS, 2021) and thus play a crucial role in the International Professional Development Schools (IPDS) programming. Specifically, assessing intercultural competence is a more complex endeavor that requires close attention to measurable learning objectives, acknowledgment of the lifelong learning aspects of intercultural competency, understanding the necessity of language fluency as a component, targeting curriculum experiences and service-learning, and engaging faculty in professional development (Deardorff, 2014, 2015).

The SUNY Buffalo State campus community is richly diverse. The college campus is in close contact with refugee and immigrant families who settle in and attend schools in Buffalo where over 80 languages are spoken. The Buffalo State PDS and IPDS connect all teacher candidates, including traveling and returning IPDS candidates, with culturally rich experiences through strategic field placements and service-learning opportunities in Western New York and on campus to continue to expand intercultural competencies and background knowledge so that their knowledge, skills, and dispositions can assist future teachers to prepare their classes for a global citizenry. Globalizing and internationalizing school–university partnerships provides many opportunities to engage in cross-cultural experiences to better understand the cultural and community assets students bring to the classroom and using them to teach and empower students (Taylor & Sobel, 2010).

Chapter 5

Evaluating Your PDS

Ways to Reflect and Examine the
Impact of PDS Endeavors

This is the final chapter of the book, but I hope it does not mark the end of your journey with PDS. As educators, we know that assessment and evaluation are important for many reasons. The data gleaned from assessments helps us to evaluate programs, knowledge, attitudes, dispositions, efficacy, confidence, and other elements of performance. This information helps us to create goals and make decisions about moving forward. The folks who do PDS tend to "know" that it is working, successful, and impactful, but if there is no data to demonstrate or prove the benefits of PDS, then the approach cannot be taken seriously or be regarded as legitimate in the field of education. As far as education models go, PDS has had a relatively long history. As educators, we realize that many educational trends can fall out of favor quickly. PDS has stuck around, but it continues to lack an abundance of impact data, particularly experimental or quasi-experimental research that can determine causal relationships. Snyder (1999) noted,

> Some may argue that there is insufficient evidence to earn the term realities. The evidence, for the most part, appears as descriptive book chapters rather than as theory-testing refereed journal articles. It is true that most of the evidence collected to this point possesses a distinctively testimonial and "anecdotal" air. It is also true that multiple anecdotes constitute data. The

> multiple testimonials create an evidentiary base that only a methodological ideologue could dismiss out of hand. There is an evidentiary base that PDSs are more than just a good idea. The worst-case scenario is that they may not be possible to sustain in many locations as institutions currently exist, but where they can be sustained, they influence teaching and teacher learning in schools and colleges. (pp. 137–138)

In this concluding chapter, I will explain the context of assessment and evaluation as they relate to PDS. We will also further explore PDS impact data.

The Impact of PDS

The evaluation of the efforts of professional development schools is important due to the fates of previous initiatives involving school–university partnerships. For instance, it has been suggested that one of the reasons for the demise of laboratory schools was the lack of school-based research, and portal schools were short-lived because there was no systematic way to document their effectiveness (Pritchard & Ancess, 1999). "Although progress has been made in defining partnerships, clarifying different types, and understanding stages of development, there has been limited progress in assessing the success of partnership efforts" (Clark, 1999, 51). Gilbert et al. (2018) determined that only partnerships that have been around for a number of years can be measured on success.

Teitel (2001) discussed many issues related to why it is difficult to assess the impact of PDS. Among other things, PDS has various groups of stakeholders concerned with different aspects of the impact of the partnership, so no one measure can likely determine the impact of the extent of the school–university partnership. In addition, most people involved in a PDS partnership are busy doing the work of the partnership and have little time to determine impact in a systematic way.

Teitel (2001) found that, in general, the most important questions regarding PDS research are related to impact, such as the impact on student learning; the impact on teacher candidates, principals, and mentor teachers; and the impact on continuing professional development of mentor teachers and university faculty. He noted that "good impact documentation needs to be carefully conceptualized and focused on products as well as processes. It needs to be well implemented and use a variety of credible outcome measures. High-quality impact documentation will allow insiders to improve what they are doing, even as it helps all stakeholders assess, well beyond a leap of faith, whether all the effort that goes into starting and sustaining a PDS is worth it" (p. 68).

Snyder (1999) proposed that in order to determine if PDSs impact P–12 learner achievement, the students of teachers prepared in PDS-based teacher education programs should be assessed. Osguthorpe (1996) recommended that any PDS evaluative efforts be a joint effort between schools and universities, which can also lead to a higher level of trust between the two institutions. Osguthorpe also thought that any type of evaluative effort of a PDS should be initiated by stakeholders and not mandated by some other source. It was recommended that evaluation of a PDS be for the purpose of accountability and in order to continue to refine practices. As well, El-Amin et al. (1999) held that "proper maintenance requires continuous assessment. Brewer and DeLeon (1983) suggested that such assessments should measure effectiveness, equity, adequacy, and efficiency. These assessments determine whether continued maintenance is needed, adjustments are needed, or the collaboration is finished" (El-Amin et al., 1999, p. 13). Similarly, Shiveley and Pribble (2001) pointed out the importance of collecting both formative and summative data, as well as demonstrating evidence of planned assessment and evaluation of all PDS areas.

In the early years of PDS (prior to 2001), the need for evidence to demonstrate the effectiveness of PDS partnerships was acknowledged. Pressure on those involved in PDS work to justify the impact was immense. Legislators and administrators from the district and state levels as well as higher education and foundations, who were being asked to put a lot of money and other resources into PDS initiatives, needed evidence. Pressure also came from university faculty from teacher education programs who were skeptical about changing teacher preparation models. Further pressure came from teachers, who were being asked to mentor teacher candidates on top of all their other duties. Journalists, parents, and researchers all sought evidence to demonstrate the positive impact of PDS on P–12 learners and teacher preparation. Teitel and Haqq (2000) agreed that evidence on the impact of PDS was necessary to enable this approach to school–university partnerships to survive.

Primarily, the focus was on evidence on the impact of PDS on the professional development of teachers and the impact of PDS on students' learning (Vare, 2004). Researchers proposed several ideas to assess different aspects of PDS (Teitel, 2001). For instance, Shiveley and Pribble (2001) gathered attributes of successful PDSs from a review of PDS literature available at that time. They found that the research focused on the themes related to issues of marginality, changing roles, reward structure, and ongoing inquiry. These areas were then used to assess ongoing PDS initiatives in an effort to assess progress in the direction of a more fully developed PDS site. In the present day, this seems like a very narrow assessment of a PDS. It is likely indicative of the type of research on PDS available at that time and how far research has developed over time, as well as where PDS research still needs to go.

Other researchers of the time were waiting for the release of standards by which to assess characteristics and activities of a PDS (Shiveley & Pribble, 2001). However, when the NCATE's PDS Standards (2001) were published, although they were a step in the right direction, they were not able to completely assess the effectiveness of a PDS. The standards could be used to determine outcomes as well as methods to assess PDSs (Vare, 2004), but they were not broadly grounded in educational literature related to assessment and evaluation. As well, the NCATE PDS Standards provided only a partial blueprint for determining a vision comprised of the PDS's mission as well as a guide for related activities. Many researchers sought for decades to develop assessments of the effectiveness of PDS. When reporting the findings of their study, Fisher et al. (2004) made an interesting observation about the usefulness of PDS research:

> While it may be impossible to establish a causal relationship between the presence of preservice teachers and student achievement, it may be unnecessary as well. Clark (1999) stated that these entanglements are to be expected in any inquiry of a PDS. "Good qualitative scholars seek to understand connections among the many variables present in a particular situation, just as good experimental researchers seek to understand the causes of a particular phenomenon . . . As one proceeds with evaluation, both qualitative and quantitative research skills can contribute" (pp. 210–211). What is certain is that achievement rose significantly among public school students with access to student teachers when compared to classrooms taught by the teacher alone. By any measure, this is a meaningful benchmark

for evaluating the benefits for the youngest stakeholders in a Professional Development School partnership. (Fisher et al., 2004, p. 54)

The constant call for more and different kinds of research on PDS and the impact of the various aspects of the approach continues today.

Despite the call for research on the impact of PDS, there have been studies regarding PDS and P–12 learners, teacher candidates, mentor teachers and university faculty. Helms-Lorenz et al. (2018) pointed out that because of the various expectations and aspects of PDS there remains little quantitative evidence that supports the notion that PDS-based programs are better teacher preparation environments. There is also a lack of longitudinal studies that evaluate the aims of PDS, particularly studies that evaluate one single aspect of the PDS approach. Back in 2001, Teitel was calling for the use of multiple measures to assess the impacts of PDS on various stakeholders, such as P–12 learners, preservice teachers, and administrators, as well as the learning and development of mentor teachers and university faculty members. However, there was a lack of emphasis on the empirical quality of the evidence, as concluded by Snow et al. (2016).

Snow et al. (2016) found that at the time of their research Abdal-Haqq (1998) and Breault and Breault (2010) were two of the larger-scale syntheses of PDS outcomes. Abdal-Haqq concluded that PDS programs usually consisted of more field hours as well as structure. School-based faculty gave support and feedback when evaluating teacher candidates, using a variety of assessment strategies in authentic classroom contexts with a focus on reflective practices. It was noted that graduates of PDS-based programs were more likely to utilize a variety of strategies, be reflective with a good sense of school-related logistics, and have more confidence working with diverse groups of learners. They also tended to have lower attrition rates. The classroom teachers working in PDS roles were likely to be bigger instructional risk takers, more stimulated intellectually, and less isolated individuals who made improvements in their practice and experienced professional growth. Abdul-Haqq's conclusions were based on some primary studies.

Breault and Breault (2010) put more emphasis on the empirical quality of the evidence than did Abdal-Haqq. They used criteria to initially screen the 300 studies they found. The studies deemed to be research had their methodologies coded as weak, acceptable, or strong, and the conclusions were coded as either valid or invalid. Based on their analysis, they came to the following conclusions. (1) PDS endeavors cannot be largely justified by the available research, (2) claims put forth in many primary PDS studies are unsupported, (3) student achievement outcomes are particularly underexamined, and (4) the perspectives of many important stakeholders have been underrepresented (p. 13). Breault and Breault (2010) also determined that much of the PDS research to that point was of poor quality and could not necessarily support Abdal-Haqq's aforementioned conclusions. Basically, Breault and Breault (2010) completed a more rigorous analysis of the existing PDS research.

The impact of professional development schools (PDSs) on preservice teachers is well documented and supports the position that interns at PDS schools achieve higher than do interns assigned to non-PDS schools (Castle et al., 2006; Darling-Hammond, 2007; Levine, 2002; Snyder, 1999). Pease (2003) studied two groups of teacher candidates who were part of two distinct PDS experiences. The first group had two PDS experiences before student teaching and a PDS student teaching experience. The other group had two PDS experiences before student teaching but completed student teaching in more traditional, non-PDS placements. In the end of student teaching, Pease found significant differences in the two groups. The all-PDS group of teacher candidates had higher role preparedness and teacher efficacy. Similarly, Guha et al. (2016) noted that when highly developed PDSs were studied, it was determined that graduates from PDS-based teacher preparation programs felt more prepared to teach and obtained higher ratings from their employers, supervisors, and researchers than other new teachers. Mentor teachers working in PDS partner schools noticed changes in their own teaching practices due to the professional development, research opportunities, and mentoring they received through being part of a PDS.

As well, Guha et al. (2016) noted that studies have reported gains in student performance connected to curriculum and instruction interventions based on PDS initiatives. Castle et al. (2008) examined student achievement on state standardized tests in a PDS site and a non-PDS control school across six years. They found that more students at the PDS school site moved up to mastery level, and more moved out of the intervention level than at the control school. These data provide good news regarding the impact of PDS on the main areas of focus: teacher preparation and student achievement.

At SUNY Buffalo State, we have experienced some difficulties when we come from a narrow perspective of impact data being measurable only by test scores. In del Prado Hill and Garas-York (2020), the way impact is typically gauged is challenged to include much more information than just test scores. The book also attempted to gather information on the impact of PDS programs and initiatives on various groups of stakeholders based on multiple data sources. The Buffalo State PDS is a vibrant consortium that consists of many busy stakeholders trying to do whatever they can to positively impact P–12 learners. There is little time to conduct full-blown research studies; however, we still need to obtain annual data to ensure the sustainability of funding and the overall network.

Some ways that the Buffalo State PDS consortium gathered information on outcomes of programming, stakeholder impact, and dissemination, to name a few areas, was by compiling data throughout the academic year. We counted the number of attendees at each event. This data can help set future goals and provide information when planning the events of the following year, such as the amount of seating needed, how much food to serve, and other elements. We keep track of the number of registrations for our online initiatives and gather evaluative data from attendees for all PDS programming in person or online. These evaluations are considered when planning and goal setting occur. We also send surveys if additional information from stakeholders is needed to better meet the needs of the entire consortium.

We also keep track of how many PDS partner agreements we have each semester. We then ask the liaison committees at each school site to compile information on the highlights of the partnership that semester. They can put everything on a presentation slide, or simply write out the data and the information is displayed in an engaging graphic on our PDS website.

Minutes are maintained for all PDS advisory council meetings and shared on the PDS website. We track all Buffalo State PDS-related scholarly activities for all stakeholders (teacher candidates, mentor teachers, school administrators, and university faculty) each year and share these details on the PDS website. The number of mini-grants and the project details are noted. The project findings are shared in PDS newsletters as part of breakout sessions at the annual PDS conference on campus or through other means of dissemination. We find that collecting different types of data allows us to make the best-informed decisions on how to best meet the strengths and needs of all PDS stakeholders. So do not fret if partner schools cannot give you access to student and other quantitative data that may help show the impact of your PDS. Consider how to best gauge impact for each initiative on all involved stakeholders in the least intrusive and time-consuming manner. Check out del Prado Hill and Garas-York (2020) for further ideas.

Sustainability

Sustainability is an important aspect to discuss when beginning and/or maintaining PDS relationships. Sustainability can be particularly tricky if initial PDS efforts are funded by grant money for a limited amount of time or if partnerships depend too much on the individual people involved and turnover ensues. According to Colwell et al. (2014), "building and sustaining quality professional development schools can be a challenge. Turnover in district and school-based leadership, changing areas of focus by universities or state policymakers, and limited financial and human resources can all place stress on a partnership. Having clear partnership expectations and lines of communication between the professional development school and the collaborating university are key to sustaining a meaningful partnership" (p. 17). Rosselli et al. (1999) also gathered themes related to PDS sustainability.

PDS sustainability themes were discussed regarding sustainability through transitions, with a focus on the use of standards for this examination (Rosselli et al., 1999). The themes included the evasive nature of PDS outcomes, collaboration levels, compatible views of pedagogy, staffing considerations, governance structures, reward systems, the essential fiscal infrastructures, the role and nature of inquiry, change in teacher education policy/practice, and time considerations. These are all to be considered when examining the sustainability of a PDS school–university partnership.

Ferrara (2014) provided several keys to PDS sustainability. She recommended ongoing professional development for stakeholders, continuous partnership evaluation, and collection of student assessment data (if possible) to foster stakeholder accountability. Ferrara also recommended that PDS relationships build slowly by first collaborating on mutually beneficial projects and leveraging resources. Her final recommendation for PDS sustainability was to embrace the NAPDS 9 Essentials.

Reflection Time

Pause

Deliberate

Share

What are simple ways to collect data on your PDS activities as well as disseminating them to foster legitimacy and sustainability?

Spotlight: Reflection

As we have discussed in this chapter, there are many ways to assess the status or impact of your PDS partnership. They range from complex research projects to checklists. It's important to find what works best for your PDS(s) and use them consistently until there is a need to rethink and adjust.

As a wrap-up, let's step back to the beginning and the reason why PDS and other iterations of school–university partnerships were initially recommended. Think back to Dewey, Goodlad, and the rest of the PDS gang. This all began in order to make education better and more equitable for children. For children to have a high-quality education, they need highly effective teachers. Decades of scholars envisioned that educational renewal would happen when universities and schools came together around the mutual goal of improved student achievement (Rutter, 2011). This was at the root of school reform, among other issues since the beginning of the 20th century, and even earlier. Clearly, there has not been widespread school reform resulting in consistent, equitable, high-quality education for all P–12 learners; however, the research reviewed in this book has demonstrated positive impact results related to the PDS approach to school–university partnerships. PDSs were touted as a means by which both schools and teacher education programs could be jointly renewed (Rutter, 2011).

Rather than "reform," Goodlad preferred the term "renewal." Simultaneous renewal is a strategy to improve both public school education and teacher education at the same time. Goodlad saw simultaneous renewal as a moral ideal situated in an understanding that the value of relationships is key to program quality and the realization of more widespread democratic ambitions. The phrase "simultaneous renewal" considers the complexity and chaos of the work of education where relationships, competence, as well as a shared and growing capacity are the priority (Bullough Jr., 2019). To effect real change, schools and universities need to renew simultaneously as opposed to individually (Rutter, 2011).

I find the PDS path to renewal appealing because it can begin at such a grassroots level to make a change in so many aspects of the field of education. In other words, we need not wait for specific legislation to continue the reform efforts of our predecessors who worked for equitable and high-quality education for all children. "Simultaneous renewal is an idea that grew out of the soil of practice" (Bullough Jr., 2019, p. 6).

Since reflection is such an important aspect of PDSs (NAPDS Essential 4 Reflection and Innovation), as you grow and monitor your PDS(s), you may choose to employ the tables below to determine the status of your partnership according to Goodlad's postulates, which basically lay out his plan for simultaneous renewal. Perfection is not expected. The goal should be growth over time. For the Buffalo State PDS consortium, I would refer to the tables at different times of the year to check in, reflect, and plan for the future. You can include your own dates and use your own symbols to indicate the status of your partnership with each postulate. This could be helpful to keep your partnership on track for renewal. As well, you can personalize the tables, where each postulate begins with "Programs for the education of educators" and insert the name of your partnership so that stakeholders can reflect on the nature of your collaborative network. Results can then be used to set goals for the future.

Goodlad's Postulates. Goodlad (1994) described his notion of educational renewal through the 20 Postulates. They are grouped sequentially based on the specifications needed for teacher preparation: (1) structural, (2) faculty responsibilities, (3) programmatic responsibilities, (4) curricular, and (5) regulatory and policy. Using the 20 Postulates (Table 5.1), Goodlad (1994) outlined his definition of educational renewal. Using Table 5.1, you can track your own renewal process season by season.

Table 5.1. Use Goodlad's 20 Postulates to Track Your Renewal Process

Postulates	Summer	Fall	Spring	Summer
1. Programs for the education of the nation's educators must be viewed by institutions offering them as a major responsibility to society and be adequately supported and promoted and vigorously advanced by the institution's top leadership.				
2. Programs for the education of educators must enjoy parity with other professional education programs, full legitimacy and institutional commitment, and rewards for faculty geared to the nature of the field.				
3. Programs for the education of educators must be autonomous and secure in their borders, with clear organizational identity, constancy of budget and personnel, and decisionmaking authority similar to that enjoyed by the major professional schools.				
4. There must exist a clearly identifiable group of academic and clinical faculty members for whom teacher education is the top priority; the group must be responsible and accountable for selecting diverse groups of students and monitoring their progress, planning, and maintaining the full scope and sequence of the curriculum, continuously evaluating and improving programs, and facilitating the entry of graduates into teaching careers.				

continued on next page

Table 5.1. Continued.

Postulates	Summer	Fall	Spring	Summer
5. The responsible group of academic and clinical faculty members described above must have a comprehensive understanding of the aims of education and the role of schools in our society and be fully committed to selecting and preparing teachers to assume the full range of educational responsibilities required.				
6. The responsible group of academic and clinical faculty members must seek out and select for a predetermined number of student places in the program those candidates who reveal an initial commitment to the moral, equitable, and enculturating responsibilities to be assumed, and make clear to them that preparing for these responsibilities is central to this program.				
7. Programs for the education of educators, whether elementary or secondary, must carry the responsibility to ensure that all candidates progressing through them possess or acquire the literacy and critical-thinking abilities associated with the concept of an educated person.				
8. Programs for the education of educators must provide extensive opportunities for future teachers to move beyond being students of organized knowledge to become teachers who inquire into both knowledge and its teaching.				

Postulates	Summer	Fall	Spring	Summer
9. Programs for the education of educators must be characterized by a socialization process through which candidates transcend their self-oriented student preoccupations to become more other-oriented in identifying with a culture of teaching.				
10. Programs for the education of educators must be characterized in all respects by the conditions for learning that future teachers are to establish in their own schools and classrooms.				
11. Programs for the education of educators must be conducted in such a way that teachers inquire into the nature of teaching and schooling and assume that they will do so as a natural aspect of their careers.				
12. Programs for the education of educators must involve future teachers in the issues and dilemmas that emerge out of the never-ending tension between the rights and interests of individual parents and interest groups and the role of schools in transcending parochialism and advancing community in a democratic society.				
13. Programs for the education of educators must be infused with understanding of and commitment to the moral obligation of teachers to ensure equitable access to and engagement in the best possible K–12 education for all children and youths.				

continued on next page

Table 5.1. Continued.

Postulates	Summer	Fall	Spring	Summer
14. Programs for the education of educators must involve future teachers not only in understanding schools as they are but in alternatives, the assumptions underlying alternatives, and how to effect needed changes in school organization, pupil grouping, curriculum, and more.				
15. Programs for the education of educators must assure for each candidate the availability of a wide array of laboratory settings for simulation, observation, hands-on experiences, and exemplary schools for internships and residencies; they must admit no more students to their programs than can be assured these quality experiences.				
16. Programs for the education of educators must engage future teachers in the problems and dilemmas arising out of the inevitable conflicts and incongruities between what is perceived to work in practice and the research and theory supporting other options.				
17. Programs for the education of educators must establish linkages with graduates for purposes of both evaluating and revising these programs and easing the critical early years of transition into teaching.				

Postulates	Summer	Fall	Spring	Summer
18. Programs for the education of educators require a regulatory context with respect to licensing, certifying, and accrediting that ensures at all times the presence of the necessary conditions embraced by the 17 preceding postulates.				
19. Programs for the education of educators must compete in an arena that rewards efforts to continuously improve on the conditions embedded in all of the postulates and tolerates no shortcuts intended to ensure a supply of teachers.				
20. Those institutions and organizations that prepare the nation's teachers, authorize their right to teach, and employ them must fine-tune their individual and collaborative roles to support and sustain lifelong teaching careers characterized by professional growth, service, and satisfaction.				

If your school–university partnership is an aspiring PDS, Table 5.2 can be used to monitor your organization's adherence to the NAPDS 9 Essentials. As noted above, you can customize the table to include your own specific examples. For instance, for the first essential, your organization might have a mission, so that can be pasted in the box next to that essential. However, your partnership may not be aligned with all elements of the first essential. The mission is there, but there is little evidence to demonstrate aims related to equity, antiracism, and social justice. In the same box as the mission, you could note that is the future goal of the partnership. I have done something similar in a presentation regarding the 9 Essentials. I pasted evidence from the Buffalo State PDS's adherence to the 9 Essentials on each slide. Remember that evidence and the sharing of results and findings is important to share to promote the legitimacy of the partnership. These tables can be used to monitor the use of other standards or to organize and keep track of the PDS partnership's goals with the 9 Essentials or the 20 Postulates.

Table 5.2. Use the NAPDS 9 Essentials to Track Your PDS Partnership Goals

NAPDS 9 Essentials	Summer	Fall	Spring	Summer
Essential 1: A Comprehensive Mission A professional development school (PDS) is a learning community guided by a comprehensive, articulated mission that is broader than the goals of any single partner, and that aims to advance equity, antiracism, and social justice within and among schools, colleges/universities, and their respective community and professional partners.				
Essential 2: Clinical Preparation A PDS embraces the preparation of educators through clinical practice.				
Essential 3: Professional Learning and Leading A PDS is a context for continuous professional learning and leading for all participants, guided by need and a spirit and practice of inquiry.				

NAPDS 9 Essentials	Summer	Fall	Spring	Summer
Essential 4: Reflection and Innovation A PDS makes a shared commitment to reflective practice, responsive innovation, and generative knowledge				
Essential 5: Research and Results A PDS is a community that engages in collabora-tive research and participates in the public sharing of results in a variety of outlets				
Essential 6: Articulated Agreements A PDS requires intentionally evolving written ar-ticulated agreement(s) that delineate the commit-ments, expectations, roles, and responsibilities of all involved.				
Essential 7: Shared Governance Structures A PDS is built upon shared, sustainable govern-ance structures that promote collaboration, foster reflection, and honor and value all participants' voices.				
Essential 8: Boundary-Spanning Roles A PDS creates space for, advocates for, and sup-ports college/university and P–12 faculty to operate in well-defined, boundary-spanning roles that transcend institutional settings.				
Essential 9: Resources and Recognition A PDS provides dedicated and shared resources and establishes traditions to recognize, enhance, celebrate, and sustain the work of partners and the partnership.				

Appendix A

PDS Agreement Forms

BUFFALO STATE
The State University of New York

Memorandum of Understanding

SUNY Buffalo State University recognizes the importance of diversity for assuring the success of students and graduates in an increasingly global environment. We seek to establish the diversity that will provide **all of our students with a learning environment to develop leaders and lifelong learners. Our efforts to attract a diverse student body will be enhanced by attracting and developing strategic partnerships with external educational partners.**

SUNY Buffalo State is committed to equal treatment in every aspect of hiring and employment. SUNY proactively reviews its policies and practices to assure that decisions with respect to every dimension of employment are made without regard to age, color of skin, disability, gender expression and identity, genetic predisposition, marital status, national origin, race, ethnicity, religion, sex, sexual orientation, veteran's status, status as a victim of domestic violence, and all other protected groups and classes under Federal and State Laws and executive orders. We recognize, too, that achieving equal treatment may require proactive measures to offset obstacles and barriers faced by the groups for whom we seek inclusion.

We affirm that our educational partners understand our commitment to equal treatment and access. We further understand that our educational partners are equally committed to ensuring equal and equitable treatment of our students who are participating in internships, externships, and other educational opportunities.

By signing the PDS agreement on the front of this document, you agree to the points outlined above.

BUFFALO STATE

The State University of New York
Professional Development Schools (PDS) Program for

Initial Stage Agreement

Initial Stage—Beliefs, verbal commitments, plans, organization and initial work are consistent with the mission of PDS partnerships. Even at the earliest stage of development PDS partners are committed to the PDS mission and their earliest work addresses how to take initial steps in that direction for the mutual benefit and learning of all PDS partners.

At the Initial Stage, Professional Development School personnel demonstrate a willingness to work with the college and college instructor(s). They assist the college instructor by providing an opportunity for EDU/ENG/MAT/MUS/SSE 200 level teacher candidates to complete the requirements of their course at their PDS school site.

These classroom opportunities for observation and shadowing for up to 25 teacher candidates will be arranged cooperatively through the liaison committee. Other opportunities for up to 25 teacher candidates might include participating in tutoring opportunities for a number of hours to be mutually established. Due to the uniqueness of each of these partnerships, the particulars of these arrangements should be worked out between the PDS school or site and the Buffalo State instructor **prior** to signing this agreement.

School representatives are welcome to attend and provide input at meetings of the PDS Consortium. School representatives are encouraged to participate in additional workshops and the annual PDS conference.

The school will be paid $\$$_____ *per* semester for each cohort of teacher candidates from a Buffalo State course; the sum is to be paid to the school at the start of the semester and to be dispersed by the building principal. This agreement is subject to revision at the end of the semester.

Initial Stage Agreement

Semester _____

_____ (school site), Professional Development School agrees to participate according to the Initial Stage Agreement with the SUNY Buffalo State Teacher Education Unit.

School Site Principal Signature _____   Date _____

Course Instructor Signature_____   Date _____

PDS Director Signature _____   Date _____

Department Chair Signature_____   Date _____

School of Education Dean Signature_____   Date_____

Financial Officer Signature_____   Date_____

Total Financial Stipend: $

Course: CRN #   Principal:

PDS Beginning Stage Agreement

Beginning Stage—Beliefs, verbal commitments, plans, organization and initial work are consistent with the mission of PDS partnerships. This means that even at the earliest stage of development PDS partners are committed to the key concepts of PDSs and their earliest work addresses how to take initial steps in that direction.

At the **Beginning Stage**, Professional Development Schools personnel demonstrate a willingness to work with Buffalo State. They assist the college instructor in preparing a cohort of up to 30 teacher candidates by providing a minimum of 40 - 50 hours of school experiences related to the requirements for a 300- and/or 5/600-level field placement course. Although course related instruction may or may not be site-based, the college instructor does work individually with each mentor teacher in the design, implementation, and supervision of each teacher candidate's school experiences during the placement time. In turn, the PDS school will receive 3 in-service hours in-kind by Buffalo State faculty and are eligible for action research mini-grants.

One school representative **should attend at least one PDS Consortium meeting** by participating at the conference or during at least one of the semester's scheduled meetings of the PDS Consortium.

The school will be paid *$_____ per* semester; the sum to be paid to the school when the agreements and vouchers have been processed during the semester and to be dispersed by the building principal according to agreements reached in conjunction with the liaison committee and the mentor teachers at the PDS. A liaison committee consisting of the principal, a mentor teacher, and the college faculty should be formed. More members may be added to the committee as appropriate.

This agreement is subject to revision at the end of the semester.

EDU/EXE/ENG/MAT/MUS/SSE 300 Level: Beginning Stage Agreement

Semester _____

_____(school site), Professional Development School agrees to participate according to the Beginning Stage Agreement with the SUNY Buffalo State Teacher Education Unit.

School Site Principal Signature _____   Date _____

School Based Liaison Signature _____   Date _____

Course Instructor Signature_____   Date _____

PDS Director Signature_____   Date _____

Department Chair Signature_____   Date _____

School of Education Dean's Signature_____   Date _____

BSC Comptroller's Office Signature _____   Date _____

Total Financial Stipend: $

Course: CRN #   Principal:

PDS Developing Stage Agreement

Developing Stage—Partners are pursuing the mission of PDS partnership through institutional support. At the developing stage, partners are engaged in PDS work in many ways. However, their supporting institutions have not yet made changes in their policies and practices that would provide evidence of complete institutionalization of all aspects of the PDS mission.

At the **Developing Stage**, Professional Development Schools personnel demonstrate a willingness to work with the college. They assist the college instructor in preparing a cohort (18 - 20) of teacher candidates by providing a minimum of 50 hours of school experiences related to the requirements for a 300-and/or 5/600-level field placement course. Although course related instruction may or may not be site-based, the college instructor works individually with each mentor teacher in the design, implementation, and supervision of each teacher candidate's school experiences during the placement time. In turn, the PDS will receive 6 in-service hours in-kind by BSC faculty and are eligible for action research mini-grants.

Developing Stage PDSs form a Liaison Committee that consists of at least three members: the school Principal, the Liaison Committee Coordinator, and the college faculty member or their designees with decision making power. All Liaison Committee members communicate the concerns, decisions and or actions of the PDS Consortium and of their own PDS staff to each other, help in identification of teacher education resource persons in the school or district, assist in scheduling teacher candidates' participation in the school according to the college instructor's schedule, and contribute to the development of PDS goals.

At least one school-based member of the Liaison Committee must attend and actively participate in each of the three yearly meetings of the PDS Consortium, as well as the annual PDS conference. Additional members of the Liaison Committee are encouraged but not required to participate in consortium meetings. **Each school has one vote.** In addition, the PDS agrees on a rotational basis to host at least one meeting at their site.

The school will be paid **$**_____ per semester; the sum to be paid to the school at the start of the semester and to be dispersed by the building principal according to agreements reached in conjunction with the Liaison Committee.

This agreement is subject to revision at the end of the semester.

Developing Stage Agreement

*Semester*_____

_____(school site), Professional Development School agrees to participate according to the Beginning Stage Agreement with the SUNY Buffalo State Teacher Education Unit.

School Site Principal Signature _____   Date _____

School Based Liaison Signature _____   Date _____

Course Instructor Signature_____   Date _____

PDS Director Signature_____   Date _____

Department Chair Signature_____   Date _____

School of Education Dean's Signature_____   Date _____

BSC Comptroller's Office Signature _____   Date _____

Total Financial Stipend: $

Course: CRN #   Principal:

PDS At Standard Stage Agreement

At Standard—The mission of the PDS partnership is integrated into the partnering institutions. PDS work is expected and supported, and it reflects what is known about the best practices. At this stage, partners work together effectively resulting in positive outcomes for all learners. Partnering institutions have made changes in policies and practices that reflect what has been learned through PDS work, and that support PDS participants in meaningful ways.

At the **At Standard Stage**, Professional Development Schools personnel demonstrate a continued commitment to work with the college. They assist the college instructor in preparing a cohort (18 - 20) of teacher candidates by providing a minimum of 50 hours of school experiences related to the requirements for a 300- and/or 5/600-level field placement course. Course related instruction is site-based, and the college instructor works individually with each mentor teacher in the design, implementation, and supervision of each teacher candidate's school experiences during the placement time. In turn, the PDS will receive 12-15 in-service hours in-kind by BSC faculty and are eligible for action research mini-grants.

At Standard Stage PDSs form a Liaison Committee that consists of at least three members: the school Principal, the Liaison Committee Coordinator, and the college faculty member or their designees with decision making power. All Liaison Committee members communicate the concerns, decisions and or actions of the PDS Consortium and of their own PDS staff to each other, help in identification of teacher education resource persons in the school or district, assist in scheduling teacher candidates' participation in the school according to the college instructor's schedule, and contribute to the development of PDS goals.

At least one school-based member of the Liaison Committee must attend and actively participate in each of the three yearly meetings of the PDS Consortium, as well as the annual PDS conference. Additional members of the Liaison Committee are encouraged but not required to participate in consortium meetings. **Each school has one vote.** In addition, the PDS agrees on a rotational basis to host at least one meeting at their site.

The school will be paid **$**_____ per semester; the sum to be paid to the school at the start of the semester and to be dispersed by the building principal according to agreements reached in conjunction with the Liaison Committee.

This agreement is subject to revision at the end of the semester.

At Standard Stage Agreement

Semester _____

_____(school site), Professional Development School agrees to participate according to the At Standard Agreement with the SUNY Buffalo State Teacher Education Unit.

School Site Principal Signature _____   Date _____

School Based Liaison Signature _____   Date _____

Course Instructor Signature_____   Date _____

PDS Director Signature_____   Date _____

Department Chair Signature_____   Date _____

School of Education Dean's Signature_____   Date _____

BSC Comptroller's Office Signature _____   Date _____

Total Financial Stipend: $

Course: CRN#   Principal:

Appendix B

PDS Student Representatives

PDS Student Representative Application

Please type or print neatly.

Name _____ Email _____ Phone _____

Address_____
street   city   state   zip code

Please answer the following questions in complete, thorough responses. Attach an additional sheet of paper, if necessary.

What experiences/insight can you provide to the PDS Consortium?

_____
_____
_____
_____
_____
_____
_____
_____
_____
_____
_____
_____
_____
_____
_____
_____
_____
_____

Why would you like to serve as a PDS Student Representative?

_____
_____
_____
_____
_____
_____
_____
_____
_____
_____
_____
_____
_____
_____
_____

Applicants must submit:
❑ Completed Application Form ❑ Letter of Interest ❑ Resume ❑ Transcript ❑ Letter of Recommendation
Please email or drop off completed forms and attachments to:

_____

The PDS leadership team will interview the most qualified candidates.

PDS Student Representative Interview Questions

1. Why do you want to be a PDS Student Representative? What do you hope to gain? What are you most eager to contribute?

2. What leadership skills do you possess that will help you be a successful PDS representative?

3. How well do you handle conflict? Stress?

4. Please give an example of a time when you experienced conflict/stress. How did you resolve the situation?

5. Are you comfortable speaking in front of large groups of people? Explain.

6. A PDS Rep has many demands on their time. How well can you handle time management? Do you have any past experiences to exemplify this?

7. What are your professional goals? How do these goals connect with becoming a PDS Student Representative?

8. All PDS Student Reps have the opportunity to conduct a research project with the support of a mentor that will be presented at the national PDS conference. Does this interest you? Please explain.

9. Are you able to give at least four hours per week to the role?

10. When would you be able to start as a PDS Rep? Would you take advantage of the summer to help out and attend PDS Advisory Council Meetings?

11. Do you have any questions for us regarding this position?

References

Abdal-Haqq, I. (1998). *Constructivism in teacher education: Considerations for those who would link practice to theory*. ERIC Digest. https://files.eric.ed.gov/fulltext/ED426986.pdf

Ackerman, K. B. (2017). Examining the efficacy of co-teaching at the secondary level: Special educators' perceptions of their Productivity as co-teachers. https://uknowledge.uky.edu/cgi/viewcontent.cgi?article=1041&context=edsrc_etds

Ariav, T., & Clinard, L. M. (1996). Does coaching student teachers affect the professional development and teaching of cooperating teachers? A cross-cultural perspective. Paper presented at the International Conference on Teacher Education, Netanya, Israel, June 30–July 4, 1996. www.semanticscholar.org/paper/Does-Coaching-Student-Teachers-Affect-the-and-of-A-Ariav-Clinard/0c8722f2363ee73b645d7cb261296d9b13ea7712

Association of Colleges for Teacher Education. (2018). A pivot toward clinical practice, its lexicon, and renewing the profession of teaching. Clinical Practice Commission. https://aacte.org/resources/research-reports-and-briefs/clinical-practice-commission-report

Badiali, B., & Titus, N. E. (2010). A study of co-teaching identifying effective implementation strategies. *International Journal of Special Education*, *32*(3), 538–550.

Badiali, B., Burns, R. W., Coler, C., Cosenza, M., Goree, K., Polly, D. . . . & Hallinger, K. (2022). Explicating essential nine of the second edition of the NAPDS Nine Essentials. *PDS Partners: Bridging Research to Practice*, *17*(3), 49–54.

Baker P. J. (2011). Three configurations of school–university partnerships: An exploratory study. *Planning and Changing*, *42*, 41–62.

Bartholomew, S. S., & Sandholtz, J. H. (2009). Competing views of teaching in a school–university partnership. *Teaching and teacher education*, *25*(1), 155–165.

Basile, C. G. (ed.). (2010). *Intellectual capital: The intangible assets of professional development schools*. SUNY Press.

Bass, B. M. (1985). Leadership: Good, better, best. *Organizational Dynamics*, *13*(3), 26–40.

Bennie, W. A. (1978). The prologue of the past. *Action in Teacher Education*, *1*(1), 3–7.

Berry, B., Boles, K., Edens, K., Nissenholtz, A., & Trachtman, R. (1998). Inquiry and professional development schools. In N. J. Lauter (Ed.), *Professional development schools: Confronting realities*, pp. 121–148. National Center for Restructuring Education, Schools, and Teaching.

Bier, M., Foster, A., Bellamy, G. T., & Clark, R. (2008). Professional development school principals: Challenges, experiences and craft knowledge. *School–University Partnerships*, *2*(2), 77–89.

Blocker, L. S., & Mantle-Bromley, C. (1997). PDS verses campus preparation: Through the eyes of the students. *The Teacher Educator*, *33*(2), 70–89.

Bolman, L. G., & Deal. T. E. (1993). *The path to school leadership: A portable mentor*. Roadmaps to Success: The Practicing Administrator's Leadership Series. Corwin

Book, C. L. 1996. "Professional development schools." In J. Sikula, T. J. Buttery, and E. Guyton (Eds.), *Handbook of research on teacher education*, 194–210. Simon & Schuster.

Bowen, G., & Adkinson, J. (1996). *Institutionalizing professional development schools: Supporting the principal*. Research Report.

Bowen, G., Adkinson, J. & Dunlap, B. (1995) *The role of the principal in the professional development school*. Paper presented at the annual meeting of the National Council of Professors of Educational Administration, Williamsburg, West Virginia, August 8–12, 1995.

Boyle-Baise, M., & McIntyre, D. J. (2008). *What kind of experience? Preparing teachers in PDS or community settings*. In J. Sikula, T. J. Buttery, and E. Guyton (Eds.), *Handbook of research on teacher education*, pp. 307–329. Routledge.

Breault, D. A., & Breault, R. (2010). Partnerships for preparing leaders: What can we learn from PDS research? *International Journal of Leadership in Education*, *13*(4), 437–454.

Brewer, G. D., & DeLeon, P. (1983). *The foundations of policy analysis*. Dorsey Press.

Brindley, R., Lessen, E., & Field, B. E. (2008a). Toward a common understanding: Identifying the essentials of a professional development school. *Childhood Education*, *85*(2), 71–74.

Brindley, R., Field, B., & Lessen, E. (2008b). What it means to be a professional development school. A statement by the Executive Council and Board of Directors of the National Association for Professional Development Schools. http://napds.org/9%20Essentials/statement.pdf

Brookfield, S. (1995). Adult learning: An overview. *International encyclopedia of education*, *10*, 375–380.

Brown, S. C., & Kysilka, M. L. (2002). *Applying multicultural and global concepts in the classroom and beyond.* Pearson College Division.

Bullough, R. (2019). John Goodlad and the origins of the idea of simultaneous renewal. *School–University Partnerships, The Journal of the National Association for Professional Development Schools*, 12(3), 7–11.

Bullough Jr, R. V., Kauchak, D., Crow, N. A., Hobbs, S., & Stokes, D. (1997). Professional development schools: Catalysts for teacher and school change. *Teaching and teacher education, 13*(2), 153–169.

Burns, R., Jacobs, J., & Yendol-Hoppey, D. (2016). Preservice teacher supervision within field experiences in a decade of reform. *Teacher Education and Practice, 29*(1), 46–75.

Burns, R. W., Badiali, B., Coler, C., Cosenza, M., Goree, K., Polly, D., . . . & Zenkov, K. (2022). Essential 2: "Clinical Practice" is what professional development schools do. *PDS Partners, 17*(1), 38–41.

Burns, R. W., & Badiali, B. (2020). The transformative nature of boundary-spanning roles: The case of a hybrid teacher educator in a professional development school context. *The New Educator, 16* (3), 187–206.

Burton, S. L., & Greher, G. R. (2007). School–university partnerships: What do we know and why do they matter? *Arts Education Policy Review, 109*(1), 13–24.

Button, K. Ponticell, J., & Johnson, M. (1996). Enabling school–university collaborative research: Lessons learned in professional development schools. *Journal of Teacher Education, 47*(1), 16–20

Carnegie Forum on Education, & the Economy. Task Force on Teaching as a Profession. (1986). A nation prepared: Teachers for the 21st century: The report of the task force on teaching as a profession, Carnegie Forum on Education and the Economy, May 1986. Carnegie Forum on Education.

Carpenter, B. D., & Sherretz, C. E. (2012). Professional development school partnerships: An instrument for teacher leadership. *School–University Partnerships, 5*(1), 89–101.

Carver-Thomas, D. (2016). *National trends in teacher attrition: An analysis of 13 stayers, movers, and leavers.* Learning Policy Institute

Castle, S., Arends, R. I., & Rockwood, K. D. (2008). Student learning in a professional development school and a control school. *Professional Educator, 32*(1), 1–15.

Castle, S., Fox, R. K., & Souder, K.O.H. (2006). Do professional development schools (PDSs) make a difference? A comparative study of PDS and non-PDS teacher candidates. *Journal of Teacher Education, 57*(1), 65–80.

Castle, S., & Reilly, K. A. (2011). Impact of professional development school preparation on teacher candidates. *Teachers College Record, 113*(14), 337–371.

Chambers, M., & Olmstead, B. (1971). Teacher corps and portal schools. *Portal Schools, 1*(1), 2–8.

Chu, Y., & Wang, W. (2022). The urban teacher residency model to prepare teachers: A review of the literature. *Urban Education* (May), 1–30. doi:00420859221102976

Clark, R. W. (1988). School–university relationships: An interpretive review. *School–university partnerships in action: Concepts, cases, and concerns.* In K. A. Sirotnik & J. I. Goodlad (Eds.), *School–university partnerships in action: Concepts, cases,* pp. 32–65. Teachers College Press.

Clark, R. W. (1999). *Effective professional development schools.* Agenda for Education in a Democracy Series. Volume 3. Jossey-Bass.

Clift, R. T., & Brady, P. (2009). Research on methods courses and field experiences. *Studying teacher education: The report of the AERA panel on research and teacher education, 309424.* In M. Cochran-Smith & K. M. Zeichner (Eds.), *Studying teacher education: The report of the AERA panel on research and teacher education.* Routledge.

Clinical Practice Commission. (2018). *A pivot toward clinical practice, its lexicon, and the renewal of educator preparation.* Washington, DC: American Association of Colleges for Teacher Education.

Cobb, J. (2000). The impact of a professional development school on preservice teacher preparation, inservice teachers' professionalism, and children's achievement: Perceptions of in-service teachers. *Action in Teacher Education, 22*(3), 64–76

Cochran-Smith, M., Feiman-Nemser, S., McIntyre, J. D., & Demers, K. E. (Eds.) (2008). *Handbook of research on teacher education: Enduring questions in changing contexts* (3rd ed.). Routledge, Taylor & Francis Group and the Association of Teacher Educators.

Cohen, S. (ed.). (1974). *Education in the United States: A documentary history.* Random House.

Coler, C., Badiali, B., West, R. B., Cosenza, M., Goree, K., Polly, D., . . . & Zenkov, K. (2022). Expanding on the revised essential 7: Shared governance structures. *PDS Partners, 17*(1), 42–44.

Colwell, C., MacIsaac, D., Tichenor, M., Heins, B., & Piechura, K. (2014). District and university perspectives on sustaining professional development schools: Do the NCATE standards matter? *Professional Educator, 38*(2), n2.

Conaway, B.J., & Mitchell, M.W. (2004) A comparison of the experiences of year-long interns in a professional development school and one-semester student teachers in a non-PDS location. *Action in Teacher Education, 26* (3), 21–28.

Connor, K. R., & Killmer, N. (2001). Cohorts, collaboration, and community: Does contextual teacher education really work? *Action in Teacher Education, 23*(3), 46–53.

Consenza, M, Brown, E., Coler, C., Derrick, K., Nardo, E. J., Silva, R., & Wagler, K. (2021). A thriving third space: California Lutheran University PDS network: Article from a 2020 NAPDS exemplary partnership award winner. *PDS Partners, 16*(4), 25–29.

Council of Chief State School Officers. (2011, April). Interstate teacher assessment and support consortium (InTASC) model core teaching standards: A resource for state dialogue. https://ccsso.org/sites/default/files/2017-11/InTASC_Model_Core_Teaching_Standards_2011.pdf

Cremin, L. A. (1959). John Dewey and the progressive-education movement, 1915–1952. The *School Review, 67*(2), 160–173.

Crow, N. A. (1996). Masters cooperative program: An alternative model of teacher development in PDS sites. Paper presented at the Annual Meeting of the American Educational Research Association, New York, NY, April 8–12, 1996.

Cushner, I. (2007). The role of experience in the making of internationally-minded teachers. *Teacher Education Quarterly, 34*(1), 27–39.

Dana, N. F., & Yendol-Silva, D. (2003). *The reflective educator's guide to classroom research: Learning to teach and teaching to learn through practitioner inquiry.* Corwin Press.

Darling-Hammond, L. (1994). *Professional development schools: Schools for developing a profession.* Teachers College Press.

Darling-Hammond L. (2005) Teaching as a profession: Lessons in teacher preparation and professional development. *Phi Delta Kappan, 87*(3): 237–240.

Darling-Hammond, L. (2007). Race, inequality and educational accountability: The irony of "No Child Left Behind." *Race Ethnicity and Education, 10*(3), 245–260

Darling-Hammond, L. (2010). Teacher education and the American future. *Journal of Teacher Education, 61*(1–2), 35–47.

Darling-Hammond, L., & Baratz-Snowden, J. (2007). A good teacher in every classroom: Preparing the highly qualified teachers our children deserve. *Educational Horizons, 85*(2), 111–132.

Darling-Hammond, L. (1990). Instructional policy into practice: "The power of the bottom over the top." *Educational evaluation and policy analysis, 12*(3), 339–347.

Deardorff, D. K. (2006). Identification and assessment of intercultural competence as a student outcome of internationalization. *Journal of Studies in International Education, 10*(3), 241–266.

Deardorff, D. K. (2011). Assessing intercultural competence. *New Directions for Institutional Research, 2011*(149), 65–79.

Deardorff, D. K. (2014). Some thoughts on assessing intercultural competence. *Viewpoints*, National Institute of Learning Outcomes Assessment (NILOA), May 15, 2014. http://illinois.edu/blog/view/915/113048

Deardorff, D. K. (2015). *Demystifying outcomes assessment for international educators: A practical approach.* Stylus Publishing, LLC.

del Prado Hill, P., Chicola, N., & Horstman-Riphahn, T. (2020). Preparing teachers for changing classrooms: Assessing the impact of an international Professional Development Schools program. In Ferrara, Nath, & Beebe (Eds.), *Exploring Cultural Competence in Professional Development* Schools, 89–105. Information Age Publishing,

del Prado Hill, P., & Garas-York, K. (Eds.) (2020). *The impact of PDS partnerships in challenging times.* Information Age Publishing.

Desimone, L. M. (2011). A primer on effective professional development. *Phi Delta Kappan, 92*(6), 68–71.

Dichele, A. M. (2016). Quinnipiac School of Education—The importance of our NAPDS association. *School-University Partnerships, 9*(2), 5–8.

Dixon, P. N., & Ishler, R. E. (1992). Professional development schools: Stages in collaboration. *Journal of Teacher Education, 43*(1), 28–34.

Doolittle, G., Sudeck, M., & Rattigan, P. (2008). Creating professional learning communities: The work of professional development schools. *Theory Into Practice, 47*, 303–310.

Duffy, G. G. (1994) Professional development schools and the disempowerment of teachers and professors. *Phi Delta Kappan, 75*(8), 596–600.

Durden, P. C. (2005). Education renewal: A path less trod: A conversation with Dr. John I. Goodlad. *The New Educator, 1*(4), 345–356.

Edelfelt, R. A., & Raths, J. D. (1998). *A brief history of standards in teacher education.* Association of Teacher Educators.

Edwards, H. E. (1961). *Building good relationships: A major role of the college supervisor* (No. 16). Association for Student Teaching.

Egeland, P. (2016). How does international student teaching shape the participants? Professional and personal perspectives and decisions. *International Education Journal: Comparative Perspectives, 15*(2), 23–37.

El-Amin, C., Cristol, D., & Hammond, R. (1999). Constructing a professional development school: A model of one school–university partnership. *The Teacher Educator, 35*(2), 1–14.

Ferguson, S. D. (1999). *Communication planning: An integrated approach.* Volume 1. Sage.

Ference, R., & Bell, S. (2004) A cross-cultural immersion in the US: Changing pre-service teacher attitudes toward Latino ESOL students. *Equity and Excellence in Education, 37*, 343–350.

Ferrara, J. (2014). *Professional development schools: Creative solutions for educators.* R&L Education.

Ferrara, J., Nath, J. L., & Beebe, R. S. (Eds.). (2020). *Exploring cultural competence in professional development schools.* Information Age Publishing.

Ferrara, J., Nath, J. L., & Guadarrama, I. N. (Eds.). (2014). *Creating visions for university school partnerships.* Information Age Publishing.

Fisher, D., Frey, N., & Farnan, N. (2004). Student teachers matter: The impact of student teachers on elementary-aged children in a professional development school. *Teacher Education Quarterly, 31*(2), 43–56.

Fleener, C., & Dahm, P. (Summer 2007). Elementary teacher attrition: A comparison of the effects of Professional Development Schools and traditional campus-based programs. *Teacher Education and Practice, 20*(3), 263–283.

Flores, I. M. (2015). Developing preservice teachers' self-efficacy through field-based science teaching practice with elementary students. *Research in Higher Education Journal, 27*, 1–19.

Florian, L. (2017). Teacher education for the changing demographics of schooling: Inclusive education for each and every learner. In L. Florian (Ed.), *Teacher education for the changing demographics of schooling*, pp. 9–20. Springer.

Flowers, J. G. (1948). School and community laboratory experiences in teacher education. *Peabody Journal of Education, 26*(2), 67–69.

Foster, E., Loving, C., & Shumate, A. (2000). Effective principals, effective professional development schools. *Teaching and Change, 8*, 76–97.

Fountain, C. A. (1997). Collaborative agenda for change: Examining the impact of urban professional development schools. Paper presented at the Annual Meeting of the American Association of Colleges for Teacher Education, Phoenix, AZ, February 27, 1997.

Freese, A. R. (1999). The role of reflection on preservice teachers' development in the context of a professional development school. *Teaching and Teacher Education, 15*(8), 895–909.

Fullan, M. (1991). *The new meaning of educational change.* Teachers College Press.

Fullan, M. (2001). *Leading in a culture of change.* Jossey-Bass

Fullan, M. (2002). Principals as leaders in a culture of change. *Educational Leadership, 59*(8), 16–21.

Futrell, M. H. (2008). Changing the paradigm: Preparing teacher educators and teachers for the twenty-first century. In J. Sikula, T. J. Buttery, and E. Guyton (Eds.), *Handbook of research on teacher education*, pp. 534–539. Routledge.

Ganser, T. (1996) The cooperating teacher role. *Teacher Educator 31*, 294.

Garas-York, K., del Prado Hill, P., Day, L. K., Truesdell, K., & Keller-Mathers, S. (Eds.). (2017). *Doing PDS: Stories and strategies from successful clinically rich practice.* IAP.

Gerlach, S. M. (2017). A Quantitative study of co-teaching as an instructional model to serve elementary students. Electronic Theses and Dissertations. 10 http://scholarworks.sfasu.edu/etds/109

Gilbert, A., Hobbs, L., Kenny, J., Jones, M., Campbell, C., Chittleborough, G., . . . & Redman, C. (2018). Principal perceptions regarding the impact of school–university partnerships in primary science contexts. *School–University Partnerships, 11*(2), 73–83.

Gimbert, B., & Nolan, J. F. (2003). The influence of the professional development school context on supervisory practice: A university supervisor's and interns' perspectives. *Journal of Curriculum and Supervision*, 18(4), 353–379

Glickman, C. D., & Bey, T. M. (1990). Supervision. In W. R. Houston (ed.), *Handbook of research on teacher education*, pp. 549–566. Macmillan.

Goldberg, M. F. (2000). An interview with John Goodlad: Leadership for change. *Phi Delta Kappan*, 82(1), 82.

Goldhammer, R. (1969). *Clinical supervision*. Holt, Rinehart, Winston.

Goodlad J. I. (1984). *A place called school. Prospects for the future*. McGraw-Hill.

Goodlad (1987). The ecology of school renewal. Eighty-Sixth Yearbook of the National Society for the Study of Education, Part I.

Goodlad, J. I. (1988). School–university partnerships: A social experiment. *Kappa Delta Pi Record*, 24(3), 77–80.

Goodlad (1990). Studying the education of educators: From conception to findings. *Phi Delta Kappan*, 71(9), 698–701.

Goodlad (1990). Better teachers for our nation's schools. *Phi Delta Kappan*, 72(3), 184–94.

Goodlad, J. I. (1990). *Teachers for our nation's schools*. Jossey-Bass.

Goodlad, J. I. (1993). School–university partnerships and partner schools. *Educational Policy*, 7(1), 24–39.

Goodlad, J. I. (1994). The national network for educational renewal. *Phi Delta Kappan*, 75(8), 632–638.

Goodlad, J. I. (1997). *In praise of education*. Teachers College Press.

Goodlad, J. I. (2000). Education and democracy: Advancing the agenda. *Phi Delta Kappan*, 82(1), 86–89.

Goodlad J. I. (2004). *A place called school*. Anniversary edition. McGraw Hill.

Goodlad, J. I. (2004). *Romances with schools: A life of education*. Rowman & Littlefield.

Goodlad, J. I., Mantle-Bromley, C., & Goodlad, S. J. (2004). *Education for everyone: Agenda for education in a democracy*. Jossey-Bass.

Goodlad, J. I., & McMannon., T. J. (Eds.) (2004). *The teaching career*. Teachers College Press.

Goodlad, J. I., Mantle-Bromley, C., & Goodlad, S. J. (2004). *Education for everyone: Agenda for education in a democracy*. Jossey-Bass.

Goodlad, S.J.I., Soder, R., & McDaniel, B. (2008). *Education and the making of a democratic people*. Routledge.

Goree, K., Badiali, B., Burns, R. W., Coler, C., Cosenza, M., Polly, D., . . . & Zenkov, K. (2022). Essential 6: Articulated agreements—foundation and guidance for PDS work. *PDS Partners: Bridging Research to Practice*, 17(3), 44–48.

Groth, L. A., Parker, A., Parsons, S. A., Sprague, D., Levine Brown, E., Baker, C., & Suh, J. (2017). George Mason University's elementary PDS program: Embracing innovation. *School–University Partnerships*, 10(1), 3–5.

Grubesky, S. (2014). *Effectiveness of co-teaching*. Student Publications. 267. https://cupola.gettysburg.edu/student_scholarship/267

Guha, R., Hyler, M. E., & Darling-Hammond, L. (2016). The teacher residency: An innovative model for preparing teachers. *Learning Policy Institute*. https://learningpolicyinstitute.org/product/teacher-residency

Guskey, T. R., & Huberman, M. (1995). *Professional development in education: New paradigms and practices*. Teachers College Press.

Gutierrez, C., Field, S., Simmons, J., & Basile, C. G. (2007). Principals as knowledge managers in partner schools. *School Leadership and Management*, *27*(4), 333–346.

Harter, A., & Jacobi, L. (2018). "Experimenting with our education" or enhancing it? Co-teaching from the perspective of students. *Inquiry in Education*, *10*(2), Article 4. https://digitalcommons.nl.edu/ie/vol10/iss2/4

Helms-Lorenz, M., van de Grift, W., Canrinus, E., Maulana, R., & van Veen, K. (2018). Evaluation of the behavioral and affective outcomes of novice teachers working in professional development schools versus non-professional development schools. *Studies in Educational Evaluation*, *56*, 8–20.

Henderson, J. I. (1918). *The distribution of a student teacher's time*. University of Texas Press.

Henning, J. E. (2018). A sustainable teacher residency: Designing paid internships for teacher education. *School–University Partnerships*, *11*(3), 1–16.

Henning, J. E., Bragen Jr, B. F., Mulvaney, T., George III, W. O., Duffy, G., Aldarelli, E., . . . & Borlan, C. A. (2018). The Monmouth University partnership: Redesigning practice. *School–University Partnerships*, *11*(1), 3–8.

Holland, H. (2005). Teaching teachers: Professional development to improve student achievement. *AERA Research Points*, *3*(1).

Holmes Group. (1986). *Tomorrow's teachers: A report of the Holmes Group*. Holmes Group.

Holmes Group. (1990). *Tomorrow's schools: Principles for the design of professional development schools: Executive summary*. Holmes Group.

Holmes Group. (2007). *The Holmes partnership trilogy: Tomorrow's teachers, tomorrow's schools, tomorrow's schools of education*. Peter Lang.

Houston Consortium of Professional Development. (1996). *ATE Newsletter* (April), 7.

Houston, W. R., Hollis, L. Y., Clay, D., Ligons, C., & Roff, L. (1999). Effects of collaboration on urban teacher education programs and professional development schools. In D. Byrd & D. J. McIntyre (Eds.), *Research on professional development schools: Vol. 7: Teacher education*, pp. 6–28. Corwin Press.

Howell, P. B., Carpenter, J., & Jones, J. P. (2013). School partnerships and clinical preparation at the middle level: Strong school–university partnerships foster valuable clinical experiences for preservice teacher candidates at three universities. *Middle School Journal*, *44*(4), 40–49.

Howey, K. R. (2011). Response to section I: What's needed now. *Teachers College Record, 113*(14), 325–336.

Hughes, C. L. (1933). A partial report of the research committee of the supervisors of student teaching. Minneapolis, MN: Supervisors of Student Teaching Annual Meeting,

Hunzicker, J. (2012). Professional development and job-embedded collaboration: How teachers learn to exercise leadership. *Professional Development in Education, 38*(2), 267–289.

Hunzicker, J. (2018). Teacher leadership in professional development schools: A definition, brief history, and call for further study. In J. Hunzicker (Ed.), *Teacher leadership in professional development schools.* Emerald Publishing Limited.

Hunzicker, J. (2019). Learning-focused teacher leadership: The professional development school (PDS) advantage. *Journal of Interdisciplinary Teacher Leadership, 4*(1), n1.

Hurd, E., & Weilbacher, G. (2017). "You want me to do what?" The benefits of coteaching in the middle level. *Middle Grades Review,* 3 (1). https://scholarworks.uvm.edu/mgreview/vol3/iss1/4

Johnston-Parsons, M. (2012). *Dialogue and difference in a teacher education program: A 16-year sociocultural study of a professional development school.* IAP.

Joyce, B. R. (1983). *The structure of school improvement.* Longman, Inc., College Division.

Judge, H., Carriedo, R., & Johnson, S. M. (1995). Professional development schools and MSU: The report of the 1995 review. Unpublished report, Michigan State University.

Kimball, W., Swap, S., LaRosa, P., & Howick, T. (1995). Improving student learning. In R. Osguthorpe et al. (Eds.), *Partner schools: Centers for educational renewal,* pp. 23–44. Jossey-Bass.

Kindzierski, C., del Prado Hill, P., & Garas-York, K. (2021). PDS bends but doesn't break: How PDS structures and processes can help schools and universities respond effectively during a crisis. *School–University Partnerships, 14*(2), 83–97.

Kleine-Kracht, P. A. (1993). The principal in a community of learning. *Journal of School Leadership, 3*(4), 391–399.

Klingner, J.K., Leftwich, S., & van Garderen, D. (2004). Closing the gap: enhancing student outcomes in an urban professional development school. *Teacher Education and Special Education, 27*(3), 292–306

Kochan, F. K., & Kunkel, R. C. (1998). The learning coalition: Professional development schools in partnership. *Journal of Teacher Education, 49*(5), 325–333.

Larabee, D. F., & Pallas, A.M. (1996). Dire straits: The narrow vision of the Holmes Group. *Educational Researcher, 25*(4), 25–28.

Larsen, C., & Rieckhoff, B. S. (2014). Distributed leadership: Principals describe shared roles in a PDS. *International Journal of Leadership in Education, 17*(3), 304–326.

Lauter, N. J. (1998). *Professional development schools: Confronting realities.* National Center for Restructuring Education, Schools, and Teaching.

Lefever-Davis, S., Johnson, C., & Pearman, C. (2007). Two sides of a partnership: Schools in partnership. *Journal of Teacher Education, 49*(5), 325–333.

Leithwood, K., Louis, K. L., Anderson, S., & Wahlstrom, C. (2004). How leadership influences student learning. Learning from Leadership Project. Commissioned by The Wallace Foundation.

LePage, P., Decker, K., & Maier, S. (2001). Using a school-wide collaborative research project to develop teacher leadership and enhance community at George C. Round Elementary School. Paper presented at the American Association of Colleges of Teacher Education (AACTE).

Levine, A. (2005) *Educating school leaders.* Teachers College Press.

Levine, M. (1992a). A conceptual framework for professional practice schools. In M. Levine (Ed.), *Professional practice schools: Linking teacher education and school* reform, pp. 8–24. Teachers College Press.

Levine, M. (1997). Can professional development schools help us achieve what matters most? *Action in Teacher Education, 19*(2), 63–73.

Levine, M. (2002) Why invest in professional development schools? *Educational Leadership, 59*(6), 65–68.

Levine, M., & Churins, E. J. (1999). Designing standards that empower professional development schools. *Peabody Journal of Education, 74*(3–4), 178–208.

Lewin (2015). John I. Goodlad, progressive educator, dies at 94. *New York Times,* January 2, 2015.

Lieberman, A. (1991). Early lessons in restructuring schools: Case studies of schools of tomorrow . . . today. Technical Report, Columbia University, New York, NY. Teachers College National Center for Restructuring Education, Schools and Teaching.

Lieberman, A., & Miller, L. (1992). *Teachers, their world and their work: Implications for school improvement.* Teachers College Press.

Lindsey, M. (1970). Teacher education: Future directions. A Report of the Fiftieth Anniversary Conference of the Association for Student Teaching, Washington, DC.

Mann, A., Reeves, E. K., McIntyre, C. J., & Curry, D. L. (2020). Co-teaching in professional development schools: The gradual release of responsibility. *PDS Partners, 15*(2), 14–17.

Mantle-Bromley, C. (2001). Collaborative action research for English language teachers. *Modern Language Journal, 85*(3), 473–473.

Marchand, G. C., Olafson, L., & Steaffens, S. (2013). Using school and university partnership resources to enhance rigor in self-assessment and evaluation at professional development schools. *School–University Partnerships*, 6(2), 7–19.

Marzano, R. J., Frontier, T., & Livingston, D. (2011). *Effective supervision: Supporting the art and science of teaching.* ASCD.

McGee, C. D. (2001) Building a professional learning community: Lessons from a university–school partnership. *Teacher Education and Practice*, 14(3), 72–95.

McIntyre, D. J., & McIntyre, C. (2020). The evolution of clinical practice and supervision in the United States. *Journal of Educational Supervision*, 3(1), 5.

Merryfield, M. M. (1995). Institutionalizing cross-cultural experiences and international expertise in teacher education: The development and potential of a global education PDS network. *Journal of Teacher Education*, 46(1), 19–27.

Metcalf-Turner, P. (1999). Professional development schools: Practices, problems, and responsibilities. *Metropolitan Universities*, 6(4), 123–138.

Miles, M. B., & Huberman, A. M. (1983). *Analyzing qualitative data: A sourcebook of new methods.* Center for Policy Research.

Milner, R. (2010). *Start where you are, but don't stay there. Understanding diversity, opportunity gaps, and teaching in today's classrooms.* Harvard Education Press.

Morris, V. G., & Nunnery, J. A. (1993). Teacher empowerment in a professional development school collaborative: Pilot assessment. Technical Report 931101.

Murphy, J. (ed.). (1990). *The educational reform movement of the 1980s.* McCutchan Publishing Corp.

Murrell Jr., P. C. (1998). *Like stone soup: The role of the professional development school in the renewal of urban schools.* AACTE Publications.

Murrell Jr., P. C., & Borunda, M. (1998). The cultural and community politics of educational equity: Toward a new framework of professional development schools. In N. J. Lauter (Ed.), *Professional development schools: Confronting realities*, pp. 65–86. National Center for Restructuring Education, Schools, and Teaching.

Myers, M., & Jenkins, A. (2020). Culturally relevant teaching in a PDS: Talking about race in an early childhood setting. *School–University Partnerships*, 13(3), 39–52.

Myers, S. D., & Price, M. A. (2010). Expanding university faculty's vision of a PDS: So this is what partnership really means? *School–University Partnerships*, 4(2), 81–91.

National Association for Professional Development Schools. (2021). What it means to be a professional development school: The nine essentials (2nd ed.) Policy statement. National Association for Professional Development Schools.

National Commission on Teaching & America's Future. (1996). What matters most: Teaching for America's future: Report of the National Commission on Teaching & America's future. The National Commission on Teaching & America's Future.

National Council for Accreditation of Teacher Education. (2001). *Standards for professional development schools*. National Council for Accreditation of Teacher Education

National Council for Accreditation of Teacher Education (2010). Transforming teacher education through clinical practice: A national strategy to prepare effective teachers Policy statement.

National Network for Education Renewal (NNER) (n.d.). https://nnerpartnerships. org

The National Research Council (2010). *Preparing teachers: Building evidence for sound policy*. Washington, DC.

Neapolitan, J. E., & Levine, M. (2011). Approaches to professional development schools. *Teachers College Record, 113*(14), 306–324.

Neapolitan, J. E., & Tunks, J. L. (2009). Exploring the "development" in professional development school research. *Action in Teacher Education, 31*(3), 3–10.

Neufeld, J. A., & McGowan, T. M. (1993). Professional development schools: A witness to teacher empowerment. *Contemporary Education, 64*(4), 249.

Newman, C., Moss, B., Lenarz, M., & Newman, I. (1998). The impact of a PDS internship/student teaching program on the self-efficacy, stages of concern and role perceptions of preservice teaching: The evaluation of a Goals 2000 Project. https://eric.ed.gov/?id=ED425164

Nolan, J. F. (2007). Five basic principles to facilitate change in schools. *Catalyst for Change, 35*(1).

Nolan, J., & Francis, P. (1992). *Changing perspectives in curriculum and instruction*. Supervision in Transition, ASCD Yearbook, pp. 44–60. ASCD.

Nolan Jr, J., Grove, D., Leftwich, H., Mark, K., & Peters, B. (2011). Impact on professional development. *Teachers College Record, 113*(14), 372–402.

Nuebert, G.A., & Binko, J.B. (1998) Professional development schools: The proof is in the performance. *Educational Leadership, 55* (5), 44–46

Orellana, M. F., Johnson, S. J., Rodriguez-Minkoff, A. C., Rodriguez, L., & Franco, J. (2017). An apprentice teacher's journey in "seeing learning." *Teacher Education Quarterly, 44*(2), 7–26.

Osguthorpe, R. T. (1996). Collaborative evaluation in school–university partnerships. Paper presented at the Annual Meeting of the American Educational Research Association, New York, NY, April 8–12, 1996.

Paccione, A. (2000). Developing a commitment to multicultural education. *Teachers College Record, 102*(6), 980–1005.

Parker, A. K., Parsons, S. A., Groth, L., & Brown, E. L. (2016). Pathways to partnership: A developmental framework for building PDS relationships. *School–University Partnerships, 9*(3), 34–48.

Partnership for 21st Century Learning. (n.d.) *Global Awareness Framework*. www. p21.org/about-us/p21-framework/256

Paufler, N. A., & Amrein-Beardsley, A. (2016). Preparing teachers for educational renewal within current contexts of accountability: Reflecting upon John Goodlad's twenty postulates. *Journal of Teacher Education, 67*(4), 251–262.

Peery, A. (2017). Co-teaching: How to make it work. www.cultofpedagogy.com/ co-teaching-push-in

Peik, W. E. (1937). Integration of the preservice curriculum for teaching separate and intensive professional courses. In J. G. Flowers (ed.), *Supervisors of student teaching: Integration of the laboratory phases of teacher training with professional and subject matter courses*. 17th Annual Yearbook, pp. 25–35. Montclair, NJ.

Pence, H., & Macgillivray, I. (2008). The impact of an international field experience on preservice teachers. *Teaching and Teacher Education, 24*, 14–25.

Pritchard, F., & Ancess, J. (1999). The effects of professional development schools: A literature review. An Information Analysis. National Partnership for Excellence and Accountability in Teaching, Washington, DC.

Polly, D., Badiali, B., Burns, R. W., Coler, C., Cosenza, M., Goree, K., . . . & Zenkov, K. (2022). Essential 3: Professional learning in the context of PDS and school–university partnerships. *PDS Partners, 17*(3), 39–42.

Quade, P. (2002). "It changed my life": Strategies for assessing student learning. In S. E. Spencer & K. Tuma (Eds.), *The guide to successful short-term programs* abroad, pp. 121–137. NAFSA, Association of International Educators.

Ravid, R., & Handler, M. G. (2001). *Models of school–university collaboration. The many faces of school–university collaboration, 3–10*. Bloomsbury Publishing.

Rexroat-Frazier, N. M. (2017). Best practices in co-teaching mathematics, teacher efficacy, and teacher and student perceptions. SMTC Plan B Papers. 51. https://repository.uwyo.edu/smtc_ plan_b/51

Rice, E. H. (2002). The collaboration process in professional development schools: Results of a meta-ethnography, 1990–1998. *Journal of Teacher Education, 53*(1), 55–67.

Richards, H. V., Brown, A. F., & Forde, T. B. (2007). Addressing diversity in schools: Culturally responsive pedagogy. *Teaching Exceptional Children, 39*(3), 64–68.

Ridley, D. S., Hurwitz, S., Hackett, M.R.D., & Miller, K. K. (2005). Comparing PDS and campus-based preservice teacher preparation: is PDS-based preparation really better? *Journal of Teacher Education, 56*(1), 46–56.

Rieckhoff, B. S., & Larsen, C. (2012). The impact of a professional development network on leadership development and school improvement goals. *School–University Partnerships, 5*(1), 57–73.

Rodgers, C., & Tiffany, P. (1997). Teacher thinking and the Windham Partnership Reflective Teaching Seminar. Paper presented at the Annual Meeting of the American Educational Research Association, Chicago, IL, March 24–28, 1997.

Ross, D. D., Vescio, V., Tricarico, K., & Short, K. (2011). *Secrets for mentoring novice teachers*. Lastinger Center for Learning.

Rosselli, H., Brindley, R., Daniel, P., Hall, A., Homan, S., & Applegate, J. H. (1999). Beyond good intentions: Using standards to examine PDS sustainability through transitions. Paper presented at the 51st annual meeting of the American Association of Colleges for Teacher Education, Washington, DC, February 24–27, 1999.

Rutter, A. (2011). Purpose and vision of professional development schools. *Teachers College Record, 113*(14), 289–305. https://doi.org/10.1177/016146811111301402

Rutter, A., & Leon, S. (2018). Teacher leadership in a PDS: Think of the possibilities. In M. Cosenza & M. Buchanan (Eds.), *Visions from professional development school partners*, pp. 217–244. Information Age Publishing.

Sachs, G. T., Fisher, T., & Cannon, J. (2011). Collaboration, mentoring and co-teaching in teacher education. *Journal of Teacher Education for Sustainability, 13* (2), 70–86.

Sandholtz, J. H. (2002). Inservice training or professional development: Contrasting opportunities in a school/university partnership. *Teaching and teacher education, 18*(7), 815–830.

Sandholtz, J. H., & Dadlez, S. H. (2000). Professional development school tradeoffs in teacher preparation and renewal. *Teacher Education Quarterly*, 7–27.

Santoro, N., & Major, J. (2012). Learning to be a culturally responsive teacher through international study trips: Transformation or tourism? *Teaching Education, 23*(3), 309–322.

Sarason, S. B. (1990). *The predictable failure of educational reform: Can we change course before it's too late?* The Jossey-Bass Education Series and the Jossey-Bass Social and Behavioral Science Series. Jossey-Bass, Inc., Publishers,

Schaefer, R. J. (1967). *The school as a center of inquiry*. Harper and Row.

Schneider, H., Seidman, I., & Cannone, P. (1996). Ten steps to collaboration: The story of a PDS. *Teaching and Teacher Education, 12*(3), 260–187.

Shandomo, H. M. (2010). The role of critical reflection in teacher education. *School–University Partnerships, 4*(1), 101–113.

Shaw, M. E. (2002). Recovering the vision of John Dewey for developmental education. *Histories of Developmental Education*, 29–33.

Shiveley, J. M., & Pribble, D. A. (2001). From pilot to program: Evaluating the progress of a professional development school. *The Teacher Educator, 36*(4), 282–294.

Silva, D. Y. (2000). Teachers' work and ethos: An ethnographic case study of the work lives of teachers in an inquiry-oriented professional development school. Paper presented at the annual meeting of the American Educational Research Association, New Orleans, LA, April 24–28, 2000.

Silva, D. Y. (2000a). Mentor teachers' ways of being and knowing in a professional development school. Paper presented at the Annual Meeting of the

American Educational Research Association, New Orleans, Louisiana, April, April 24–28, 2000.

Sirotnik, K. A. (1990). On the eroding foundations of teacher education. *The Phi Delta Kappan*, *71*(9), 710–716.

Sirotnik, K. A. (1991). Improving urban schools in the age of "restructuring." *Education and Urban Society*, *23*(3), 256–269.

Sleeter, C. E. (2008). Preparing white teachers for diverse students. In J. Sikula, T. J. Buttery, and E. Guyton (Eds.), *Handbook of research on teacher education*, pp. 559–582. Routledge.

Smedley, L. (2001). Impediments to partnership: A literature review of school-university links. *Teachers and Teaching*, *7*(2), 189–209.

Snow, D., Flynn, S., Whisenand, K., & Mohr, E. (2016). Evidence sensitive synthesis of professional development school outcomes. *School–University Partnerships*, *9*(3), 11–33.

Snyder, J. (1999). Professional development schools: What? So what? Now what? *Peabody Journal of Education*, *74*(3–4), 136–144.

Soard, L. (2018). *The top ten qualities of a good teaching candidate*. Chron.

Sosin, A., & Parham, A. (1998). *An urban public school and university collaboration: What makes a PDS?* Paper presented at the annual meeting of the American Educational Research Association, San Diego, CA, April 13–17, 1998.

Spillane, J. P., Diamond, J. B., & Jita, L. (2003). Leading instruction: The distribution of leadership for instruction. *Journal of Curriculum studies*, *35*(5), 533–543.

Stallings, J. A. (1991). Connecting preservice teacher education and in-service professional development: A professional development school. Paper presented at the annual meeting of the American Educational Research Association, Chicago, IL, 1991.

Stallings, J. A., & Kowalski, T. (1990). Research on professional development schools. In J. Sikula, T. J. Buttery, and E. Guyton (Eds.), *Handbook of research on teacher education*, pp. 194–210. Simon & Schuster.

Stoddard, T. (1993). The professional development school: Building bridges between cultures. *Educational Policy*, *7*, 5–23.

Stoicovy, D., Badiali, B., Burns, R. W., Coler, C., Cosenza, M., Goree, K., . . . & Zenkov, K. (2022). Essential 4: A shared commitment to reflection, innovation and generative knowledge. *PDS Partners*, *17*(1), 41–42.

Stratemeyer, F. (1937). Reactions to the papers of Dr. Flowers and Dr. Peik. In J. G. Flowers (Ed.), *Supervisors of student teaching: Integration of the laboratory phases of teacher training with professional and subject matter courses*. 17th Annual Yearbook, pp. 36–40. Supervisors of Student Teaching.

Stroble, B., & Luka, H. (1999). It's my life, now: The impact of professional development school partnerships on university and school administrators. *Peabody Journal of Education*, *74*(3–4), 123–135.

Stumpf, J. A. (2015). A case study of co-teaching practices in Minnesota. Culminating projects in education administration and leadership. https://repository.stcloudstate.edu/edad_etds/9

Swennen, A., Jones, K., & Volman, M. (2010). Teacher educators: Their identities, sub-identities and implications for professional development. *Professional Development in Education, 36*(1–2), 131–148.

Sykes, G. (1997). Worthy of the name: Standards for the professional development school. In M. Levine & R. Trachtman (Eds.), *Making professional development schools work: Politics, practice, and policy*, pp. 159–181.Teachers College Press.

Taylan, R. D., Tunç-Pekkan, Z., Aydın, U., & Birgili, B. (2022). Teacher educators in K–12 classrooms: How to nurture professional development and research. *Journal of Higher Education Theory and Practice, 22*(1).

Taylor, S. V., & Sobel, D. M. (2003). Rich contexts to emphasize social justice in teacher education: Curriculum and pedagogy in professional development schools special issue: Partnering for equity. *Equity & Excellence in Education, 36*(3), 249–258.

Teitel, L. (1997). Changing teacher education through professional development school partnerships: A five-year follow-up study. *Teachers College Record, 99*(2), 311–334.

Teitel, L. (1997). Understanding and harnessing the power of the cohort model in preparing educational leaders. *Peabody Journal of Education, 72*(2), 66–85.

Teitel, L. (1998). *Designing professional development school governance structures.* American Association of Colleges for Teacher Education [AACTE] Professional Development

Teitel, L. (2001). An assessment framework for professional development schools: Going beyond the leap of faith. *Journal of Teacher Education, 52*(1), 57–69.

Teitel, L. (2003). *The professional development schools handbook: Starting, sustaining, and assessing partnerships that improve student learning.* Corwin Press.

Teitel, L. (2004). *How professional development schools make a difference. A review of research* (2nd ed.) National Council for the Accreditation of Teacher Education.

Teitel, L. (2004) Two decades of professional development school development in the United States. What have we learned? Where do we go from here? *Journal of In-Service Education, 30*(3), 401–416.

Teitel, L. (2008). School/university collaboration: The power of transformative partnerships. *Childhood education, 85*(2), 75–80.

Teitel, L. (with Abdal-Haqq, I.). (2000). Assessing the impacts of professional development schools. American Association for Colleges of Teacher Education Publications.

Tidwell, M., & Thompson, C. (2008). Infusing multicultural principles in urban teacher Preparation. *Childhood Education, 85*(2), 86–90.

Tilford, K. (2010). A phenomenological study of professional development schools: How principals make sense of their role. *School–University Partnerships*, 4(2), 60–73.

Torres, R. (1992). Evaluation of the professional development school effort. In C. Woloszyk & S. Davis (Eds.), *Professional development school handbook*, pp. 1–11. Routledge.

Trachtman, R. (1996). The NCATE professional development school study: A survey of 28 PDS sites. Unpublished manuscript. (Available from Professional Development School Standards Project, National Council for Accreditation of Teacher Education, Washington, DC 20036)

Trubowitz, S., & Longo, P. (1997). *How it works—inside a school-college collaboration. The series on school reform*. Teachers College Press.

United States. National Commission on Excellence in Education. (1983). *A nation at risk: The imperative for educational reform*. The National Commission on Excellence in Education.

Valli, L. (1997). Listening to other voices: A description of teacher reflection in the United States. *Peabody Journal of Education*, 72(1), 67–88.

Van Scoy, I. J, & Eldridge, D. B. (2012). NCATE's blue ribbon panel report and NAPDS: Working together. *School–University Partnerships*, 5(1), 7–12.

Vare, J. W. (2004). Empowerment, vision, and voice: Building an assessment system for professional development schools. *The Teacher Educator*, 40(2), 133–148. https://doi.org/10.1080/08878730409555356

Vélez-Rendón, G. (2002). Second language teacher education: A review of the literature. *Foreign Language Annals*, 35, 457–467.

Villegas, A. M. (2008). Diversity and teacher education. In J. Sikula, T. J. Buttery, and E. Guyton (Eds.), *Handbook of research on teacher education*, pp. 550–558. Routledge.

Wahlstrom, K., & Louis, K. (2010). *Learning from leadership: Investigating the links to improved student learning*. The Wallace Foundation.

Walling, B., & Lewis, M. (2000). Development of professional identity among professional development school preservice teachers: Longitudinal and comparative analysis. *Action in Teacher Education*, 22(supp. 2), 65–72.

Wait, D. B. (2000). Are professional development school trained teachers really better? Paper presented at the annual meeting of the National PDS Conference, Columbia, SC.

Walmsley, A., Bufkin, L., & Rule, A. (2009). Developmental stages of a professional development school: Lessons from a long-term partnership. *School–University Partnerships*, 3(2), 69–79.

Ware, B., del Prado Hill, P., & McMillen, S. E. (2017). The PDS student representative: leadership development that benefits everyone. *PDS Partners*, 13(1), 1–20.

Webb-Dempsey, J. (1997). Reconsidering assessment to be reflective of school reform. In N. Hoffman, W. Reed, & G. Rosenbluth (Eds.), *Lessons from restructuring experiences: Stories of change in professional development schools*, pp. 269–294. SUNY Press.

Weber, S., & Klein, D. (2021). Structures that promote self-confidence in PDS undergraduate student representatives *The Impact of PDS Partnerships in Challenging Times*, 135.

Weiss, E. M., & Weiss, S. (2001). Doing reflective supervision with student teachers in a professional development school culture. *Reflective practice*, *2*(2), 125–154.

Wheatley, M. J. (1992). *Leadership and the new science: Learning about organization from an orderly universe*. Berrett-Koehler Publishers.

Whitford, B. L., & Metcalf-Turner, P. (1999). Of promises and unresolved puzzles: Reforming teacher education with professional development schools. *Teachers College Record*, *100*(5), 257–278.

Whitford, B. L., & Villaume, S. K. (2014). Clinical teacher preparation: A retrospective. *Peabody Journal of Education*, *89*(4), 423–435.

Whitford, E. V., & Barnett, B. E. (2016, June). The professional development school approach to teacher education: Identification of a model. In *Conference Proceedings. The Future of Education*, p. 457.

Willard-Holt, C. (2001). The impact of a short-term international experience for preservice teachers. *Teacher and Teacher Education*, *17*(4), 505–517.

Williams, R. B. (1996). Four dimensions of the school change facilitator. *Journal of Staff Development*, *17*(1), 48–50.

Winitzky, N., Stoddart, T., & O'Keefe, P. (1992). Great expectations: Emergent professional development schools. *Journal of Teacher Education*, *43*(1), 3–18.

Wiseman, D. L., & Cooner, D. (1996). Discovering the power of collaboration: The impact of a school–university partnership on teaching. *Teacher Education and Practice*, *12*(1), 18–28.

Wolf, M. (2021). Getting started: Art educators stepping into PDS. *PDS Partners*, *16*(4), 39–42.

Wong, P. L., & Glass, R. D. (2005). Assessing a professional development school approach to preparing teachers for urban schools serving low-income, culturally and linguistically diverse communities. *Teacher Education Quarterly*, *32*(3), 63–77.

Yendol-Hoppey, D., Gregory, A., Jacobs, J., & League, M. (2008). Inquiry as a tool for professional development school improvement: Four illustrations. *Action in Teacher Education*, *30*(3), 23–38.

Yendol-Hoppey, D., & Smith, J. J. (2011). What do we know about accountability and resources in professional development schools? *Teachers College Record*, *113*(14), 531–566.

Yopp, R. H., Ellis, M. W., Bonsangue, M. V., Duarte, T., & Meza, S. (2014). Piloting a Co-Teaching Model for Mathematics Teacher Preparation: Learning to Teach Together. *Issues in Teacher Education, 23*(1), 91–111.

York-Barr, J., & Duke, K. (2004). What do we know about teacher leadership? Findings from two decades of scholarship. *Review of Educational Research, 74*(3), 255–316.

Young, M. D., Crow, G., Orr, M. T., Ogawa, R., & Creighton, T. (2005). An educative look at educating school leaders. *UCEA Review, 47*(2), 1–5.

Young, M. D., Peterson, G. T., & Short, P.M. (2002) The complexity of substantive reform: A call for interdependence among key stakeholders. *Educational Administration Quarterly, 38*, 137–175.

Zenkov, K., Shiveley, J., & Clark, E. (2016). What is a PDS? Special Issue. *School–University Partnerships 9*(3).

Zenkov, K., Badiali, B., Burns, R. W., Coler, C., Cosenza, M., Goree, K., . . . & Lague, M. (2021). The revised nine essentials. Article Series Essential 1: Justice is our Comprehensive Mission. *PDS Partners, 16*(4), 21–24.

Index

Milton Keynes UK
Ingram Content Group UK Ltd.
UKHW030040261024
450168UK00006B/89

9 781438 499932